LEADING
PEOPLE

LEADING PEOPLE

Transforming Business
from the Inside Out

ROBERT H. ROSEN
with Paul B. Brown

VIKING

VIKING
Published by the Penguin Group
Penguin Books USA Inc., 375 Hudson Street, New York, New York 10014, U.S.A.
Penguin Books Ltd, 27 Wrights Lane, London W8 5TZ, England
Penguin Books Australia Ltd, Ringwood, Victoria, Australia
Penguin Books Canada Ltd, 10 Alcorn Avenue, Toronto, Ontario, Canada M4V 3B2
Penguin Books (N.Z.) Ltd, 182–190 Wairau Road, Auckland 10, New Zealand

Penguin Books Ltd, Registered Offices:
Harmondsworth, Middlesex, England

First published in 1996 by Viking Penguin, a division of Penguin Books USA Inc.

10 9 8 7 6 5 4 3 2 1

Healthy Companies® is a registered trademark of
Healthy Companies, Inc.

Leading People℠ is a service mark of RHR Enterprises.

LIBRARY OF CONGRESS CATALOGING IN PUBLICATION DATA
Rosen, Robert H.
Leading people: transforming business from the inside out / by Robert H.
Rosen with Paul B. Brown.
p. cm.
Includes index.
ISBN 0–670–85874–9
1. Leadership. 2. Entrepreneurship—United States. 3. Management—
United States. I. Brown, Paul, 1954– II. Title.
HD57.7.R66   1996
658.4'092—dc20   95-32360

This book is printed on acid-free paper. ♾

Printed in the United States of America
Set in New Baskerville

To Barbara, Dick, and Randi
for all your love and support over the years

ACKNOWLEDGMENTS

So often we forget that who we are and how we see the world are influenced by the many people we touch over our lifetime. This book is a wonderful story of these many minds at work. I am deeply grateful for the inspiration and wisdom I have received over the years from family, friends, and colleagues. This book is for you.

To Jay for your principles and insights about people. You are a true leader.

To my family for their love, encouragement, and sense of humor—Jay, Barbara, Dick, Randi, Rick, Chris, Ryan, Devon, Margot, Jerry, Lynne, Mark, Erin, Amanda, Michael, Sergio, Paul, Nancy, Karlyn, and Stanley. Special thanks to Snapper, my eight-year-old Labrador Retriever, who sat under my feet and provided companionship, keen insights, and unconditional support of the manuscript.

To my fellow journalists, Paul Brown for your brilliant story-telling abilities, and Mark Schoofs for your keen sense of style.

To my agent, Gail Ross, for your warm guidance and friendship.

To my business colleagues, who inspire and challenge me every day—Ted Malloch, Anne Kahn, Janet Moyer, Peter Carlson, Jill Klobucar-Logan, Peter Ross, and Judy Brown. And to those who worked hard to support this project—Jennifer Beams, Toni McIntosh, Virginia Dickey, Mary Boylen Wichansky, David Obstfeld, and Wanda Rappaport.

To my family of friends for your love and candor—Marshall Singer, Tom Mader, Jim Mathews, Glen Fischer, Helen Mills, Susan Spriggs, Amy Cunningham, Linda Scott, Sam Paschall, Polly Agee, Maria MacKnight, and Bill Oyler.

To Jane von Mehren and her team at Penguin USA for your enthusiasm and commitment to this project.

To the Healthy Companies Research Council for your keen intellect and guidance on this journey—Elsa Porter, Dennis Jaffe, Jim O'Toole, Ernie Savoie, Doug LaBier, Bradley Googins, John Aram, Marilyn Gowing, Irving Bluestone, Diana Chapman Walsh, Edgar Schein, John Harris, Bob Caplan, Louis Laguardia, Bill O'Brien, and Dennis Young. My warmest thoughts go to Alan Westin, chairperson of the council. Alan, you are a true friend, colleague, and mentor.

To my clients who teach me every day about courage, humility, and the challenges of leading people.

To Raymond Ho at Maryland Public Television, and my friends at PBS, Eric Sass, Fran Levey, and Carol Dickert-Scher for believing in this project.

To my colleagues at Leadership Washington—"The One of Only Ninth"—you truly were an inspiration as I wrote this book.

To the Healthy Companies Learning Network, who taught me about the real world and kept my faith in the principles of healthy companies.

To the Collegial Network for your wise and honest friendship—Suzanne Allford, Laura Avakian, Tim Burns, Hank Feir, Bill Hargreaves, Karen Hollenbeck, Kay Hubbard, Michele Hunt, Gloria Nemerowicz, Penny Pestle, Gene Rosi, Craig Schrotenboer, and Barbara Walker.

To my colleagues at the MacArthur Foundation for your intellectual creativity and unwavering support of our work—Denis Prager, Bob Rose, Lauri Garduque, Ida Gittelson, Ruth Runeborg, Adele Simmons, Victor Rabinowitz, Paul Lingenfelter, Ray Boyer, and my fellow network directors.

To the editorial board of the Healthy Companies newsletter for your quiet credibility. Special thanks to Jossey-Bass Publishers for working with us on this project.

To our communications alliance, especially Tim Westerbeck, and Sarah and Bob Steck, for your commitment to this work.

To the various federal agencies, particularly the Departments of Labor and Commerce, for taking the lead in the promotion of high-performance workplaces.

To the organizations taking the lead in promoting these principles—Association for Quality and Participation, Healthcare Forum, Human Resource Planning Society, American Psychological Association, Businesses for Social Responsibility, Social Venture Network, National Association of Women Business Owners, Society for Human Resource Management, Council on Economic Priorities, and the National Association of Manufacturers.

To the people who came before me I owe an intellectual debt of gratitude: Richard Walton, Michael Maccoby, Ed Lawlor, Warren Bennis, Max DePree, Peter Senge, Peter Drucker, Rosabeth Moss Kanter, John Gardner, Harry Levinson, James Autry, Bob Waterman, Bob Kaplan, Peter Block, Tom Peters, Donald Clifton, John Kotter, and John O'Neil.

And finally to the leaders in this book, and to all the other leaders—known and unknown—around the country who are leading people every day. You are my greatest inspiration. Thank you.

CONTENTS

LEADING IS

HARD WORK

LEADING IS

HARD WORK

Ironically, it was the effects of casting darkness that first sparked my interest in leadership. Back in 1980, I was working as a young psychologist at the George Washington University School of Medicine, treating the families of executives in business and government. A mother and her thirteen-year-old son came to see me. The son's performance in school had been deteriorating—he was having trouble concentrating and, in frustration, was growing increasingly unruly.

From my sessions with the boy and his mother a portrait emerged of a father who was charismatic, smart, and, as the head of a growing and profitable company, extremely successful. Indeed, he was so engrossed in his business that he gave little time to his family.

Later, I came to realize that despite all the time this man put in at the office, he treated his employees exactly as he did his family. He ignored them. Oh, he spent a lot of time supervising them, inspecting their work, and mistrusting their intentions. He rode them extremely hard, demanding late nights and frequent weekend stints. In short, he treated his employees as tools to make a profit, but he refused to recognize their family and community lives. He ignored them *as people.*

As it turned out, this was one of the major reasons his firm eventually went bankrupt. Turnover and morale problems got out of hand. Bitter infighting divided his top leadership cadre, and, not surprisingly, the firm couldn't develop long-term customer relationships.

Extreme though this story is, I realized that to paint a true portrait of thousands of American managers one would have to use many of the same stark colors. I also saw the profound and critical connection between this man's inner life and his leadership of his family and business. He was casting his shadow side—his insecurities and self-absorption and excessive ambition—on everyone around him, with disastrous effects. I wanted to understand how this vicious circle worked, and to help others reverse it or avoid it altogether. I set about interviewing and studying leaders from all walks of life.

Almost immediately, I encountered leaders who were mature and effective, who were casting brightness rather than darkness on those around them. One of the first such leaders was Max DePree, CEO of Fortune 500 furniture manufacturer Herman Miller, and a renowned writer on leadership. In our interview, DePree recounted how an employee came to him and complained that two coworkers had been wrongly fired. Taken aback, DePree investigated and confirmed the complaint. He reinstated the fired employees and gave the offending supervisor the boot.

But what sticks most prominently in my mind is not the decisive action DePree took, but how deeply he was affected by the episode. I remember sitting in his office—which was remarkably spare and unassuming for a person of his position—as he told me how thrilled he was that his employees had the confidence to approach him, the top boss, with the expectation of fairness. I had spent several hours with DePree, and found him to be pleasant but reserved. Now, for the first time, passion flowed forth: his greatest achievement was not his company's high profit margins, he told me, nor even the quality of its products. Instead, it was his creating of a culture where people were treated right, where the open-door policy was not an empty phrase but a reality. "My job," he said, "is to oversee fundamental principles, like fair play and honesty. If I do that, the profits will follow."

As he said this, I felt a twinge of skepticism. Could a person under the kind of pressure Wall Street imposes on CEOs really believe that his duty was to watch "principles" as closely as quarterly earnings? But the more time I spent with leaders, the more I realized that the best of them did exactly that.

In the early years of my career, I worked mostly with entrepreneurs. And I noticed that those who were able to grow their businesses were the ones who, like DePree, understood human nature and how to tap the best in people. They understood that the bottom line is, ultimately, the result of human endeavor.

I noticed the same dynamic when I was consultant to the Washington Business Group on Health, a national group of Fortune 500 companies. There I saw how some of the most prestigious businesses in America managed—and mismanaged—their human capital. I was dismayed at how many of these corporations undervalued and underinvested in their people.

But something else surprised me: the corporate leaders who did understand the human side of their businesses and who were most effectively motivating and mobilizing their people were operating mostly by instinct. Just like the entrepreneurs, these leaders were acting from the profound intuition that profits follow principles. Why were these leaders, with all the immense resources at their disposal, going with their gut? Because almost no solid data existed to make the case for investing in people.

Corporate accounting, so sophisticated when it came to finances and hard assets, was downright primitive when it came to measuring human assets. It couldn't prove how different management techniques affected employee performance, and it certainly couldn't tell leaders how to maximize their workers' creativity and commitment. It was as if clocks had not yet been invented, and people could only guess the time.

By now I was engrossed in these issues. I began to explore a new concept: the "healthy" organization, a high-performance enterprise that nurtures and taps the talents, ideas, and energy of its people. Healthy enterprises start from core human values, such as trust, integrity, and teamwork, and they balance the needs of all their stakeholders—employees, customers, shareholders, and the larger community. They don't do this merely because it's right or fair. They do it because it's better business, because it gives them the profound and enduring competitive advantage of a fast, flexible work culture, where employees act like they own the business, learn on the job, and care deeply about quality and service.

With a growing network of colleagues from business, academia, government, and labor, I pursued key questions: How do we develop robust, successful enterprises? Where and how do people create the most value for business? What investments in people will really make a difference in performance? How can we unleash the full potential of our workers?

In 1990, the John D. and Catherine T. MacArthur Foundation helped me delve even more deeply into these questions by giving a charter grant to the not-for-profit think tank I founded, called Healthy Companies Institute. We surveyed the dominant philosophies and practices of American management, and as we did so it became clear that American organizations face two profound crises.

The first is a crisis in commitment. People are not working at their full potential. Competitive advantage comes from the effort workers put in above and beyond "just doing their job." If a line worker in a factory sees a better way to reuse scrap but doesn't share it with the company, that worker is, technically, still doing his job. He's earning his pay, fulfilling the letter if not the spirit of his contract. But in a competitor's factory down the road—or across the ocean—another worker comes up with the same recycling idea and pushes to get it implemented. Suddenly the second factory gets more out of its raw materials than the first—and not because of superior technology or training, but purely because an employee gave more than was strictly required.

We call this "discretionary effort" because no leader can *force* an employee to give it. Employees provide it at their discretion, and if they choose to give it often enough, the power it gives an enterprise is truly awesome. But across the country and in every sector of the American economy, I saw people withhold their discretionary effort.

Sometimes people were downright passive-aggressive. Other times they were indifferent, as if their spark had been snuffed out. And often they blamed management. The bureaucracy was too cumbersome. The company didn't invest in learning opportunities. Top leadership hoarded information, especially financial figures, that would clarify the big picture and enable workers to suggest improvements. The glass ceiling kept women and people of color "in their place." Technology was implemented without any thought to the workers who used it, causing health problems like repetitive stress syndrome. A relentless demand for extra work hours ate into precious time for family and leisure.

Sometimes these complaints were baseless bellyaching. There are always a few bad apples in any bin. But in many cases, the workers were right. Leaders had created environments that undermined motivation and discouraged discretionary effort. I saw the worst of these companies go out of business, brought to their knees by employee burnout, rampant mistrust, missed market opportunities and resistance to change—in short, by a colossal waste of human potential.

I saw other companies stumble along by taking partial measures. Management strategies such as total quality, reengineering, and empowerment programs helped these enterprises, and deepened my own understanding of healthy, high-performing organizations. But unfortunately, they were only fragmentary approaches that didn't inspire people to consistently contribute discretionary effort, and so didn't resolve the commitment crisis.

In fact, employees in these companies were often jaded, quick to deride the new management techniques as "fads." These workers would often tell me that, yes, the management "flavor of the month" made sense and even improved things. So what was their gripe? That the new technique seemed like a ploy to jack up short-term profits. What these people sensed was something awfully close to hypocrisy. They felt that their leaders were merely tinkering with rhetoric and style, but that deep down they were still operating from the same old assumption: namely, that work is something to be extracted from people, as though employees were a kind of fuel to be burned up and reduced to waste. In short, workers sensed that they were still being managed as costly liabilities, not as valuable assets.

But buried in the complaints of such workers lies an urgent—and surprising—message. People want to be led. They don't want the old authoritarian leadership style. Nor do they want some clever new management technique. Instead, they want leaders with deeply held human values who respect people's unique talents and contributions. They want leaders who will create an environment that nurtures excellence, risk taking, and creativity. They reject intimidation or manipulation, but they positively yearn for inspiration.

Similarly, in the misguided efforts of leaders is hidden another message: leaders need followers. Leaders don't want docile, do-only-as-ordered employees. Instead, they want responsible, mature, forward-looking associates. They want partners who are as committed as they are to the success of the enterprise.

The simple fact is that leaders and followers need each other, but they are not working well together. As I travel around the country, I see tensions between them as severe as a chronic ache. These rifts divide not just employers and employees, but also politicians and constituents, doctors and patients, teachers and students. Everywhere, our leader-follower relationships are tense, cynical, confused, and mistrustful. This dysfunctional relationship is the primary cause of the crisis in commitment.

But the responsibility for mending the relationship lies with leaders. Leaders must take the first steps, for it is leaders who set the rules, create the culture, and determine the values and principles that guide the organization. Indeed, fostering mature and robust leader-follower partnerships is what leading people is all about. But most leaders aren't pulling their weight. To put it another way, followers aren't following because leaders aren't leading.

A 1995 national survey found that 98 percent of executives agreed that improving employee performance would significantly increase company productivity, and 73 percent claimed that employees were their company's most important asset. But when asked to rank business priorities, these same executives relegated investing in people to fifth place on a six-item list.[1] Such dissonance between rhetoric and reality is almost deafening, but it's only one example. Over the last two decades, employees have watched the salaries of top executives rise much faster than those of the average worker, and they have seen failed executives jump with golden parachutes worth tens of millions of dollars. Is it any wonder that workers cock a cynical ear when management asks them to make sacrifices, such as paying part of their health insurance or shouldering more responsibility?

Yet, in a small but growing group of enterprises, I found little such cynicism. These were organizations that had leaders committed to ethical values, frank talk, and deep listening. Some used the latest management innovations, others didn't. Some of these leaders were well into their sixties, some were surprisingly young. Indeed, they had little in common, except for what really counts: a profound understanding of themselves, of the motivations and aspirations of the people around them, and of the external challenges their enterprises faced.

These leaders knew their business inside and out, and were fiercely committed to reality and results. But they defined success broadly. It included making a profit, of course, and it also included making their enterprise valuable to the larger society through quality products and services, healthy and challenged employees, and environmental stewardship.

In their enterprises—which ranged from huge multinational corporations to small family businesses, which were scattered across industry, government, and the nonprofit sector—I didn't find perfection. That doesn't exist. But I did find excellence, innovation, resilience, and optimism.

I found labor-management relations marked by candor and mutual responsibility. I found workers who wanted to be challenged and stretched by their jobs, and who wanted to be identified with their organization because they knew it was doing good, meaningful work. I found work cultures in which information was shared rather than hoarded, and in which learning and development were valued rather than shortchanged. I found management structures that were flexible and responsive rather than rigid and stifling. I found enterprises steering their way through today's conflicting demands: innovate but avoid mistakes, think long-term but increase productivity now, downsize but improve teamwork.

And I found profit. But as the leaders of these enterprises were always quick to point out, their profit was the result of creating an environment that liberated people's creativity, nurtured their commitment, and inspired their discretionary effort.

In short, I found healthy, high-performance enterprises, models of the organizations that will succeed in the twenty-first century. In every case, the key was leadership. Healthy, mature, self-aware leaders were unlocking the best in their employees, and therefore the best in the enterprise as a whole. But where leaders were still projecting more of their dark sides, leadership acted as a jailer rather than a liberator, confining creativity and enthusiasm, and keeping the best prospects of the organization shut away.

With growing conviction, I realized that the only way to transform an organization in the deep, long-term ways that inspire people and invigorate their efforts is to transform an organization's leadership. What America needs to thrive in the next century, I realized, is not a new management practice or productivity program. What we need, in all walks of life and all endeavors, is new leadership. This book is both a call for and a lesson in this new leadership.

SUCCESS DEPENDS ON PEOPLE

We live in a time of chaos, marked by breathtaking technological advances, tectonic cultural and political shifts, and vigorous international competition. Our workforce grows more diverse every day, while our attitudes about work are constantly changing. At the same time customers are demanding intensive service and near-perfect quality. Everything has to be better, cheaper, faster.

That kind of continuous innovation and improvement cannot come from technology alone, which nowadays turns obsolete as quickly as a mayfly. It comes from human creativity and commitment, from employees giving their best at all levels of the organization. In short, success depends on people—and in order to achieve success, people depend on leaders.

It's a simple idea, but one with sweeping consequences. It opens up tremendous opportunities, but also gaping pitfalls. In order to succeed, leaders will have to reinvent their organizations to get the most from their people. But to do that leaders must take a deep look inward and discover the ways they influence their enterprise and their people. More important, they will have to reinvent themselves.

We have not had an honest conversation in this country about leadership, about what we want and expect from our leaders, and about the real-life experience of leading. Instead, leading gets inflated to a John Wayne caricature or deflated to a bloodless "manager." This isn't surprising. As a robust, action-oriented society, we usually look outside for answers—to competitors, other countries, new techniques. We mistrust introspection, dismiss our emotions, and generally neglect the "soft" side of business. This cultural bias has given us leaders who are comfortable with operations and marketing but not with inner emotions and human relationships, leaders who are good at manipulating numbers but not at developing people.

That's a real problem, because the only way to succeed in the lightning-quick Information Age is to nurture independent, motivated people and to build healthy, high-performing organizations. We've known this for a while. The importance of people has become a cliché of annual reports. And more profoundly, a whole new social contract is evolving.

This contract requires more from both employees and employers. Workers must pitch in with more than their hands; they must also contribute with their minds and their hearts. They must "own" their work and act as mini-entrepreneurs. The old paternalistic contract rewarded effort and loyalty, long hours and doing what the boss asked. The new contract rewards results and self-reliance, smart solutions and taking responsibility without having to be asked.

For their work as whole people, workers need to be treated as whole people. But in survey after study after poll, people tell us they're not getting this from their companies. They want a say in workplace decisions, as voters have in a democracy, but too often they're still treated as children and told what to do. They need the opportunity for camaraderie and teamwork and excellence, but they are often frustrated by rigid hierarchies. They want their labor to have meaning and they want to learn on the job, but they're often stuck in companies that offer scant opportunity to grow and develop. Leaders must live up to their end of the new contract and offer their people respect, dignity, and fairness.

This results in smart business. The leader's job is to maximize the organization's most valuable asset, people. Their "intellectual capital" is the most appreciable asset in the knowledge economy. Yet a recent national survey of more than ten thousand workers found that current leadership is costing American companies more than *half* their human potential. To put that another way, improved leadership alone could double worker productivity.[2]

To do this, leaders must build organizations that help employees strengthen their competence, creativity, and commitment. Leaders must create healthy environments where people are excited about their work, take pride in their accomplishments, and contribute to their colleagues doing the same. Their task, in short, is to foment ideas, skills, and energy. *This* is leading people.

But for the last decade American business leaders have focused not on appreciating their human assets, but on cutting costs. In order to increase productivity, they have pared their organizations down to the bone. Companies have stripped out management layers, "reengineered" work units, linked computer networks. And most commonly, they have laid off workers, sometimes in massive one-time reductions, often in protracted downsizing.

The result? Lean enterprises, some of which have emerged healthier and more robust than ever. But where enlightened leadership has been absent, cost cutting has left a demoralized workforce, prone to cynicism, mistrust, and resentment. In these companies, stressed-out employees end up putting in more work in less time with fewer resources, and then withhold their full potential from executives, who reap excessive bonuses from short-term financial performance. Such organizations—and there are too many of them—are like anorexics; lean, yes, but so thin that they are unable to withstand competitive assault. They are financially solvent, but emotionally bankrupt. And in the long term, they are extremely vulnerable.

The current internal malaise affecting our companies is bound to come to a head. All indications reveal that by the year 2000, the competitive advantage will go to companies that most effectively mobilize their people. Organizations with the best ideas, the most skills, and the most dedicated workforce will succeed. But developing human assets is a whole different ball game from cutting costs. New management practices, such as employee involvement and organizational learning, come closer to what's needed, but still fall short. After reengineering, retooling, and restructuring, many companies wonder why they're still lagging behind. Frustrated, they look around for some new technique or management practice. Instead, they should look inward. They should look at the way they are leading their people.

Leaders shed light or impose darkness. This is the most profound power they have. Because people look to leaders for guidance and purpose, their every action and word carry extra impact. In fact, leaders project their attitudes and personality onto the people around them.

The danger is that all personalities have a dark side—secretiveness or insecurity or arrogance. That's part of being human, as is a tendency to cling to old concepts of power, motivation, and diversity.

But if leaders lack a deep understanding of themselves, they will cast too much of their shadow side onto their enterprise, with chilling effect. A 1994 study at the Center for Creative Leadership identified the most common reasons why managers derail on their careers. The four most enduring explanations were: interpersonal problems, inability to meet business demands, failure to lead a team, and the inability to adapt to change.[3] The fact is they all had to do with leading people.

This translates directly to the bottom line. The single biggest influence on employee commitment and performance, according to a sweeping national study of more than 25,000 workers, is the leadership skills of their managers.[4] To inspire their people, leaders need to cast brightness, to project confidence and humility. Doing so will liberate the best in other people, their talent and enthusiasm. It is only when leaders learn more about themselves that they will be able to avoid casting their shadow side onto their enterprise.

Does this mean that leaders must shirk painful decisions or must be preoccupied with employees' needs? Of course not. Leadership has always required tough choices, and always will. The difference lies in how leaders make and carry out these decisions.

Consider two methods—both of which have been used in the real world—to lead a company through the same difficult change. In one scenario, top management huddles together, decides that the financial figures call for drastic action, and delivers termination to 10 percent of the workforce one Friday afternoon, without warning.

In the other scenario, top management shares the dire economic news with the entire company, janitor through CEO, and asks for creative ways to cut costs and boost productivity. As many suggestions as possible are implemented, reaping real improvements. But the situation still looks bad. Top management again communicates this to workers and lets them know that some people will need to be let go—although, thanks to employee suggestions, not as many as management had feared. It offers a combination of options to reduce the workforce by 7 percent, including early retirement, employee buyouts, and, for those involuntarily laid off, job training.

If you survived the cutbacks, which leaders would you rather work for?

Same problem, different leadership. In the first instance, the leaders hoarded information and power; in the second case they shared it. In the first scenario, the leaders acted *on* their people; in the second case they acted *with* them. In the first case, the leaders cast a pall of secrecy and fear over their enterprise; in the second, they cast a light of candor and common purpose.

This idea—that leadership is the casting of light or darkness—is simple to understand, but hard to master. It requires constant introspection, peeling back layers of oneself, learning about one's strengths and weaknesses. But it also requires real-life experience: interacting with colleagues and customers and competitors, coping with hard economic realities, balancing the tensions and trade-offs that leadership decisions inevitably demand. In short, it requires both contemplation and challenge, hard thinking and hard knocks.

In my case, it has taken fifteen years to understand leadership, most of my adult career as a psychologist and business consultant, and I'm still learning. This book shares what I've discovered, and it also shares the lessons of thirty-six of my best teachers: outstanding, real-life leaders from every field of work. In this book, we'll look at leaders such as Paul Nolan of the Ford Motor Company and Richard Greenfield of the United Auto Workers, who together have forged a new breed of labor-management partnership. We'll learn how Wal-Mart Vice Chairman Don Soderquist has opened the corporate books to all his employees, and reaped higher productivity as a result. We'll look at James DePreist, who overcame polio and racial prejudice to become the conductor of the Oregon Symphony, and Barry Alvarez, who led the University of Wisconsin football team to its first-ever Rose Bowl victory. We'll see how Carla Gorrell created—from nothing—a charity that delivers nourishing meals each day to eight hundred homebound people with AIDS, and we'll examine how Air Force General Michael Loh met the awesome logistical challenge of the Persian Gulf War.

The leaders in this book come from all three sectors of the American economy: business, government, and nonprofit. Each of these sectors has its special strengths and challenges, and each sector can learn from the others. Business is expert in efficiency, technological innovation, and profitability. Government can teach us about balancing constituencies for the larger public good, and about justice and equal treatment. The nonprofit world knows the value of public trust, volunteerism, and the motivational power of a larger purpose. As we'll see, the best leaders adapt traits from the other sectors to their own enterprises.

There are many books on the subject of leadership. I openly acknowledge that I stand on the shoulders of those who wrote before me. But this book is uncommonly practical. Because it draws its lessons from actual people and experiences, it does not hold out an unattainable, theoretical ideal. These leaders are successful, yes, but they make trade-offs. They wrestle with tensions and dilemmas, and they stumble and fall along the way. This book does not paint what is perfect. It portrays something more complex, more authentic, and ultimately more inspiring. It paints what is possible.

THE LEADER'S NEW WORK

So what exactly is this new leadership? First off, it is not a status. Forget about all the paraphernalia of the high and mighty down the centuries, from scepters and crowns to limousines and corner offices. Just as clothes do not make the man, trappings never made a leader. They just stroked someone's vanity. Such trappings also intimidate people—which is good if you want to be a dictator or run a personality cult, but bad if you want to create an open, vibrant, high-performing team. Leaders inspire rather than intimidate, motivate rather than monitor, mobilize rather than manage. And these activities don't require the totems of rank and position.

Rather than a status, leadership is an activity. To emphasize this I prefer to use *leading* instead of *leadership,* a verb instead of a noun, a process rather than a position. Leading is like marketing or manufacturing or accounting—it *does* something. What it does is enable a group of people to pursue a shared vision and create extraordinary results.

Leaderless organizations don't work. Some people have argued that self-managing organizations don't need leaders, that they can operate strictly through an organic, participative, bottom-up process of collaboration and consensus. But my fifteen years of working with all manner of organizations, large and small, refutes that. At some point, even small, self-managing firms need leaders. People can rotate into the leader's position, or a leader can develop *de facto*, without a title or job description. But leading is a necessary function, as vital to the life and prosperity of an organization as speaking is to communication.

This function can be learned. Leaders are made, not born. Leading is not some mystical charisma that you either have or you don't. It is more like a language: we all have a capacity for it, some more and some less, but with experience virtually everyone can learn to lead people effectively.

The analogy goes further. For the most part, language isn't learned in a classroom. Indeed, we talk before we ever see our first blackboard or scribble our first grammar lesson. We learn it from the people around us. We listen, and we imitate what we hear. So too with leading. We emulate those around us: parents, bosses, coaches, teachers. Like kids picking up a language, we learn leadership without even being conscious of it.

Unfortunately, most of our leadership role models reached their positions by climbing up traditional hierarchies. They watched leaders before them hoard control, play politics, and issue edicts, so they do the same. In a truly blighted cycle, that's the style of leadership they're passing on to the next generation. In order to learn a new and better leadership, we need better role models, people who connect fundamental values to their work.

That's exactly what this book presents: real-life individuals who broke the cycle and created a new way of leading. From their stories, I extract a grammar of leadership: not tips or quick fixes, but precepts that, with time and practice, make for fluent leading.

But there is much more than grammar in this book. There is also poetry. The poetry is in the lives of these leaders, in their actions and struggles. Becoming a leader is a lifelong adventure, much the same as becoming a healthy, integrated person. Some of us mature into leadership smoothly, others bleed into it through a crisis. But leaders are always made—through experience on the job and in their family and community lives. All of the leaders in this book had key teachable moments in their lives, moments when they leapt to a new level of understanding.

For many of them, one of those moments was when they realized that leaders are not heroes or villains. That's how our society thinks of leaders. We love them or hate them, idolize or demonize them, in much the same way as the press portrays our Presidents. But this conception of leaders as larger than life, as the organization's all-knowing Big Brain, undermines leaders and followers alike. It puts tremendous stress on the leaders, who know they can never measure up. The result? Frustration and workaholism—or the arrogance of someone who has begun to believe this fantasy of omnipotence. Both responses are psychologically corrosive.

This impossible ideal makes it all too easy to snipe at a leader's "failures" and "shortcomings." It also infantilizes workers, putting them in the role of children who must depend on the adult leaders. The new leader-associate relationship is not adult-child, but adult-adult. Workers have to shoulder more responsibility and independence, and leaders must step down from their pedestals.

But humanizing is a tricky task. We expect both too much and too little of our leaders. On the one hand, we must learn to be more forgiving and gentle, to allow our leaders to be human rather than heroic. We have to recognize that leaders often face dilemmas that pit important interests and parties against one another and that lack a single clear answer. In such cases, decisions can involve painful, even wrenching, trade-offs. But even as we humanize leaders, we must hold them to new and higher standards. Leaders must share power and information. They must speak candidly, and they must "walk their talk." They must listen carefully. They must recognize that their personalities get magnified and projected onto the organization, and so they must work to be more aware of their inner lives. They must be willing to admit mistakes, to say they don't know, to express their feelings, to ask for help.

But above all, leaders must cultivate healthy adult-adult relationships. Why is this so critical? Because in our fast-paced, complex, highly technical world, people need to work together and share a common vision to produce high-quality work. Their relationships, therefore, are crucial. Indeed, these relationships are the glue that holds the enterprise together, connecting its strategy, structure, systems, and technology.

This couldn't be more different from the traditional workplace. The old glue was formal boundaries. Rules, hierarchy, walls, policies, and authority held the old organization together. The new glue is shared values, a common purpose, clear responsibilities, and the relationships between the adults who make up (indeed, who *are*) the organization.

Effective leaders know this, and so they pay careful attention to these relationships. They manage the "space" between their people, keeping it close enough for collaboration but not for complacency, wide enough for friendly competition but not for conflict.

This is a messy business. Humans aren't like technology or numbers. They feel things. They get jealous and angry. They retreat into disappointment. They swell up into overconfidence and arrogance. They play politics. They take drugs. They act thoughtlessly, and sometimes meanly. And they're always *changing.* Just when you think someone's okay, content and confident, suddenly she's not.

Of course, people also act nobly and generously, shoulder responsibility, show joy and satisfaction. They help each other, and they laugh together. And often their unpredictable changes are for the better. Just when you think you ought to can someone he pulls off a spectacular performance.

Yes, people are any organization's most valuable asset—but like divas and racehorses, people are very high-maintenance. They demand constant attention. Indeed, the everyday work of the leader is human interaction. Building on strong ethical principles, the leader partners with her employees. She shares power and lets others shine. She challenges people to stretch. In short, she recognizes that people have a deep drive for competence and achievement. People yearn for respect and want to feel good about themselves. They want to be full members of a team. They want to know what's going on, and to be surrounded by healthy relationships founded on honesty and reciprocal responsibilities. It is the leader's job to create an environment which will liberate the talents and energies lying dormant in people and tap their deep desire for excellence.

Of course, employees are not a leader's only concern. In business there are three fundamental values: a commitment to satisfying customers, a commitment to developing a mature and motivated workforce, and a commitment to earning excellent returns for stockholders or the public. Research shows that companies that focus on all three of these values outperform their competitors. Too narrow focus on employee satisfaction, for example, can be just as destructive as squeezing out short-term profits to satisfy stockholders.

Keepers of the big picture, leaders have to make sure that all the elements of the business are in synch. Just as a conductor must hear in his mind's ear how all the instruments should harmonize, a leader must visualize how all those with a stake in the organization—employees, customers, stockholders, and the community at large—should interact. It is the leader's job to balance and align people and systems in such a way that all will benefit.

This broad perspective stems from a profound business logic. AT&T, a company I work with, put it this way: If an enterprise invests in its human side—in values, respect, pay, learning—then it will reap a healthy productive workforce. This is People Value Added. That high-performance workforce will then delight the organization's customers with excellent service, high-quality products, and reputation capital. That's Customer Value Added. In turn, those satisfied customers will reward the company with profits—Economic Value Added. That allows the enterprise to reinvest in its people and keep the cycle going. It also allows the company to benefit the community at large with a stable vibrant workforce, as well as donations and volunteers. That's Society Value Added. The diagram below sums up this idea.

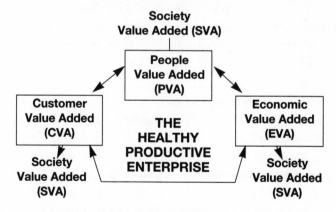

In the healthy, productive enterprise, leaders are always looking for their critical sources of competitive advantage, whether it be their financial capability, their marketing skills, or their state-of-the-art technologies. They know they must build an efficient infrastructure, reengineer their work processes, and continuously manage change.

But it's no accident that this cycle begins with an organization's people. A company's people are the prime movers, the first among equals, the leading indicators. Why? Because people operate the technology and machinery, manufacture the products, provide the services, interact with customers, make the sales, order the supplies, plan for the future, and hold the institutional memory. They are the asset that makes all other assets possible. People are the nerve center of the organizational body.

The best leaders see themselves as the Chief People Officers of their enterprise, and that's why they spend so much of their day leading people.

And the very best leaders, the kind of leaders we'll meet in this book, know that none of this happens without reinventing themselves and their organizations. Great leaders begin by looking inside themselves. They work to become comfortable with the whole range of human emotions, from happiness and joy to anger and jealousy and insecurity—for they know they will feel all those emotions themselves, and they will encounter them in others.

They search for the secret ways by which they sabotage their own efforts. They scrutinize their biases and prejudices. They acknowledge their blind spots: perhaps a narrow definition of success or an excessive competitiveness or a tendency to blame others. They know that the higher they climb the less supervision they receive and the more self-confidence they get—which puts them in danger of the pride that goeth before a fall. Instead, they pursue humility and maturity.

They seek out reality checks to counter isolation and arrogance, and to allow a constant flow of information. Enlightened pragmatists rather than ideologues, they constantly dart back and forth between the internal and the external, between their own minds and the outside world, challenging their ideas and beliefs. And always they look for ways to learn and grow, for they know that their own development—intellectually, emotionally, and spiritually—is their greatest leadership tool. Self-awareness allows them to gauge their effect on people, and to calibrate it to diverse individuals with diverse needs. It allows them to tap more effectively the spirit and creativity of their people, and to inspire high performance. And self-awareness leads to wisdom.

An all-embracing concept, wisdom includes character as well as intelligence, empathy as well as insight. It implies maturity, the importance of balance, and the necessity of trade-offs. It has depth—of understanding, of caring, of commitment. With abundant common sense, it recognizes the implacable limitations of the real world, such as money, time, and logistics. But it also knows that the key to transcending those limits—to making possible tomorrow what was impossible yesterday—lies in the unseen world of the human mind and heart.

Leading people is wisdom in action.

In this book, the individuals putting wisdom into action come from all walks of life, from all backgrounds and all regions of the country. Their fields of endeavor are just as diverse: they work in business, charity, music, the military, and religion. They espouse no single philosophy. But because the world is changing so fast, and because the old models of leadership don't work anymore, they all know they can't look to past practice as a guide to the future. So instead of looking backward, these leaders all look inward—to human values and psychological insight. These leaders are putting their faith (and their money) into creating organizations that nourish people and promote open, fair, adult relationships. And their healthy, high-performing organizations are living proof that this wisdom works.

THE EIGHT PRINCIPLES OF LEADING PEOPLE

In studying and working with these kinds of leaders, I've come to recognize eight principles that run through all their stories, eight strands that, when woven together, form wisdom in action. They are:

- **Vision.** Leaders see the whole picture and articulate that broad perspective with others. By doing so, leaders create a common purpose that mobilizes people and coordinates their efforts into a single, coherent, agile enterprise.
- **Trust.** Without trust, vision becomes an empty slogan. Trust binds people together, creating a strong, resilient organization. To build trust, leaders are predictable, and they share information and power. Their goal is a culture of candor.
- **Participation.** The energy of an organization is the participation and effort of its people. The leader's challenge is to un-

leash and focus this energy, inspiring people at every level of the enterprise to pitch in with their minds and hearts.

- **Learning.** Leaders need a deep understanding of themselves. They must know their strengths and shortcomings, which requires a lifelong process of discovery, and they must be able to adapt to new circumstances. So too with their organization. It must promote constant innovation, and the leaders must encourage their people to refresh their skills and renew their spirits.

- **Diversity.** Successful leaders know the power of diversity and the poison of prejudice. They understand their own biases, and they actively cultivate an appreciation of the positive aspects of people's differences. In their organizations, they insist on a culture of mutual respect.

- **Creativity.** In a world where smart solutions outpace excessive work, creativity is crucial. Leaders pay close attention to people's talents, leaning on their strengths and managing around their weaknesses. They encourage independent, challenging thinking, and they invest in technologies that facilitate the efforts of their people.

- **Integrity.** A leader must stand for something. As a public citizen and a private person, she knows what is important in life and acts by deep-seated principles. Every wise leader has a moral compass, a sense of right and wrong. Good leaders understand that good ethics is good business.

- **Community.** Community is mutual commitment, and it inspires the highest performance. It's human nature to go the extra mile for one's neighbors and fellow citizens, and a mature leader stresses the organization's responsibility to the surrounding society. A leader also acts as a steward of the natural environment.

As the chart below makes plain, these eight principles are the components of leading people. They are the DNA of wisdom at work.

This book devotes a chapter to each of these principles, illustrating them with profiles of four or five leaders who tell their own stories. Each leader exemplifies a special skill. When combined with the other leaders, you can see how they work together. A graphic describes this

in detail. Their tales bring the principles to life, showing how they work in specific real situations. Of course, none of the leaders in the book are one-dimensional. I tried to focus on an outstanding quality, but any of them could have exemplified several of the principles.

At the same time, no single leader was equally gifted in all the principles. Nobody could be. It is the composite of all these leaders, therefore, that provides a model for leading. No one I know has fully attained it, but the best leaders constantly strive for it, getting ever closer with age and learning and experience.

In the meantime, they compensate by team leadership. Knowing their shortcomings and dark sides, they manage around themselves by assembling a cadre of leaders with diverse talents and backgrounds and outlooks. And in the ultimate act of leadership, they create a culture of leading, nurturing at every level of the organization healthy, ethical, mature employee leaders. In short, the best leaders try not just to become wise themselves, but to institutionalize wisdom.

Leading People is written as a personal guide for leaders. Each person will experience the book in his or her own way. Some will read from cover to cover. Others will pick out chapters that reflect their own interests. Still others will use it as a reference as they deal with specific problems. You might want to sit down with a pad and pen and ask yourself some tough questions as you read. Do you like the people you are reading about? How does their story resonate with your own situation? What are you doing that is working and not working? And what can you do to change? I hope you enjoy getting to know these leaders as much as I have.

Do Healthy Enterprises Perform Better?

Yes, they do. An overwhelming amount of research indicates that organizations that incorporate many of the leading principles outlined in this book gain a definite advantage over companies that remain mired in the traditional ways of managing people. Here is a sample of these findings:

- An MIT study comparing automotive plants with similar technology found that plants with innovative work practices (including extensive training, work teams, pay for performance, and participative management) manufactured vehicles in an average of 22 hours with 0.5 defects per vehicle. Traditional plants took 30 hours with 0.8 defects per vehicle.[5]

- A 1993 survey of 700 publicly held firms from all major industries found that companies utilizing a greater number of innovative human-resource practices had higher annual shareholder returns from 1986 to 1991, and higher gross return on capital. The most "progressive" 25 percent of firms had an 11 percent rate of return on capital, more than twice as high as the remaining companies.[6]

- A 1993 report by the U.S. Department of Labor indicates that healthy management practices (open communications, teamwork, employee involvement, extensive training) are associated with increases in productivity and long-term financial performance. The study further found that these effects are most pronounced when they are implemented together.[7]

- A 1994 study examining *Fortune* magazine's annual survey on corporate reputations found that companies that were well respected for their employee practices also had excellent reputations for quality of products and the ability to innovate. These companies also scored highest on long-term corporate performance.[8]

- Firms listed in *The 100 Best Companies to Work for in America* in 1993 had higher total return (the sum of stock price appreciation and dividends paid) over the previous eight years than did the 3,000 largest companies in America. The difference was substantial: 19.5 percent for the 100 Best Companies compared to 12 percent for the others.[9]

- The Domini Social Index—comprised of 400 corporations with good records on employee relations, quality, community involvement, and the environment—has outperformed the Standard & Poor's Index since its inception in 1990, returning 70.11 percent while the S&P has gained 58.29 percent.[10]

- A survey of 150 Forbes 500 firms found that the most "progressive" firms (defined by participation, creativity, reward systems, flexibility, culture, and structure) fared considerably better than "nonprogressive" firms in profit growth, sales growth, earnings per share, and dividend growth.[11]

- Cooperative labor-management relations help company performance. One major study in a manufacturing industry found that innovative workplaces had 75 percent fewer worker hours lost to waste and scrap, 42 percent fewer defects per worker, and 17 percent higher labor productivity.[12]

- A 1994 review of studies on pay and compensation showed a strong connection between productivity and compensation linked to performance. The use of profit sharing was generally associated with 3.5–5 percent higher productivity. The increase for small and midsize firms topped 11 percent.[13]

- Americans favor socially responsible products and companies. A 1990 Roper poll found that over two thirds of Americans are concerned about a company's social performance and that 52 percent would pay up to 10 percent more for a brand made by a socially responsible company.[14]

- Firms with cultures emphasizing all the key stakeholders (customers, stockholders, and employees), and leadership at all levels, outperformed those that did not by a huge margin. Over an eleven-year period, revenue increased 682 percent for healthy enterprises, compared to 166 percent for unhealthy companies. Net income increased 756 percent versus 1 percent.[15]

THE EIGHT
PRINCIPLES OF
LEADING

Vision

Leadership is the art of creating a working climate that inspires others to achieve extraordinary goals and levels of performance.

GENERAL JOHN MICHAEL LOH, U.S. AIR FORCE

People are not inspired by a higher net margin. They are not inspired by increased market share. And they are not inspired—at least not for very long—by a bigger paycheck. None of these things will cause them to achieve extraordinary goals or superior levels of performance.

Something to believe in will.

A leader's first job is to articulate a clear, compelling vision for his organization. What does this enterprise stand for? What does it believe in? And where is it going? The best leaders know that a vision with a single voice never amounts to much. So they share the vision across the organization, enlisting the input and participation of all employees. By letting everyone shape the vision, the leader inspires people and builds commitment.

Everyone in the organization needs to believe in the vision. It can't be vague, and it can't be simple to achieve. Not only must the vision inspire people, it must stretch them as well. It is the guiding light that leads the organization forward.

Every leader develops his own vision, based on who he is and where he wants to take his organization. Although it's impossible to predict exactly where the vision will lead, the leader must be absolutely clear in his own mind about what he believes, because his purpose and principles will comprise the foundation on which everything in the organization will be built.

The leader's vision is the organization's blueprint. It's the mental picture of the possible, of a better future. It shows how a local savings-and-loan can become a world-class bank, how a small not-for-profit health clinic can become known for providing state-of-the-art medical care, or how a large manufacturing company can become the envy of its competitors, both here and overseas. The vision must clarify direction, instill a sense of common purpose, and clearly present what the organization should strive to become.

But a vision is only as good as its execution. That's why leaders must always be thinking about outcomes, and results, and about what it will take to translate the vision into reality. The benefits of outcome thinking are clear. It increases speed, efficiency, and effectiveness of action. It makes the organization's mission easier to understand, and becomes a rallying point for mobilizing the workforce.

Having articulated a mission for the organization, it is vital to keep the organization moving forward. Making that happen means institutionalizing the vision inside the organization. That's also the leader's job. He must become the champion of the organization's vision and values to ensure they take hold. Only then will people be active partners in the enterprise, working together to establish a standard of excellence.

The leaders you are about to meet do an excellent job at that.

James DePreist, the conductor of the Oregon Symphony, begins by painting the whole picture. He lays out his vision in a way that people can rally around.

After explaining the vision, the leader needs to enlist the support and cooperation of the whole organization in order to turn that vision into a reality. Creating a common purpose is critical to success. Bill Pollard of ServiceMaster is a master at it. His values, principles, and beliefs provide the foundation for his company's common purpose.

Terry Larsen, chairman of CoreStates Bank, understands that

one of the leader's toughest jobs is to navigate the organization through chaos and unpredictability. A solid vision keeps people pulling in the same direction. If everyone knows what the organization is trying to accomplish, it makes the road from here to there less treacherous.

To ensure that this effort creates results, the leader must get her employees to focus on outcomes. This is the specialty of Anne L. Bryant, the executive director of the American Association of University Women. Bryant helps her employees imagine the doable and create results.

This new way of doing business needs to become a way of life, in which the policies, systems, rewards, and measurements all support the new operating style. There is no one better at doing this than General Mike Loh. He links his vision to performance measures, which he monitors constantly to ensure that the vision is becoming a reality.

If you were to follow the examples of these five leaders, the result would be an organization in which employees understand the business, understand where they fit, and understand their leader's sense of urgency. People would focus on their work and on achieving results. They would stay flexible, and adapt easily to the inevitable changes that occur. In a high-performance organization, people perform to the best of their abilities and get excited about the opportunity to measure the results of their work.

Leaders who pursue the principle of vision lay the foundation for building a high-performance company.

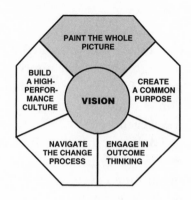

PAINTING THE
WHOLE PICTURE

Leaders see the whole organization, thanks to their singular vantage point.

Successful leaders make the whole greater than the sum of its parts. They take charge of the organization and feel a sense of obligation and responsibility for making things happen. This can only occur if the leader has a mental image of the ideal organization he wants to create.

To come close to the ideal, he must share his vision with others, enlist their ideas and support, and help people see where they fit in.

Leaders must celebrate—and balance—the diverse voices within their organization. The voices must blend; otherwise there is just noise. Creating this harmony is the challenge of any leader.

When James DePreist arrived in Portland, after serving as a guest conductor for orchestras throughout the world, he found a provincial ensemble. The Oregon Symphony played a limited number of concerts a year in a crumbling facility, and the musicians needed outside jobs.

Confronted with this situation, DePreist could have said, "I am a maestro; money-raising concerns are beneath me." But instead he took the symphony out into the community, to raise its profile. The orchestra played in parks, county fairs, colleges, and even shopping centers. DePreist lobbied the city and state for a new facility, and he and his wife went out into the community and sold "Symphony Shares," certificates of "ownership" for contributions of any kind. By "sharing" the symphony, DePreist was able to touch people with his

---

JAMES DePREIST
Oregon Symphony Orchestra

TITLE: Conductor and Music Director

AGE: 58

FAMILY SITUATION: Married

EDUCATION: B.S. and M.A. from the University of Pennsylvania

HISTORY: Born in Philadelphia, 1936; studied composition with Vincent Persichetti at the Philadelphia Conservatory; European debut with the Rotterdam Philharmonic (1969); Associate Conductor, National Symphony Orchestra (1971); Music Director and Conductor, Quebec Symphony (1976); Music Director and Conductor of the Oregon Symphony (1980); Music Director, Monte Carlo Philharmonic (1994)

HEADQUARTERS: Portland, Oregon

NUMBER OF FULL-TIME MUSICIANS: 86

NUMBER OF SEATS: 2,776; Arlene Schnitzer Concert Hall

APPROXIMATE TOTAL ATTENDANCE PER YEAR: 300,000+

BUDGET SIZE: $8.4 million

FACTS: First and oldest orchestra in the West, founded in 1896

HOBBIES: Writes poetry; published two books, *This Precipice Garden* and *A Distant Siren*

---

music, and eliminate artificial barriers of snobbism. His vision of the whole included the entire community.

Today, the orchestra rehearses and performs in a new concert hall, musicians' salaries have more than doubled, and the symphony is one of the first things that residents rave about, when you ask them about their state.

How was DePreist able to accomplish this, and in the process turn what was once a small regional orchestra into one that is recognized around the world? The answer has a lot to do with the man himself, his ability to paint the whole picture, and the environment he creates to make fulfilling his vision a reality.

Let's start with the man.

He's tall, six feet three, and sounds a little like James Earl Jones, the actor who supplied Darth Vader's voice in *Star Wars*. Although both his size and his voice can be intimidating, almost everyone calls him Jimmy. "It's possible to be open, to be accessible, to be informal, without losing authority," DePreist explains.

But what is more striking than his authenticity is his optimism. There is little that DePreist can't imagine either himself, or his employees, accomplishing.

This approach to work is a direct result of his upbringing and life experiences. DePreist was raised in a musical Philadelphia household. Growing up, he saw what his aunt, Marian Anderson, the first African American to sing with the Metropolitan Opera, was able to accomplish. And he saw the obstacles she had to overcome when she was forced to sing on the steps of the Lincoln Memorial after being denied the chance to perform in Constitution Hall.

That belief in what is possible was reinforced by DePreist's successful battle to overcome polio. The battle was a difficult one, and not surprisingly, DePreist put off accepting the fact that he had polio for as long as possible. He contracted the disease while on a goodwill tour for the State Department in the 1960s, shortly after he had finished college. Rather than returning home in triumph, as he had imagined, DePreist found himself on a military cargo plane headed for Clark Air Force base in the Philippines.

"On the plane directly in front of me is a young marine on a stretcher," DePreist recalls. "The marine had a stomach wound, and I remember thinking, 'I'm glad I'm not in his shoes.' We ended up sharing a room at Travis Air Force Base in California.

"Suddenly, I heard water running in the bathroom. I knew without looking it was the marine. So, I told this corpsman, who was taking my history, to see what was going on. He found this guy on the floor, just about dead. He was so thirsty that he took a drink, even though he knew he shouldn't have.

"The next day, the marine is lying in bed, and he says the nurse told him that I had saved his life," DePreist continues. "He asked me to come over, so he could shake my hand. That was the first time I ever had to admit to anyone that I couldn't walk."

DePreist had always held himself to the highest standards, and overcoming polio would be no different. But this time he had to be more generous with himself. He had to accept his limitations, acknowledge reality, and still maintain his faith in what was possible. The gap between the ideal of walking and his current situation was crystal clear. Today, DePreist has regained some use of his legs, walks proudly with crutches, but conducts the orchestra sitting down, because he finds it less stressful.

But while he has come to grips with his physical limitations, he still does not give himself much slack. After he recovered, DePreist served as Leonard Bernstein's assistant in the early 1960s. In writing a glowing letter of recommendation for DePreist in 1965, Bernstein equated DePreist's being black and having polio as equal afflictions. "I saw Lennie the next day, and I said thank you so much for your letter," DePreist recalls. "But could you take out the businesses about polio and being a Negro, I don't want either one to be a reason for people to engage me." Bernstein made the changes.

As a result of the life he's led, DePreist believes "things can be better than they are, and individuals can make that happen." Yet, despite this idealism, DePreist is a realist, living and working in the gap between his ideals and his current reality. He has a deep appreciation for the humanness of life, the fragility and courage of people. His own generosity of spirit enables him to give the people who work for him the benefit of the doubt.

"It's counterintuitive that an inept soloist would be playing for a world-class orchestra. So when a conductor has reservations about [a musician's] performance, it's probably because he is not having a good day, is nervous, or there are other mitigating factors. One might view that as indulgence, or being overly tolerant. But my feeling is if the person can be helped through the problem—and there are limits—then the end result can be glorious."

Clearly, DePreist feels his job as a leader is to create an atmosphere in which people can give their best. This allows great visions to become reality. But even with all the respect DePreist gives to his employees, he is not afraid of the power of leadership. He believes the leader needs to exert "power with compassion," because of the effect he can have on the people who work for him.

"You're making decisions that impact people's lives," DePreist says. "They impact their monetary future, their psychological well-being, their families, as well as their performances. One has to be really circumspect, because an idle word, an ill-chosen word or gesture, carries the cumulative effect of all the baggage they see the leader possessing. So one tries to be conscious of the impact of the position, never being cavalier, never being thoughtless. And if by some accident you forget to acknowledge a person's contribution, or just forget something that could be interpreted as a slight, it's very important to make clear to everyone that it was unintentional, and you accept responsibility for it. You must do that and not assume that the person will get over it."

Because he understands the power a leader has, and because he has his generosity of spirit, DePreist takes great pains to see that his employees succeed.

"I think it is the function of a leader to create an atmosphere in which individuals want to give their best," DePreist says. "If I see that is not being produced, I'll ask if there's any way in which I can be helpful in bringing from them, or having them produce for us, the kinds of results I believe they are capable of."

This approach, as he is quick to point out, has "a dual function." "It identifies me as being on the side of the best that is within them. It might enable them to see something they might not have seen, in terms of their capacity to reach a higher level. But it also stops them—if in the final analysis I have misjudged their abilities—from saying they could have developed the necessary skill, or they could have reached the goal, had they been presented with the challenge in a less confrontational, or less threatening way." In short, it prevents employees from taking advantage of the leader's goodwill, or blaming the leader for their own shortcomings.

Since he is thoughtful and compassionate, DePreist has earned the right to be angry and direct. "Every opportunity is given for the person to flower and develop," he adds. "If they don't, then I feel very, very confident in making a decision that may lead to their termination from the organization."

Notice the relationship that DePreist has established. In exchange for doing everything in his power to create the right environment, he makes demands. Employees must perform and they must make their individual talents blend in with, and support, the goals of the organization.

CREATING A SHARED VISION

When James DePreist is on the podium, he has a mental picture of the ideal performance. He "hears" in his mind exactly what the music should sound like, whether he is conducting Beethoven or a concert for children. Through sharing his vision, soliciting cooperation and participation—from both his musicians and the community— and creating an atmosphere that brings out the best in people, DePreist creates a very special performance.

How does running an orchestra relate to running a business? Perhaps surprisingly, the organizations are similar. Not only does DePreist have financial responsibilities to manage within a budget, he has the same problems of any business person. In a traditional company, sales must talk to marketing; in the symphony violas and violins must work together. Both corporations and symphonies must delight customers. And while they are not typically thought of this way, musicians—even symphony musicians—are employees who look to the leader for direction. DePreist supplies that direction. For him, creating a shared vision involves a four-part process.

First, he must have a vision and paint a picture of the possible. He must know what he, as leader, wants to accomplish. He has to have the whole picture in mind at all times.

Second, DePreist must communicate his vision to everyone involved, and do it in a way that inspires people and builds commitment to his goal. As people share in the plan it evolves from "my vision" to "our vision."

Third, his job is to enable those independent, distinct voices within his organization to be heard, and to weave them together into a collective whole that is bigger than the sum of its parts.

And finally, he must create an environment that allows his vision to become a reality. That takes us full circle, so it is best to start with DePreist's vision.

"This is not a free-for-all," DePreist says, talking about the orchestra. "In any kind of interplay there are rules, either implicit or explicit, and the rules within the symphony orchestra are clear. There is one person who is in charge, and that person is the musical director. In charge of what? In charge of the artistic vision, and in charge of fulfilling that vision by putting together all the separate parts."

What makes DePreist unique is that he is constantly comparing the ideal performance in his head with the actual performance of his orchestra. "This is going on simultaneously, and you're changing the idealized performance based upon the feedback that you're getting from the orchestra. Where is it falling short? Where is it exceeding expectations?"

"The musicians come with their individual parts; they are not reading from the scores," DePreist says. "I'm the only person using a score, seeing how all the parts go together."

But how can a leader get disparate people with disparate talents to blend as one? And how does he weave each person's individual vision into a collective one that everyone can get excited about? For DePreist, this tricky task is accomplished in two steps. He explains his vision, outlining what he is trying to accomplish with a particular piece of music. Next, he explains to individuals where they fit into the vision. By providing this focus he can align the energies of his diverse musicians. He knows each person must own and personalize the vision. They all must understand where DePreist is going and they must see exactly where they can contribute. Having done all this he then asks for the musicians' finest performance.

"There are many conductors who have been known for imposing a performance. They say this is the way it shall be, because I am telling you this is the way it should be," he says. "I would rather make manifest the direction in which we're going, and solicit willing cooperation. Musicians want certitude, and some kind of vision, so you have to provide that. But they are making the music. A conductor without an orchestra is much like Marcel Marceau on radio.

"It is essential that they feel they are producing the music, which in fact they are," he adds. "They are producing the work. They are producing the sound. The initial vision is mine, but we are doing the interpretation together."

Instruments are like people; each is unique and each comes with its own ego and insecurities. In the orchestra, violins are seen as the orchestra's elite, woodwinds as disadvanged, and cellos, everyone agrees, come to the job with chips on their shoulder. The goal is to blend their unique perspectives into a shared vision. To create this vision, DePreist points out how the results can be extraordinary if everyone does his job well. The musicians, DePreist says, will be able to leverage not only their own talents, but also those of their colleagues. In the process, they turn DePreist's vision into "our vision."

Everyone is urged to express himself, within the context of the vision. Shared vision helps unify the organization. Suddenly a hundred large egos can be pulling in the same direction, and the result is a deeper, richer performance. As a result of this approach, the interests of the individual—and of the organization—are brought into complete alignment. The musicians get a chance to be the best they possibly can be, in the context of helping to fulfill the organization's goals. DePreist's vision, which is the integrating force, propels the organization to a higher level.

DePreist understands people need a vision to be inspired by. That vision must be focused on the future, but rooted in reality. It needs to be perceived as achievable, challenging, and inspirational. It must come from the heart, as well as the head.

As Jimmy DePreist knows, the leader's job is to celebrate the independent, unique voices of his employees and weave them together into a collective vision that is bigger than any one of them. That is exactly what he has done with the Oregon Symphony for the last fifteen years.

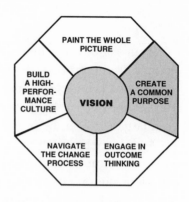

CREATING A
COMMON PURPOSE

Every organization needs a North Star, a purpose to believe in, something that inspires and stretches the workforce.

A common purpose incorporates the organization's traditions and memories. It gives the organization stability, a foundation, and a reason for being. It helps employees focus their efforts, resolves tensions, and provides a purpose for their work. It lets people know where the company wants to go and how it wants to get there. It is a road map.

All of this starts with the personal purpose of the leader. He knows what he believes in and what kind of person he wants to be. His principles and beliefs provide the foundation for the company's common purpose. When people become part of something greater than themselves, amazing things can happen.

Service, not surprisingly, is what ServiceMaster is all about. From Terminix, which controls pests, to Merry Maids, which provides residential maid service, to TruGreen, provider of lawn care, or any other of its divisions that offer cleaning or maintenance to companies and residences around the world, all of ServiceMaster's employees are in the business of serving people.

Given this, it's not surprising that Bill Pollard, chairman of ServiceMaster, talks a lot about what it means to serve.

"I believe that you can't really serve unless you are humble, and I don't think you can be humble unless you are successful," Pollard says. "That's why it's so important for us to recognize people when they've done a good job, so they in turn can serve others."

C. WILLIAM POLLARD
The ServiceMaster Company

TITLE: Chairman

FAMILY SITUATION: Married; 4 children; 8 grandchildren

EDUCATION: Graduate of Wheaton College; J.D., Northwestern University of Law

HISTORY: Practiced law (1963–72); Vice President of Wheaton College (1972–77); joined ServiceMaster (1977); Chief Executive Officer (1983–93)

HEADQUARTERS: Downers Grove, Illinois

BUSINESS: Provider of supportive management services to approximately 1,300 health-care facilities and 500 educational institutions, and provider of a variety of consumer services to over 4.9 million home owners

NUMBER OF COMPANY-OWNED AND FRANCHISED BRANCHES: 5,700

NUMBER OF DIRECT EMPLOYEES: 34,000

CUSTOMER LEVEL REVENUE: $4.2 billion (1994)

PROFIT: $140 million

HONORS: Recognized by *Fortune* magazine over the past 10 years as the #1 service company among the Fortune 500

But how do you create a culture of service in which everybody lives by the same principles? The leader can write down a credo, but if he doesn't follow it, nothing much will happen. People spend an awful lot of time watching what the boss does, and if he doesn't walk the talk there is no way that his credo will take hold.

ServiceMaster's company purpose is reinforced by the personal purpose of its leader, Bill Pollard. "The leader must be prepared to serve. He must be willing to do what he asks others to do. To listen and to learn before he talks. To be a giver, not a taker. To be a role model."

How does he do that? In part, Pollard draws on what he learned from his predecessors. He keeps their pictures, along with those of their wives, displayed on the company walls.

"But frankly the starting point for me is God," says Pollard. "I ac-

cept a basic truth that every individual has been created in God's image and has dignity and worth, regardless of position, intelligence,
sex, religion, race, or education. As a result, I believe it is wrong for
someone to secure a benefit at the expense of another, and it is fun-
damentally right to serve and help another." These concepts are
summed up in ServiceMaster's company credo "We serve." You see
that phrase everywhere inside the company.

This belief in service is the foundation for building the common
purpose. From there, Pollard and his senior managers work hard to
see that those beliefs are institutionalized. They want to ensure that
the corporate purpose becomes the foundation out of which everything else grows—strategies, product lines, policies, plans, practices,
and promotions.

To make sure that the members of the executive team themselves
had internalized these values, Pollard took them on a retreat, where
one of the exercises was for every manager to create a collage of
magazine pictures depicting himself. Those pictures were then
placed in a company mosaic. The mosaic was deliberately too small
to accommodate all the collages, so, after they had completed their
artwork, each executive figuratively had to cut off pieces of himself
to make everyone fit. The exercise was designed to make two simple
points: everyone has a special gift to offer, and everyone must make
sacrifices to serve the common good.

Inside the company the concept of service is stressed in many different ways. During "We Serve Day," everyone spends a full day delivering one of the company's services. "It doesn't matter if you're an
officer, a computer operator, or a secretary, you are going to spend
one full day out in the field," Pollard says. "You can choose the day,
and what you are going to do, but it's part of your job."

There are a couple of benefits that flow from this approach. Not
only do employees get to serve, they discover why the company does
business in a certain way. For example, when Pollard spent a day
working for Terminix, he was surprised to discover that the extermi-
nators would go from a private residence to an office to a restaurant,
instead of concentrating on just homes or businesses.

"We do this, I found out, so that people see pests occasionally.
Most offices are clean, and if all you did was go around spraying

places where there were no bugs, after a while you would get to wondering if your work had meaning."

In a company founded on purpose, knowing your work has meaning is important. So are symbols, because they tangibly illustrate
what the company stands for.

At ServiceMaster, office walls are glass—to underscore the need
for open communication—and tables in many conference rooms
are round—so that there is no head of the table. But the most important symbols pertain to the service workers, who are held up as
examples. In the lobby of ServiceMaster's headquarters is a six-by-
four-foot mural, composed of twenty-four fluorescent panels showing real ServiceMaster employees going about their jobs. It is this
powerful image of its employees that is featured most prominently,
not a chart showing the performance of the company's stock, or a
picture of the board of directors.

And just as it's obvious who the company believes is most important, it is equally obvious what the company believes. Underscoring
their permanence, the company's values are literally carved in stone.
On a marble slab in the lobby you can read the company's objectives:

- To honor God in all we do.
- To help people develop.
- To pursue excellence.
- To grow profitably.

The company has all these symbols here for a reason. Pollard believes that searching for purpose is part of human nature, that people want meaning in their work. They want to identify with their
company and understand what it stands for, and how they, and their
jobs, fit in. He knows employees want to be part of something
greater than themselves.

Companies change overnight. Leaders come and go. But what
ServiceMaster believes is permanent. That is why its values are
carved in stone.

"Our objectives are not there to hang on the wall and be wor-
shiped," Pollard says. "They've got to be implemented. And there is
often a tension between them. You don't have the option of saying,

I'm going to honor God, and I don't care about making money. And you can't say, I'm going to make money, and I don't care about developing people. You have to fit all those things into what you are doing. And if they don't fit, you better stop, because the decision you are about to make is probably not right."

If the systems and relationships within the organization undermine or conflict with its purpose, people become disillusioned and unhappy. But if the purpose gets woven into the fabric of the company, then it can shine a guiding light.

"I'll give you an example," Pollard says. "I got a phone call from a manager who was running the maintenance department at a hospital. It turned out his boss, who was our employee as well, was padding the payroll. He had created three fictitious people and was pocketing their checks. The boss told the manager not to say anything, but he just couldn't live in that environment. He went home all frustrated. He called me, and we took care of it. This is a fantastic audit system."

FINDING AND DEVELOPING THE RIGHT PEOPLE

One of the great challenges for a company like ServiceMaster is to find and develop the right people, who will live by the common purpose.

Today's workforce is diverse. People come from different backgrounds and beliefs. Says Pollard, "You've got to take all the differences that people bring to the job, and get them to work together. We have found that when you give people a mission and purpose that goes beyond money, they buy into it, are excited by it, and are willing to participate. Take, for example, the housekeeper cleaning a patient's room. Her work must go beyond cleaning the floor, and actually touch patient care. She must become part of the wellness program that's going on inside the institution."

But there is a fine line between believing and forcing your beliefs on others. Pollard warns, "People will either say, 'I want to be part of this,' or they will reject it. We are creatures of choice. We're not dealing with robots." Pollard, and his senior managers, work hard to be inclusive, not exclusive. But in doing so they set limits. As a result, not everyone is welcome at ServiceMaster. At a senior-management meeting recently, Pollard showed a video of different types of people applying for jobs, to underscore that point.

"In the video we presented someone who came to us saying, 'I'd like to work for you, but I have a problem. I can't tell the truth. I mean I just lie regularly. I'm a different kind of person, I certainly fit under the concept of diversity. I just lie.'

"I asked our managers if that kind of person fits," Pollard recalls. "We concluded he didn't."

"On the other hand, we talked about a woman who said, 'My sexual preference is that I'm a lesbian, and I want to work at ServiceMaster,' " Pollard continues.

"Is she going to be allowed in ServiceMaster? Do we have to wait for a law to be passed for her to work here? After talking about it, we concluded that she can contribute provided her purpose is to perform, not promote her difference. She is part of God's mix.

"We had another person on the video say, 'I want to come and work at ServiceMaster, but I really don't like serving.' That person doesn't fit in, that's our ruling. So there are boundary limitations to our inclusive environment."

Not everyone will accept the company's purpose and values, and that's fine, says Pollard. For people that don't, ServiceMaster is not the right place, and both the company and they should know that. There is a responsibility on both sides to create a shared purpose. Leaders can't do it alone. Employees must also make an effort to tie their personal skills and desires to the company's objectives.

"Our values force people to think," Pollard says. "When somebody applies to work for us, and sees what we believe, he has to think about whether this is the right place for him, and whether he is comfortable with our values. If he is, he has to think about how he is going to implement them. I don't think you can run a good business today without thinking people."

So when it comes to building a common purpose, hiring the right people is the most important business decision a company can make. Pollard is fond of quoting Peter Drucker on the point. Drucker defines management as "getting the right thing done through others." And you won't get the right things done if you hire the wrong people. Still, most companies spend far too little time identifying the kind of people they want inside their company. They don't invest sufficient time determining the full range of skills—technical, interpersonal, character traits—they want in a new employee.

To ensure that his company doesn't fall into this trap, Pollard insists that several ServiceMaster employees interview every potential hire. This idea is part of the company's devotion to personal development. For ServiceMaster, developing people and unleashing their potential to fulfill themselves—and the corporate mission—is key to the company's success.

"Our real business is developing people," Pollard says. "We are in the service business, and you can't deliver service without people, and you can't deliver quality service without trained, motivated people. The task before us is to train, motivate, and develop people so that they will be more productive in their work, and—yes—even be better people.

"Our philosophy is that everybody is a teacher/learner, so if a manager is too busy to teach, he is probably too busy to work here. People work for a cause, not a living, and if a person hasn't caught the fun and enjoyment of seeing somebody develop and grow as part of our investment in her, and if she doesn't get some kind of intangible reward out of that, well, then it's awfully hard to incent her. Another five percent in the paycheck is not going to do it."

As employees grow, they also develop skills that can help offset the deficiencies of their colleagues. "We all have strengths and weaknesses, and when the firm is operating correctly, my weaknesses are covered by someone else's strengths, just like shingles on a roof," says Pollard. "But for this to work, it requires an openness and honesty on my part to recognize that I have certain strengths here, but I don't have strengths over there."

The concept is present in everything ServiceMaster does, including picking Pollard's successor, Carlos Cantu, who had been president and CEO of ServiceMaster's consumer service unit. "He has great strengths on the operational side of the business, far greater than I do," says Pollard. "We are going to need that as we add more and more businesses." And so when it came time for Pollard to pick a successor, he looked for someone whose skills offset his own. The purpose was so well understood in the company that when Pollard announced his selection, ServiceMaster's senior executives stood up and cheered.

By every standard, Pollard has been successful at his job. Employee satisfaction is high, turnover low, and *Fortune* magazine consistently names ServiceMaster one of the stars of its Service 500.

By making a personal commitment to ServiceMaster's common purpose, and by communicating that mission and modeling it every day in what he says and does, Pollard has become the champion of the purpose. As a result, the company's four principles have become the touchstone for employees. By accepting those principles, and acting upon them, the employee becomes part of something greater than himself. Helping employees achieve that state, Pollard will tell you, is the true job of a leader.

SERVICEMASTER'S LEADERSHIP PRINCIPLES

1. We are opportunity seekers, not entitlement takers. We create and earn and cannot afford to sit and inherit.
2. We are value driven and performance oriented.
3. We eat our own cooking. We bet the egg money on our own performance.
4. We train and run for both the sprint and marathon. We rest, have fun, never quit, and always seek to learn.
5. We plan for succession and develop our future leaders.
6. The truth of what we say is told by what we do. "If you don't live it, you don't believe it."
7. If we cannot serve and sell with a passion for excellence, we cannot lead.
8. We believe in what we sell and deliver.
9. As we provide extraordinary service, we bring value-added to the customer that cannot be duplicated.
10. There are no friendly competitors.
11. We believe in a lean and disciplined organization.
12. We pay based on performance and promote based on potential, not belief, tenure, gender, race, or friendships.
13. Those who produce the profits should share in the profits. Those who produce more should share more.
14. We make and beat budgets.
15. We seek to know and increase our market share so that we can grow and increase the profitability and value of our business.
16. When we are wrong or fail, we admit it. Truth cannot be compromised.
17. We promote others, not ourselves. We shoot against par.
18. We must have a spirit of independence without the malady of autonomy.
19. The customer comes first and should be our friend.
20. We are all prisoners of our hope. It is our hope that sustains us, and it is our vision for what could be that inspires us.
21. We have all been created in God's image and the results of our leadership will be measured beyond the workplace. The story will be told in the changed lives of people.

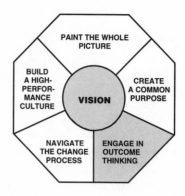

ENGAGING IN
OUTCOME THINKING

There are two aspects of vision. In part one, the leader stands before her people and paints a picture of the possible. But if she stops there, nothing will ever be accomplished.

The second part of vision is just as important as the first. Here the leader focuses on outcomes, on the execution of the vision. She imagines and implements the doable, and creates results.

The benefits of outcome thinking are clear. It increases speed, efficiency, and effectiveness of action. It makes the organization's mission easy to understand and becomes a rallying point—for both leaders and followers.

A true leader is a master of outcome thinking. She focuses attention—hers, her employees', and her organization's—on what needs to be done in order to accomplish the task at hand.

Anne Bryant began applying outcome thinking to the American Association of University Women (AAUW) even before she became part of the organization. She started when she was interviewing for the job of executive director of the organization, which promotes education and equity for women and girls. The organization, which is based in Washington and has assets of over $80 million, was having problems. Although it had a membership of over 100,000 college and university women graduates, and local chapters in 1,700 communities, the situation was deteriorating. Membership was falling, and the mission was not clear.

"I remember at one of the first meetings I attended, a board

ANNE L. BRYANT
The American Association of University Women

TITLE: Executive Director

AGE: 46

FAMILY SITUATION: Married; 2 stepchildren

EDUCATION: Ed.D., University of Massachusetts; B.A., Simmons College

HISTORY: Vice President of P. M. Haeger and Associates (1978–86); Director, National Association of Bank Women Educational Foundation (1974–78)

OTHER ACTIVITIES: Board Member: Education Commission of the States, Simmons College, The Washington Center, and the United Nations Association of the USA; Board Chair, National Association for Women and Girls in Education; Vice Chair, Independent Sector

HONORS AND SPECIAL ACCOMPLISHMENTS: Fellow, American Society of Association Executives (1987); ASAE's Key Award (1992); Who's Who in America (1988–89); University of Massachusetts Alumnae Achievement Award

HEADQUARTERS: Washington, D.C.

BUSINESS: Association devoted to advancing education and equity for women and girls

NUMBER OF EMPLOYEES: 105   NUMBER OF MEMBERS: 150,000

TOTAL BUDGET: $14.6 million (1994–95)   TOTAL ASSETS: $80.4 million (1993)

---

member brought in a very pretty colored membership kit that she had made at home. She presented it as an example of the kind of membership tools we needed to give to attract new members. I thought I was going to croak. I said to myself, We have big problems here.

"But then I thought about it for a moment and said the real issue isn't the member's home-made kit, which is not exactly a twentieth-century recruiting tool. The real issue is that we have a staff problem. This woman had created the kit because she didn't see the staff doing it. The organization had all this friction between members and staff because no one knew who was supposed to be doing what."

And so figuring out the day-to-day mechanics of running the organization, along with determining a clear, coherent mission for the AAUW, became the subject of Bryant's focus even before she got the job. When Bryant arrived at the AAUW, she immediately began meeting with her board and staff—one on one, in small groups, and on retreats—to start determining what needed to be done.

"We began by saying we cannot afford to be all things to all people," Bryant recalls. "Besides, nobody knew who we were anyway. When we did research, people said, 'The AAUW is a good organization, but I'm not sure what it does.' " Part of the reason was that each year by charter the organization was required to adopt a new issue to support. One year it might be women in the workplace, and the next making sure women's work was valued, and the year after that it would change again.

Bryant worked with her board to clarify what the AAUW should be.

"We began by focusing on four areas: leadership, valuing women's work, education, and equity." Bryant says. "A year later we said we are going to drop valuing women's work, because it was too amorphous a concept. Then we eliminated leadership, since it is part of what we have to do to accomplish the mission. That left our mission as education and equity issues."

And so the AAUW had a focus. The organization, as its new slogan said, would take the lead in "promoting education and equity for women and girls." With a clear mission and focused strategy, the AAUW was positioned to create exceptional results. Bryant's next task was to find projects that would achieve the organization's goals and rally its members.

Bryant knew the AAUW needed to represent a specific image in the marketplace, one that its employees and members (who are also its customers) could support. A unifying mission is critical to an organization of over 100,000 people spread throughout the country.

Bryant, together with her volunteer leaders, commissioned a national assessment of how well girls were being served by schools. This was the issue that both the staff and members would rally around. This was the thing the AAUW would focus upon. This was the product of outcome thinking. The organization was beginning to reflect the personality of its executive director and her team of outcome thinkers.

How did Bryant know this was the right project? Because every time a new issue or opportunity comes up, Bryant asks four specific questions. The questions are designed to make sure the AAUW stays focused on its mission.

- *Is this needed?* Will it improve the lives of girls and women?
- *Is it credible?* If you were to say that the AAUW is about to undertake this issue, would people say, "What?" or "Of course."
- *Do the members/customers want it?* In a not-for-profit organization, if you're not doing what the members are interested in, you are going to find yourself not supported.
- *What can we uniquely contribute?* In our case, it is a combination of being about women and equity issues, and a strong history and interest in education.

Says Bryant: "Every time I think about how to accomplish a goal or fulfill our mission, I go back to these four issues: need, credibility, unique contribution, and member interest, and it clears away the clutter. It clarifies what we should do, and what we shouldn't."

Another way Bryant determines what the organization should be doing is to fantasize about the outcomes she wants. "This helps me, because usually one's fantasies or dreams are a lot more exciting than reality," she says. "It helps to generate within my own head excitement about what I am doing.

"If you envision the President of the United States calling up and saying we're going to do a major education conference, and we just can't have it without the AAUW's being there, that is a fantasy. However, if you think about what it would take for that fantasy to become real, you realize that you have to be a policy player, you would have to have lots of influence in Congress on education. So by allowing your mind to drift toward the crazy idea of the President calling you up and begging you to come to a conference, you can actually start to do some creative thinking about what would have to happen to get you there."

This approach to business allows Bryant to take decisive action on emerging opportunities. Becoming part of a highly visible national education conference served as a real-life case in point.

The timing could not have been better. Bryant wanted to let the world know what the new AAUW stood for, and the conference was the perfect chance to do that. Simply talking about how the organization's mission had changed wouldn't attract much attention. What was needed was a newsworthy project that could be unveiled at the event. A team of staff, volunteers, and consultants came up with an idea: a nationwide poll on girls and their self-esteem.

The poll satisfactorily answered Bryant's four questions about outcome thinking. It was needed. No one had done it. It was credible for the AAUW to do it, and the AAUW had a unique contribution to make, given the new focus of the organization.

But for the AAUW to achieve national visibility, there were obstacles to be overcome. First, the AAUW needed major educational and girls' organizations at the conference. Bryant worked doggedly behind the scenes, to make sure their views would be valued. They would know what was in the report, and would be able to comment on it at the press conference. But, while their views would be represented, the AAUW's poll would be the focus of the media event. And that's exactly what happened.

One year later, the AAUW held a second national conference, this time based on a major research report. But this time the obstacle proved to be as tough as it was unexpected. On the very day that the AAUW expected to be thrust back into the limelight, the power failed at the Washington hotel where the conference was to be held. At 3 A.M., Bryant and her staff learned they needed to find another facility, arrange for buses to transport people from the first hotel to the second, and alert both participants and a hundred reporters that the venue had changed. There had never been a clearer example of the need for outcome thinking.

Bryant and her staff mastered the logistical nightmare, and the conference went off without a hitch. A packed room of press and education leaders learned about *The AAUW Report: How Schools Shortchange Girls*. The report documented how girls were being cheated in learning science and math, and in pursuing careers in fields such as engineering, in which those skills were key.

"The beauty of outcome thinking," says Bryant, "is that it enables you to create the result you want." More than anything else, that report raised the profile of the organization.

SHARING THE LEADERSHIP

Like so many leaders, Bryant's biggest challenge was to get her people to follow her lead. In her case, it meant she needed them to engage in outcome thinking. Clearly focusing on what the organization should become was a good beginning, but for Bryant to optimize her impact, she needed to share her perspective with the entire association.

The leader must distinguish between what she can do alone and what she can enable others to do. The best way to leverage the organization was to draw on the talents of everyone in the AAUW. Instead of having a single leader, Bryant decided to share leadership, so that everyone would have the ability to represent the AAUW to the outside world.

You can't share leadership until you have a clear focus. And sharing leadership can only occur when leadership is real on both sides. Leaders must make room for others, and know when to challenge, confront, buffer, or get out of the way. In return, the other members of an organization must be willing to come forward and take the responsibilities that come with leadership.

"Our public-relations firm is always after me to become the single spokesperson for the AAUW," Bryant says. "The press understands an organization better, they keep telling me, when there is one spokesperson. Well, they are now getting used to the fact that AAUW President Jackie DeFazio speaks for the AAUW. Alice Ann Leidel, the president of the AAUW Educational Foundation, speaks for the AAUW. I can speak for the AAUW, and so can a staff person.

"My leadership style can be summed up this way: I may have empowered us to do the work, but we all must share the credit," she adds. "All of us helped achieve the goals. We need to find ways to tap the inherent leadership potential within each member. The AAUW will grow stronger as we develop a wide range of leaders. In an era in which time has become a precious commodity, leadership can rarely be a one-person show."

But if everyone is going to be capable of representing the organization, then everyone must know what is going on, and what the organization is trying to accomplish. By focusing on outcome thinking, Bryant has taken steps to ensure that is the case.

Some people believe that leaders who engage in outcome thinking are being manipulative or controlling because they think the leader already made a decision about the outcome, even before the project begins. Bryant admits she struggles with this issue. "Sometimes staff members believe I have a predetermined agenda when I honestly don't." Bryant is not forcing issues down anyone's throat. She is constantly testing new ideas on her staff and the organization's members, changing those ideas as the feedback requires. By engaging in outcome thinking, she is simply stating, "Here is where I stand. This is where I want to go."

She adds: "I have high expectations of the people around me, yet I know you can't make people do anything. You have to help them figure out what they want to do."

That is what the constant meetings, gathering of information, and refining of mission are all about.

"One of my best leadership experiences was a very internal one, and probably nobody else noticed it," Bryant recalls. "It was in a staff meeting and I heard my dream and my direction articulated by others. I will remember that for as long as I live, because one of the speakers was someone who had resisted those ideas initially. I was so proud that I could have screamed, but I didn't. I just sat there and listened and said, 'What a great idea.' "

In less than seven years Bryant and her team have transformed the AAUW from a meandering, rudderless organization with a declining membership into a model of efficiency. She has been so effective a leader that the American Society of Association Executives gave her their Key Award, their highest accolade. Not surprisingly, when notified of the honor, she made it a condition of acceptance to share the award with Sharon Schuster, then president of her board of directors.

What drives Anne Bryant is her unwavering commitment to excellence. A strong, energetic person, she is always "aiming for the stars." She sets high standards for herself and others, and by her own admission can be impatient and a perfectionist.

Bryant has an uncanny ability to engage in outcome thinking. She is able to "fantasize" about desired outcomes and direct organizational energy toward a specific goal in order to make successful, lasting, and profitable change possible. She pursues a few goals at a time, pursues each one with her full attention, and eliminates activities that don't contribute to her strategy or desired outcomes. What you get with Bryant is her undivided attention on a few specific goals that produce terrific results.

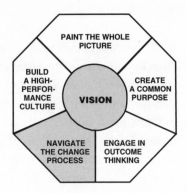

NAVIGATING THE
CHANGE PROCESS

Change. It's constant. It's also very difficult to lead.

The successful leader understands the complexity of change. He's a change agent who mobilizes his workforce.

He starts by convincing the organization that there is an urgent need to change. He creates a vision that is clear, compelling, and shared by others. People then must step up to the plate—understand the challenges, and take responsibility for solving them. Often this means changing the way the company is structured and the way people behave. The leader continually challenges the organization to keep the momentum going.

In the process he must assess the emotional climate of the organization and deal with the complex emotions that change triggers. If he doesn't, employees—either consciously or not—will shut down the process.

Dealing with the human side of change includes something else: the leader himself. He must be aware of his own feelings and reactions—and act to facilitate, not sabotage, the process.

It would be hard to imagine a more difficult set of circumstances than the situation Terrence (Terry) A. Larsen found himself in, in the late 1980s. Larsen, who runs CoreStates Financial Corporation, a regional bank based in Philadelphia, watched as his company was squeezed from all sides. De facto deregulation had brought the international banks—such as Citicorp and Chase—into his territory, and had also prompted nonbanks, such as Merrill Lynch and Paine Webber, to go after his customers as well. At exactly the same time, small local banks were expanding, sensing that they now had to

---

TERRENCE A. LARSEN
CoreStates Financial Corporation

TITLE: Chairman

AGE: 47

FAMILY SITUATION: Married; 2 children

EDUCATION: B.A. from University of Dallas; Ph.D. in Economics from Texas A & M University

HISTORY: Vice President and Economist, Philadelphia National Bank (1977), Senior Vice President (1980); President and Chief Operating Officer (1986); Chairman and Chief Executive Officer (1988)

HONORS AND SPECIAL ACCOMPLISHMENTS: Board member: Greater Philadelphia Urban Affairs Coalition, Greater Philadelphia First, the United Way, the University of the Arts, the Pennsylvania Academy of Fine Arts, the Committee to Support Philadelphia Public Schools, the Greater Philadelphia Chamber of Commerce, and the Pennsylvania Opera Theater

HEADQUARTERS: Philadelphia, Pennsylvania

BUSINESS: Multibank holding company, marketing diversified financial services in the mid-Atlantic states

NUMBER OF EMPLOYEES: 13,000

ASSETS: $23.7 billion

FACTS: CoreStates Bank is the oldest in the country, tracing its founding back to 1781.

COMPANY HONORS: Among the 25 banks identified by the *American Banker* as a "superregional"; in return on assets, ranked sixth nationally

---

either grow or die. The middle market dominated by CoreStates was being squeezed from all sides.

Larsen needed to develop a new business strategy. But what? How can you stand out in the banking business? The cost of money is the same for everyone, so there is no way to compete on price. All banking products are basically the same, so product differentiation is difficult. And even if you develop a new product—such as the cash management account, which links all of a customer's financial assets—it can be copied within months.

Larsen realized he had only one source of competitive advantage: his people.

"What else could it be?" he asks simply. "If your people aren't feeling good about things, then it's pretty hard to come out with a good result. Pushing power down the line, and supporting one another, is a nice mixture of things that work, and feel right."

Larsen's challenge was to leverage his people in order to respond to the changes in the marketplace. He decided the only way to do that was by transforming his company from the inside out. There were bumps, tensions, and many lessons learned along the way. And while CoreStates has made remarkable progress over the last four years, the journey continues. Here's what happened.

1990

Word that Larsen wanted to gather everyone together had spread through the company. Major addresses by CEOs are rare anywhere, and guessing what Larsen would say would become the number one topic of conversation in the halls. Few people guessed right.

"Who are we? What are we? Where are we headed?" is the way Larsen began. With these three questions, the transformation of CoreStates was under way.

Larsen stressed that the company would manage change by playing to its strengths. It would rely on its financial assets, use technology to stay ahead of the competition, and draw upon its people as its biggest source of competitive advantage. Said Larsen: "People are at the core of CoreStates."

As Larsen spoke publicly, he was also having a private conversation in his head: "Do people really understand this vision? Are these people excited or are they really scared? Do they have the right skills and resources to carry it out? Will our company culture support or undermine it?"

Many of us are naturally suspicious or fearful of change. The leader has to prove credible when he talks about change. He must back his words with action. So Larsen immediately elevated the human-resource department so it reported directly to him. And he formed a people task force staffed by senior bank managers that would be charged with creating the new CoreStates.

"Changing an organization is always a moving target," Larsen says. "There are always new issues, new chances to get it right or wrong. Where people are concerned, there's always volatility."

There is also a lot of resistance. People bring their own emotional skills and baggage to the table when it comes to change. And it didn't take Larsen long to realize that much of the resistance was at the top, including one Terrence A. Larsen, chairman. It was not easy to admit, but Larsen realized he would have to change as well. This is no small point. Leaders sometimes feel they can stand apart from their organizations, and somehow not be affected as the company evolves. But because leaders are people too, they can either be facilitators or saboteurs of change.

Larsen admitted that changing was difficult for him. He had "grown up" as a manager within the traditional business model, in which leaders told employees exactly what to do. But Larsen was committed to changing. In making that commitment he was far ahead of most leaders.

"The way we interact with people has to be different," he says. "Twenty years ago, there was a rigid environment with given regulations, given competitive conditions, and given expectations of our employees and customers."

No more. Today, companies that build healthy, long-term relationships with their customers, and especially their employees, are the ones that succeed. American business has not handled its relationships with employees particularly well. CoreStates would have to do better. What was happening inside Larsen's heart and head would be a model of what happened inside CoreStates.

1991

Larsen's annual speeches became the touchstones for the company and would tell the story of the CoreStates transition. They would present the organization with honest, realistic dialogue about the change process.

"We are now positioned for success," Larsen told his employees as the second year began.

The people task force he appointed had developed "Core Values," principles to govern how CoreStates would operate. These principles would serve as the glue that would hold the organization together during the chaos and unpredictability of a changing marketplace.

CORESTATES VALUES

We value people. We will treat all people with respect and courtesy and create an environment that supports the attainment of their personal and professional aspirations.

We value performance. Exceptional contributions by individuals and teams are critical to CoreStates' successful performance. Such contributions at all levels will be appreciated and recognized.

We value diversity. We will actively promote an atmosphere of mutual respect for each other's differences, recognizing that our diversity creates a breadth of perspective that strengthens our organization.

We value teamwork. Teamwork is critical to our success. Trust and mutual respect for each other's responsibilities, functions, skills, and experience are essential ingredients.

We value communication. Open, candid communication flowing in all directions will be the norm. We emphasize that listening is a crucial component of the communications process.

We value integrity. We will strive to be recognized as an organization of the highest ethical standards and unquestioned integrity.

Change is a long, continuous process. It unfolds on many different levels, and there are many setbacks along the way. Larsen's strategy of developing—and relying on—a set of values made perfect sense. A leader cannot anticipate every change. He can't draw up contingency plans for every possible situation. There are just too many variables, and he must rely on others to take the lead. Indeed, if we are really honest with ourselves, leaders control very little. So how does a leader lead when he can't control the organization? Exactly the way Larsen does. He gives his people something to hold on to, the principles that CoreStates believes in. They can use the Core Values as a guide to steer them in the right direction.

But any good leader would say that you need to do more. You need to keep your hand on the pulse of the organization. Since people can either derail or support any change effort, it is crucial to understand how they are feeling about the organization, and to enlist their support. As one way of doing this Larsen instituted regular companywide employee surveys.

The initial results were not good. The surveys showed that employees believed they didn't have enough decision-making authority, and didn't feel sufficiently valued. While they agreed with the Core Values, they thought they were given lip service by some senior managers. This was distressing. One of Larsen's personal goals was to reach people who felt disenfranchised in CoreStates. He needed them to be fully engaged, productive employees, and he viewed each one of them as an untapped asset.

Acting on the results of those surveys would give him the chance to tap into that asset. But the survey data was just the beginning. Larsen knew he had to dig deeper and start a dialogue with his people. Skilled managers called together focus groups of employees to get them to talk more honestly beyond the numbers. Did the information feel right? Were the results consistent with their perceptions?

Venting feelings was the first step. People then were asked to help solve the problems—"What do you need from senior management? What do you need from your manager? And what are you personally going to commit to?" Larsen knew the responsibility for change had to reside in the hands of people at every level of the organization.

Larsen was determined that the reality in his organization would reflect the rhetoric. He addressed the survey findings—and the corrective steps he planned to take—in public meetings. "You must be willing to confront directly the inevitable conflicts between behavior and goals," Larsen says. Most important of all, these moves added to Larsen's credibility.

1992

The challenge now was to transform the organization so that it was consistent with the Core Values. Year three was spent acknowledg-

ing the personal challenges required to implement the new way
of life. The focus was on showing how the values applied to Core-
States' four stakeholders: its employees, shareholders, customers, and
communities.

"We need to ensure that each of these groups is treated with honesty
and respect and is afforded all the ingredients it needs to succeed,"
Larsen says. "If any one of them is not thriving, or is receiving poor
treatment, then the other groups cannot survive." While all four groups
are equal, Larsen made clear that employees come first, and that the
values are absolute and are to be followed in the case of conflict.

"We said to our employees, You have some rules of thumb—our
values—and if you think there is a conflict between finances and values, and there probably isn't a real conflict, but if you think there is,
go with the values. If you do, it will work out for the finances as well."
More and more people at CoreStates are willing to stand up and say,
"I don't think this thing or that system is right," Larsen told his employees during 1992. "People are challenging inconsistencies with
our Core Values and that is a wonderful sign."

Why? Because it showed the values were being internalized and
the company was being honest. But it also put pressure on the company's leaders to listen. How CoreStates now goes about handling
acquisitions shows the company is learning, and the gap between
what the company says and what it does is narrowing.

The typical model for bank acquisitions is this: you buy a bank,
then close some branches, and eliminate positions, to get cost savings
to justify the price paid. But, as Larsen warns, "there is an apparent
conflict here in taking on a bunch of new employees and then laying
them off right after you have said, 'Welcome to the CoreStates family.' We have the conflict of reducing the cost of the acquisition—
which is important to our shareholders—and treating people right,
which is central to our Core Values. A lot of people would say that the
people we acquired were never really on board, so the layoffs never
really counted. That would be an easy way out, but we don't take it."

Larsen has resolved the conflict. Following an acquisition, a companywide freeze is put into effect. That opens up jobs for some of
the people from the acquired bank. People from the new bank are
also hired as consultants, to help figure out ways their bank can
blend with CoreStates' way of doing business. As a result, employees

from acquired banks usually end up with jobs. Why take this approach? First, it's humane. Second, it's profitable.

"Customers have very strong ties to people they know in the organization, and they don't like seeing those people treated badly," Larsen explains. "So you have alienated some customers if you treat the new employees badly. Second, employees have strong ties to one another, so if you go laying off 25 or 50 percent of a workforce, they are going to feel bad.

"So we think you have gotten this thing off to a terrible start, when you follow the standard hard-hearted approach," he adds. "Actually from a financial approach, it's more effective to do it our way."

It's also a way to show that all this talk about valuing employees is not some touchy-feely thing. It is, as Larsen says, an effective financial strategy.

1993

With the pieces in place, "creating a culture for success" became the focus in year four. Unlike the many companies that in the early 1990s went through a massive reengineering process—slashing labor costs and changing their organizations from the outside in—Larsen worked from the inside out, focusing first on his employees.

He is quick to stress that the hard part had already been done. Some 20 percent of quality improvement comes from instituting new techniques, Larsen says. The other 80 percent comes from changing the culture. CoreStates started where others are willing to quit. Since the new culture at CoreStates was value driven, free of most old-style management attitudes, and filled with empowered employees, the "new" CoreStates was substantially closer to its customers.

Still, Larsen continued to acknowledge and confront obstacles to success: a lack of respect and integrity, bureaucratic turf fighting, and inertia. Equally important, he was quick to appoint new leaders who reflected the Core Values. And Larsen once again offered his personal commitment to change. "I underestimated how long it would take, and how hard it would be for everyone—including myself," he says.

"I always thought I was pretty aware and sensitive, but when you start looking inside and start delving a little deeper it's amazing that

you could miss some things for so long. I have a problem empowering and I sometimes have a problem avoiding a blame mentality,"
Larsen told his employees. "I keep my emotions under wraps normally, so it is often impossible for people to know where I stand on
developing issues. I need to change. I need to find out more. When
we first started the change process, it was scary how much I didn't
know. I struggle with issues, and at times I lose the struggle."

But he has won more often than he has lost. You can see that in the
company's financial results. By year four, with the program of putting
people first clearly in place, CoreStates was firmly established as a
"superregional" in the banking industry. Not only had its profits
grown impressively, but the company was clearly a better place to
work. Employee satisfaction was steadily rising, and that was translat-
ing into higher profits and a greater return on assets. Larsen's in-
stincts were right; it was possible to differentiate a financial-service
firm on the basis of its people. And while his timing for doing so—in
the midst of industry chaos—appeared odd at first, in retrospect it
turned out to be just right.

Terry Larsen understands the human side of business. He had a vision. He saw people as the principal asset in his company, and he had
the courage to invest in that vision. He developed a business strategy
that supported that vision and had staying power. He understood the
value of relationships and the need to listen to his people, since they
were his source of competitive advantage. They knew his customers best.

He also had a deep understanding of organizational change. He
knew he had to open up Pandora's box, to dig deeply into the root
causes of his organization's problems. But he had confidence that
his people could understand the problems and help solve them. Unlike other leaders, Larsen did not assume the responsibility by rush-
ing in with promises. That would have disempowered his people and
reinforced a feeling of dependence and resentment. Instead, he
asked his people to look at their own roles and contributions, which
ultimately encouraged them to take more responsibility.

Larsen navigated the change process year by year. In 1990, he
communicated the need for change, simply and with a sense of urgency. He persuaded his people to disengage from the past and work
toward a new vision of the future. In his second year, he created a
clear, exciting new business vision that was easy to understand, yet

challenged people to a new level of working. In year three, Larsen re-designed the organization with new processes and systems that were aligned with the company's new objectives and values. By 1993, Larsen was able to talk about his successes, yet continued to be honest about the need for improvement.

Larsen understood something else. He realized much of the culture change started with him, and that he would have to walk the talk, closing the gaps between rhetoric and reality. He did. And his company prospered.

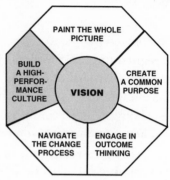

BUILDING A HIGH-
PERFORMANCE CULTURE

The ultimate challenge of any leader is to create a world-class organization, one that is both highly productive, and able to withstand competitive assault.

To make that happen, the leader must unify the organization into one holistic, integrated business. His approach to leading must be embraced throughout the organization. All policies, systems, and rewards must support the vision and goals. And the climate must inspire people to achieve extraordinary results.

In this kind of environment, the leader must manage by facts, not gut feel. Clear, quantifiable goals are indicators of success. In high-performance organizations, measurement is a way of life. And the leader must link those measurements to high-performance outcomes. It is not enough to measure things; you must measure the right things.

Only then can vision become a reality.

"Tennnnn Hut!"

The leader—be he a general, captain, or noncommissioned officer—enters the room, and everyone snaps to attention. They listen attentively to what he has to say, then follow his orders to perfection. "If only my business could be run like the military," more than one executive has been heard to say, "my life would be so much easier."

Back when competition was less, and strictly local, simply ordering people about might have been an effective strategy. But that is no longer true. Ironically, one of the people who understands this best is a thirty-five-year veteran of the U.S. Air Force, General John

---

GENERAL JOHN MICHAEL LOH
United States Air Force Air Combat Command

TITLE: Commander

FAMILY SITUATION: Married

EDUCATION: U.S. Air Force Academy (1960); M.S., Aeronautical Engineering, MIT

HISTORY: Commander, Aeronautical Systems Division, Air Force Systems Command; Air Force Vice Chief of Staff; Commander, Tactical Air Command

HONORS AND SPECIAL ACCOMPLISHMENTS: More than 4,300 flying hours, primarily in fighter aircraft; flew 204 combat missions in Vietnam

BUDGET: $9.5 billion annual operating budget—$5.1 billion payroll

PHILOSOPHY: "No one is more or less important than anyone else."

HEADQUARTERS: Langley Air Force Base, Langley, Virginia

NUMBER OF PEOPLE UNDER HIS COMMAND: 135,000 at 32 bases

Michael Loh. For the past four years, Mike Loh has served as commander of the Air Combat Command (ACC), the primary provider of combat air forces for the U.S. Air Force worldwide. His position draws on all the skills Loh is known for: those of a warrior (he was a fighter pilot in Vietnam); those of an R & D expert (he has a master's in aeronautical engineering from MIT); and those of a businessman (he has had numerous staff positions, with profit-and-loss responsibility, during tours in the Pentagon).

In his new command, Loh finds himself running an organization with an annual operating budget of $9.5 billion. If the ACC were an independent entity, it would be the third-largest member of the Fortune 500. In fact, with the exception of not having to turn a profit, running the ACC is basically identical to running a major corporation. Indeed, as Loh is quick to stress: "It doesn't matter whether you are in business, education, government, or public service, the globalization of our economy and the stress of competition have strained your organization."

In the ACC's case, the strain has come from combining the Air

Force's Strategic Air Command with the Tactical Air Command, and being pressured to reduce costs and cut personnel at a time when modernization is an absolute necessity.

"The problem we now face is adapting to support our customers—the American people—in a new security environment with far fewer people and planes than we had in the past," Loh says. "Instead of relying on the physical presence of our people and weapons near the most likely areas of conflict, we rely on the demonstrated ability of our forces to respond quickly to conflict when and where it arises."

In his new command, Loh figured he knew exactly how to run his organization to achieve the leaner, more efficient structure that is required today. His idea was far from the old-style, hierarchical military structure he grew up with.

"I had a vision of a leader being one who is on top of everything, someone who has total control," Loh recalls. "But after I was in the job a while, I realized that as your responsibilities grow and you become head of a much larger organization, you can't have control. You don't even know what's going on. To think you could direct and control activities from the top is incorrect. It is a false concept of leadership."

Loh gives a simple example. "The crew of a B-52, with nuclear weapons on board, goes off and is expected to perform their mission halfway around the world and come back safely and land. I can't be with them on that mission. I need to have a certain amount of trust and confidence in their ability to do the work."

What Loh realized, as he moved up through the ranks and had to confront traditional views about power, status, and control, was that his success, and the success of his organization, would be determined by the performance of people who would be operating free of his direct supervision. When you are responsible for 135,000 people in your command and another 100,000 in the reserves, you can't supervise each one. So Loh decided to take a very unmilitary course of action: He would give up control. He would make clear roles and responsibilities, and then he would let the people who were doing the work be responsible for the work.

"I decided that we ought to organize our work in such a way that the squadron—the unit of production in our case—could operate in a fairly autonomous fashion. They needed to have the responsibility, and accountability, to do their job.

"You find a lot of companies like to talk about delayering their organizations, but when it comes to leaders giving up real power, it doesn't happen," Loh adds.

It's easy to understand why. Pushing responsibility down the line is a far cry from the command and control model that Loh—and indeed most senior managers—grew up with. Still, Loh realized the change was necessary. He came to that insight by realizing that people follow you into battle—either literally, or in the corporate marketplace—because they respect you, not because you order them to. If employees or soldiers don't want to follow you, they won't. They will do the absolute minimum, on the surface, and probably work to sabotage you behind the scenes. Leadership, Loh now understood, meant creating an environment where people could do their best.

Given that he now had a new vision of leadership, Loh realized he would need to develop a new operating style that reflected his new ideas. Those beliefs would have to be deeply felt, because "the troops can spot a phony a mile away."

Nothing will happen unless the leader fully embraces it. Loh understood that. Still, changing the way he viewed his job was difficult.

"First, I had to realize that getting promoted to a higher rank didn't mean that I had suddenly become any smarter," he says. "I had to listen, and that was hard, because I like to talk, direct, and give orders. I'd have to tolerate mistakes—honest mistakes—because in this new organization you're giving power and responsibility to people at a much lower level, and if you don't tolerate their mistakes, your people will say 'the hell with it,' and go back to the old ways of doing things."

This change in leadership style was challenging for Loh and his managers. Still, these changes needed to take place, and Loh needed to make sure that all the people who worked for him accepted them. That is, he says, an important part of his job.

"I need to establish a set of values among my senior managers that will inspire people, and can be passed down through all levels of the organization," Loh says. "The leader has a responsibility to articulate and transfer this perspective and framework to the organization. We call it operating style. We have 591 squadrons and they all need to learn about our new operating style."

And the most important thing they have to learn is that no one in the organization is more important than anyone else. "When I first said that three years ago, everybody laughed," Loh recalls. "They said, what the hell are you talking about? Obviously, a general is more important than a captain, and the captain is more important than the sergeant. But you cannot have a working environment where people don't believe everyone is important to the overall mission. The positions we hold are not a matter of importance, but of our responsibilities.

"We expect a jet-engine mechanic, who just completed training, to perform a certain set of tasks," he adds. "She knows how her job links together with the overall mission of the organization, because we have explained it to her. She says to herself, 'I'm repairing this engine that goes in the turbine that goes into that F-15 that is part of our combat troops' readiness. If I don't do my job properly, then the mission will be adversely affected.'

"Everyone is critical to the outcome, and that is why everyone must have a stake in the organization. It is also why no one in the organization is more important than anyone else."

Not surprisingly, not everyone in the organization accepted Loh's new approach. "There are lots of people, with old attitudes, who just don't like to operate in this new environment. They are uncomfortable with sharing power. It's difficult to work with them. I call them saboteurs. They are the ones who don't believe in what we are doing, and try to undermine the operation. They are at every rank and level. They are probably five to ten percent of the organization and you just have to let them go, if they are unwilling to change. Otherwise, your operating style is never going to take hold."

Once you have an operating style, it is important to institutionalize it. "You want to go from having an operating style to 'This is the way this company operates,' " Loh says. And this kind of change cannot be accomplished piecemeal. Partial solutions produce partial results. "Given what I now believed about leadership, it was important for me to create a new working climate," Loh says. "The typical autocratic, hierarchical organization is too inefficient."

The first step in creating this new style of leadership was to figure out what he wanted ACC to become. Loh concluded he wanted to create a high-performance organization, one where not only every airman was performing to the best of his ability, but where their efforts together would be unmatched.

"High-performance organizations are decentralized, rather than centralized," Loh says. "They set very high standards, and invariably meet them. That was the kind of environment I wanted to create. It would mean changing just about every system and procedure the ACC had.

"When organizations try to change their leadership from top down to one that is decentralized, they fail, or they are unable to sustain it for a long period of time, if they don't take a holistic, integrated approach to it," Loh adds. "It needs to become a way of life, where all the policies, the leadership, the systems, the rewards, and all the measurements support this new operating style."

Loh's new operating style is based on two critical principles. The first is *quality*. Convincing people that the Air Force needed to be interested in quality was one of Loh's hardest jobs. Quality, in the ACC, is vital for four reasons, he says. First, the ACC's success during the Gulf War established a new standard. "We know the American people expect us to win quickly, decisively, and with few casualties. That demands maximum efficiency and effectiveness from all our people." Second, "Quality keeps us competitive. We compare ourselves internally squadron by squadron, wing by wing. We also compare ourselves to performance in the private sector." Third, "The armed services are in a severe drawdown. We must be extremely efficient with fewer resources." Fourth, "Quality makes people feel good about who they are and what they do." Loh sums up quality this way: "It's a leadership commitment to an operating style which fosters genuine trust, real teamwork, and a quest for continuous improvement in all we do."

The second principle is *measurement*. "I used to believe that if it doesn't get measured, it doesn't get done," Loh says. "Now I say if it doesn't get measured it doesn't get approved. The world is now too complex—and the leader's job is too encompassing—to manage by the seat of your pants. You need to manage by facts, not gut feel." And performance measurements are the means to provide you with those facts.

Many of today's organizations are sending mixed messages about their basic values and strategic vision. Efforts to refocus their missions are frequently undermined by old measurement systems rooted in outmoded assumptions about the business. The leader may say he wants new behaviors, but the way people are paid and rewarded supports the old ones. New measurement systems can help clarify the organization's mission and strategy by reinforcing the right behavior. Measurement systems affect how managers and employees behave. They provide incentives to bring organizational practices into alignment with organizational objectives. But deciding to measure performance is just the beginning. Loh explains that, first, you have to figure out what you are going to measure. "You don't want to measure activity, you want to measure outputs and productivity," he says. "For every one of our operating units, we created a set of output measures that tracks everything from the utilization rate of our aircraft to how long you have to wait to get a prescription filled in the pharmacy. We have 162 output measures across all our businesses, and every quarter I look at the results, and ask if we are measuring the right thing."

Intriguingly, Loh says the goal behind the measurement system is not to keep constantly "raising the bar." The risk of constantly raising standards, he says, is that ultimately you may set the objectives so high that they are unachievable.

"Let's use our mission capability rate as an example," he says. "I expect our aircraft to be in commission 83 percent of the time. You might say, If your people can reach that, why not raise it to 85 percent or even 90 percent? The reason is there is no need to. With an 83 percent capability level, we can win decisively the next Gulf War. That level meets our peacetime training as well. So instead of raising the bar, we try to achieve the same output with less input. Achieving 83 percent with one and a half shifts instead of two becomes our goal."

All the goals that Loh sets are quantifiable, and they are all directly linked to his overall plan for achieving peak performance. But Loh stresses, "We don't compete with each other. We compete against the ACC standards. When we do that we are not divided into winners and losers. We all win." The high performers get most of the attention, but there is positive reinforcement for all. "When you start achieving your productivity goals, you must provide a way to give people an incentive to continue doing their job well. In industry, they'd get a salary increase or a bonus. I can't do that." Instead, at the very least, Loh gives people time off for achieving their goals. It is possible for a soldier to achieve as many as sixteen days a year off with pay. And if the goals produce quantifiable cost savings—a squadron cuts its fuel consumption by $1 million a year—he gives them half, to be used by the unit to improve the quality of life at the base.

As a result of this approach, there have been enormous savings, as well as increased efficiency. And everyone is involved. In a recent twelve-month period, ACC members suggested 3,732 detailed ideas for saving money—everything from using worn aircraft landing tires on trucks to buying off-the-shelf parts to fix "hopelessly damaged" high-tech equipment. Two-thirds of the ideas were approved. The total savings: $60 million. Wal-Mart has benchmarked the base pharmacy's ability to fill virtually every prescription in less than ten minutes, and GE executives have come to study how Loh's quality standards make merging divisions easier.

It is not surprising that when Vice President Al Gore's task force on reinventing government was searching for models of efficiency, Loh's ACC was singled out. What impressed the task force were the quantifiable gains that the ACC had produced, as well as the fact that virtually every single component of performance was being measured. For example, when the Secretary of Defense asked Loh, "How is the morale of the troops," Loh pulled out the most recent survey of his people.

There is no way to overstate the importance of measurement. For General Loh, measurement is an interactive process with his people, not a form of control. But without some way of measuring change, managers are groping in the dark. Measures can shine a light into organizational shadows to guide change.

General Mike Loh has a keen sense of strategy and a passion for performance. He sets high standards, implements goals from start to finish, and knows exactly where he stands at all times. He leads by "soft" principles, but measures by "hard" facts. And he loves the excitement of measuring himself and his organization.

Ultimately, Loh is trying to create a system of high productivity by linking his goals to his business strategy and his business strategy to performance outcomes. The idea is simple, the execution is not. Loh, who says he'd rather be known for his personality than for his title, knows it comes down to institutionalizing the vision and building the proper environment.

"We have done well because of the culture. It's not because I stand on Mount Sinai and preach."

TRUST

If you don't trust your associates to know what is going on, they'll know you don't really consider them partners.

DON SODERQUIST, VICE CHAIRMAN OF WAL-MART

Upward communication only takes place when leaders are trusting—and trustworthy.

DOUGLAS G. MYERS, EXECUTIVE DIRECTOR, SAN DIEGO ZOO

Trust is the glue that holds relationships together. Without trust, no vision ever becomes a reality. In fact, without trust nothing works very well. Unless there is trust within an organization—between employee and employer, between employees, between the customer and the company—productivity, quality, sales, and earnings all suffer.

Trust takes a long time to earn, and is lost in a moment's thoughtlessness. Although we rarely talk about it, we all need to trust our leaders. We know in our hearts when we do and when we don't. If we trust them and each other, the process of building relationships and a high-performance company are that much easier.

74

Trust has two parts. Being trusting—the ability to believe in others—and being trustworthy—being worthy of others' belief in you. It is the leader's job to make sure both elements are present throughout the organization.

Healthy leaders are:

- Genuine. It's important for people to touch and feel them as real people.
- Believable. Their word—whether spoken or written—is credible.
- Dependable. They make good on their promises, whether declared or implied.
- Predictable. Being consistent makes it safe for people to be vulnerable and work together.
- Benevolent. They have the capacity to put aside self-interest for the good of the group.

When leaders act this way people feel valued as human beings, which enables them to be trusting in return. They participate in honest dialogue and respect the confidence of the information they receive. They give the leader the benefit of the doubt. They know the leader believes in them, so they believe in the leader in return. This is not a seamless process. There are many missteps and misunderstandings along the way. A true leader navigates through the range of human behavior and emotion and stays committed to the end result.

How do you create trust within an organization? It is a three-step process that begins from the top and moves down, expanding as it goes, filling the organization with an atmosphere of shared trust. It starts inside the leader. He understands that first you must be honest—both about yourself and about what is going on inside the business—and then trust others. Mutual trust is critical. When this exists, relationships and commitments become more authentic.

These leaders know that people need to be aware of what's going on, want to be told the truth—the good news and the bad news—and need to know where they stand. Deep inside themselves, leaders understand that sharing information will increase trust. And they know that the more they share the greater the trust will be.

The second step in building trust occurs when leaders put their beliefs into practice. The best leaders are honest, consistent, direct, and empathic. By exhibiting these qualities, the leader creates a safe foundation for people to make and meet commitments to each other, to customers, and to the company.

Building on these beliefs and behaviors, the leader next creates an open, trusting culture, one in which the company communicates about its condition, operations, choices, and financials. This sharing occurs at all levels. In the best companies, the leader takes the trust that is inside him and institutionalizes it within the organization. The result is increased commitment and productivity. This positive outcome allows the trust to continue and grow.

In the four portraits of leaders that follow, what emerges is a commitment to the crucial elements necessary to building trust in the workplace: authenticity, deep listening, predictability, and communication. Jack Stack, chief executive at Springfield Remanufacturing, will show us that being honest about yourself and the business builds a sense of trust and safety in the workplace. That sense of trust intensifies, Gun Denhart, the head of Hanna Andersson believes, when leaders listen deeply to the people being led and teach them the art of dialogue. That listening makes work relations more real. The relationships will stay that way if the leader remains predictable, according to Doug Myers of the San Diego Zoo. In a world of chaos and complexity, being predictable makes it safe for people to take risks. The story of Don Soderquist at Wal-Mart will take us full circle. Soderquist, a Sam Walton disciple, believes that sharing information and communicating in all directions builds trust and commitment in the organization.

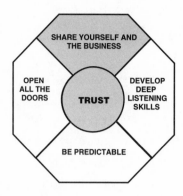

SHARING YOURSELF
AND THE BUSINESS

We use distance as a way of dealing with our insecurities. People hide their emotions and identities when they are uncomfortable. Insecure managers hoard information in the belief that it strengthens their position as leader.

If leaders hold themselves too far apart from the people they lead, people won't apply themselves fully—they won't reach within themselves for that extra bit of creativity or commitment. Subliminally but powerfully, these leaders communicate to people that they are better than others. That's hardly an inspiring message.

Being honest is the first step toward building trust in the workplace. Sharing yourself tells people you are authentic, and they are more than just numbers. Sharing information increases trust and accountability. If people had better relationships with their leaders, and more numbers about the business, they would contribute more to productivity.

The situation was daunting to say the least. Jack Stack's supervisors at International Harvester had just put him in charge of the division that had the worst productivity in the entire company. The move was designed to cure Stack of his happy-go-lucky ways.

Raised in a Roman Catholic family, Stack first thought he might become a priest. He entered a seminary, but, not surprisingly, he found it was less than a perfect fit.

"I failed there," Stack says bluntly. "Then I went to college," he continues, "but got kicked out. From there I went into the military, but they didn't want me. And so I decided to try business."

JOHN P. (JACK) STACK
Springfield Remanufacturing Corporation

TITLE: President and CEO

FAMILY SITUATION: Married; 5 children

EDUCATION: B.A., Elmhurst College

HISTORY: Native of Chicago; kicked out of the seminary, dropped out of college and the military, and fired from GM; started with International Harvester in the mailroom; with 12 other employees, bought the almost bankrupt Springfield branch and turned it into Springfield Remanufacturing Company

HOBBIES: Coaches baseball and soccer; fishing, golf, pool, and poker

HONORS AND SPECIAL ACCOMPLISHMENTS: Wrote *The Great Game of Business* (1992); Entrepreneurial Leadership Award for western Missouri and Kansas (1991); Business Ethics Award (1992); Business Enterprise Trust Award (1993)

HEADQUARTERS: Springfield, Missouri

BUSINESS: Rebuilding engines and engine components

NUMBER OF EMPLOYEES: 700

GROSS REVENUE: $93 million (1994)

PROFITS: $2.4 million (1994)

FACTS: Sales growth over 40% per year

COMPANY HONORS: SRC named as one of the 100 Best Companies to Work for in America (1993)

That career almost fizzled as well. Stack was fired from General Motors, after he was caught playing poker on company time. But soon he landed another job as a mail deliverer in an International Harvester plant just outside Chicago.

This time he did not get fired and quickly moved up through the ranks. Suddenly, at age twenty-six, he was a factory supervisor responsible for five sullen foremen, all of whom were more than twice his age. Clearly, Stack couldn't order these guys around. His youth precluded any natural authority, and since they already considered him an upstart, any attempt at using his title would have simply increased their resentment.

But Stack was still in charge of raising productivity. And if he wasn't comfortable ordering people to do things, he still needed to find a way to get things done. He decided to do it by appealing to his employees' egos.

Each day he gave the foremen the results of how well their people had done the day before. The report showed how many units were produced and how many defects they contained. Stack also gave the foremen the daily productivity score for the division as a whole, compared to the other six departments within the plant. Suddenly, all five foremen were aware of how they were doing individually, and how well they were doing as a group. They began to motivate each other. Productivity soared.

The first time the division broke its previous productivity record, Stack gathered his foremen together, bought a round of coffee, and let them take some time out to talk, laugh, and feel good about their accomplishment. The second time they set a new mark, Stack treated them to coffee and donuts. The third time, he invited them to his house for pizza and poker. Within three months of taking over, Stack's division was leading the factory.

What made this possible, Stack says, is his core belief that, no matter what title he has, he is no better than anyone else.

That is more than a moral or spiritual epiphany. It is also a key to effective leadership, as Stack so vividly proves. Instead of trying to use his title and status as a wedge to split himself off from the people he was managing, Stack did just the opposite. He used his common, unassuming bond with people as a powerful management tool. "International Harvester probably told me that I wasn't allowed to associate with my employees, but I associated anyway. We went out drinking, we had picnics, and we celebrated victories."

Many leaders get entangled in the trappings of power, in the pomp and the prestige. These leaders lose sight of their own imperfections. Such leaders would never admit their job is just a desk and title. They try to retain the job's mythology, its aura and power. In doing so, their own job becomes ever more separate from the jobs of their employees. The synergy of a common purpose dissolves. When leaders take themselves too seriously, the result in the ranks is almost always resentment, disillusionment, and apathy.

Jack Stack, CEO of Springfield Remanufacturing, is anything but a detached leader. Stack doesn't change who he is when he walks through the office door in the morning. He is open and real, and his employees respond in kind.

When Stack invites his foremen over for pizza and poker, or when he picnics with their families, he and his coworkers are mingling as equals. He is sending the message that there are neither little people nor little jobs, and that the common effort of each team member will result in common benefit to all.

Underneath his playful and open demeanor, Stack is a man with strong gut beliefs about himself and others—namely that people are created equal, that we all pay taxes and eventually die, and that everyone needs both physical and emotional nourishment to succeed. Stack laughs *at* himself, but *with* other people. He's the kind of person who feels fortunate to be alive, and eager to share his talents and insights with others.

"I always felt that I was lucky because I was given the opportunity to see things other people weren't able to see," he says. "I always promised myself that if I ever got the chance I'd tell everybody what it looked like. For example, I said that if I ever got a job that people really admired, the kind of job where people think the guy who's got it is practically a god, I would tell them, 'It really doesn't feel like that when you're in it.' And that's what I did. I opened up my job to everyone and let them see what it looks like. I showed them that it is just a desk and a chair and a title, and nothing more than that."

But can't leaders go too far in aligning themselves with their followers? Don't their jobs, in fact, differ from the jobs of their employees, and not just in terms of office furniture? The answer, of course, is yes. The job of leader carries responsibility for the well-being of those being led. And although Stack doesn't take himself seriously, he takes his job very seriously. He calls this "a sense of obligation," and it's what propelled Jack Stack to go from factory manager to entrepreneur.

In 1979, four years after Stack turned around the last-place division, International Harvester sent him to a lagging factory in Springfield, Missouri. They ordered him to decide within six months whether the plant should be saved or closed down. When Stack arrived at the engine remanufacturing plant, the division was losing $2 million a year, on revenues of $26 million.

With his customary lack of pretentiousness, Stack says he "literally begged" the workers to give him a chance. They did, and nine months later the plant had turned a $200,000 profit. By 1981, profits were more than $1 million.

But the joy was short-lived. International Harvester was diving ever deeper into its tailspin and threatening to drag the Springfield plant down with it. The prospect of the plant's slow death was agonizing. "To me the biggest failure in my life would have been to lay people off at the factory," says Stack. So Stack and his top twelve managers decided to buy it. Clearly, managers buying a factor in order to save their workers' jobs would be a drastic move under any circumstances, but it was especially drastic in this case. The terms of the sale left Stack's new company with a crushing 89 : 1 debt-to-equity ratio.

The sheer bravado of the purchase testifies to Stack's sense of obligation. The same person who loves playing poker and drinking beer is also willing to step up to his responsibilities even under the most dire of circumstances. It is precisely this balance of obligation and camaraderie that enables Stack to take charge of a project without acting superior to his people. The key is that Stack takes seriously his function—his contribution to the common effort—but not his status. He takes his job seriously, but doesn't allow it to feed his ego. And that balance, and the strong partnership it helped Stack form with the 119 employees of the now independent Springfield Remanufacturing Corporation, allowed him to lead an amazing turn-around. Ten years after he bought the company, SRC had sales of $73 million, almost triple what they were when he took over, and the firm has hired almost 600 additional workers.

SHARING THE BUSINESS

What allowed Stack's success was his creation—through trial and error—of a simple but brilliant strategy for motivating people. He would make their work meaningful by engaging them in what he called "The Great Game of Business." Stack taught the people who worked for him how their individual jobs fit within the company. "I'm completely obsessed," says Stack, "with trying to teach people the big picture."

"The underlying idea," he explains, "is to take the job of CEO down to every level of the organization. We're trying to turn employees into employers. In the past, management never asked employees to generate cash flow. We just said, 'Do this little process here and don't think about anything else.' Even today, most business theories focus on just one piece of the pie, like product quality, and only require the employee to think about that single piece. These theories don't ask employees to consider the whole company, and how their piece fits into it." The Great Game of Business was designed to teach every employee about the entire company—including its financials—and inspire them to take as much responsibility as possible for its success.

Part of Stack's psychological impetus for doing this was his humility, his desire to demystify his job as CEO. But another ingredient was a deep passion to communicate, to demonstrate how any given job contributes to the large order of things. He wanted to show—vividly and clearly—how business and capitalism work.

"If I can get people to really understand business," Stack says, "it changes their lives forever. It makes them much more productive, and it gets them to believe in themselves.

"I can't tell you the number of people whose lives have changed in the eleven years we have been opening all our books and explaining every number and how each one connects to all the others, and how they all affect people's livelihood. Here's an example. We have one guy, who never finished high school, who shot his eye out with a pistol and had his brother die in a penitentiary, who's now a plant manager at one of our factories. I can see every day how teaching business changes people."

This passion to communicate benefited Stack tremendously when he and his top management purchased the Springfield plant. "I had to make people understand that the stakes were no longer win or lose, they were win or die," says Stack. "We were playing for our survival."

Crisis tends to push leaders into whatever style they feel most comfortable with, and unfortunately most leaders today are comfortable either with paternalistic control or hierarchical power. A lot of CEOs, facing that monstrous 89 : 1 debt-equity ratio, would have looked to trim labor costs any way they could. Extra education for factory laborers? They would never even have considered it. They would have begun looking at their workers as a liability to be pruned back rather than an asset to be invested in and built up. But Stack, who had begun his egalitarian and communicative style in his earliest management days, turned back to it with renewed vigor in this crisis. Every supervisor and manager took courses in understanding financial reports, and they in turn taught classes to their employees.

"The balance sheet is a thermometer," says Stack. "It tells you when you have a fever or a variance of any kind. Can you imagine what would happen if people asked to review balance sheets before they accepted a job offer? We have people who are going out into the workforce every single day, establishing lines of credit and buying houses, and they don't even know the health of the company that they're going to work for. They don't even know how to evaluate the health of that company, and yet they're willing to spend the next twenty to thirty years of their life there. It's unfair. It's stupid. I really think that if the workforce looked at balance sheets first, there would be a better impetus to make healthier companies, because everyone would be focused on optimizing that balance sheet."

That's certainly true at SRC. "We try to give as much information to our people every day as publicly held companies give to their shareholders every quarter. There isn't a number that isn't available. From any terminal anywhere in the organization you can access everything. Any employee at any given time can put together an income statement for the whole company. And every single Wednesday we do the complete analysis of the entire company—income statement, balance sheet, cash flow for the month that we're in—and it goes to all seven hundred employees."

By institutionalizing Stack's urge to communicate, SRC has reaped two major benefits. One is morale. "When you say, 'Okay, I want you to understand the whole picture first, and then we're going to teach you your job,' people tend to be much happier with their work," Stack says. The second benefit is excellence. "When you appeal to higher levels of thinking, you get higher levels of performance. I've seen that all my life, in job after job."

It sounds easy, but there's an emotional snag. Leaders like Jack Stack can appeal to higher levels of thinking because they are not afraid. Stack lays everything out on the table: his vision, goals, and intentions, plus the nuts-and-bolts information about the business. For many leaders, this would be agony, because they interpret any question as an attack, any improvement as a blow to their status. Not Stack.

"I've got a vision that capitalism is really neat," he says. "Very few people want to take the time to understand it. The majority of people think it's dirty, rotten, and promotes cheating. But, in fact, you can only beat it by performance. You can't cheat, because there's a way of finding out. There's all these different checks and balances, so if somebody does something wrong you catch it. In this sense, it's no different than a baseball game or a hockey game. That's why we call it 'The Great Game of Business.' It can actually be played like a board game. It can be a unifying factor, when you can bring everyone together around the same board, and it's fun. It's really neat to be able to generate profits and then take some of those profits and give bonuses. I mean, who doesn't like to give out a bonus? It's one of the greatest things you can do."

Back when Stack was at International Harvester, he was in charge of an engine assembly line. "If they built 300 engines, 150 of them would have major defects. So you'd have to bring in a repair group, and that meant you needed an extra layer of overhead. I went out and talked at great length to the guys on the line, and it dawned on me that to them their job was just a paycheck. They didn't know they were building engines that go into trucks that move America's goods. They didn't know they were building engines that went into tractors that produced food that goes on people's tables. They didn't have any idea what the hell they were doing, because we had stuck them into this one little box, this one little section of an assembly line.

"So I went to the marketing department and got a bunch of the posters we were sending out to customers. In those days, those posters were kind of sexist. They'd have these beautiful girls with big busts standing by trucks, or they'd have American emblems on huge trucks and tractors, you know the propaganda. I started to put those posters on the end of the assembly line, and started parking trucks and tractors that had our engine there as well. The more of that I did, the fewer defects we had.

"My greatest thrill from that was the day a guy on the line told me a story. He said he was driving along with his kid and he pulled up to a stoplight, and next to them was a big truck with our engine emblem, DT466. He tapped his kid on the shoulder and he said, 'Do you know who built that engine? Your daddy built that engine.' And that is the whole concept of the big picture. Right there. That's it."

Stack isn't just communicating facts and information, he's communicating purpose and emotions—and himself. People value authenticity and they want the truth. No one expects the leader to be perfect—only genuine and honest. Jack Stack is both. He tells the truth about himself and the business, and the trust he creates forms a special bond inside the company. Employees will work a lot harder for people than they will for robots.

Stack knows that "being real" is a two-way street. You have a right to demand honesty if you are treating people honestly. It's all about trust.

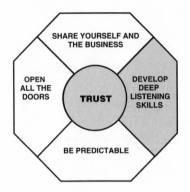

DEVELOPING DEEP LISTENING SKILLS

Businesses, customers, and employees know what they need and want. They'll tell you, if you're willing to listen and listen hard.

Most of us don't listen well. We are moving too fast. We are too preoccupied with where we are going. We spend too much time thinking about how to respond to, or one-up, the person talking to us.

Good leaders listen well. They understand that people have a need to see, touch, and feel their leaders, and that leaders have a need to see and understand the business.

Leaders use these listening skills to dialogue with others. They engage in conversations for learning and possibility, seeking to deepen understanding, clarify perspectives, and find new ways of solving problems.

To them, the link between deep listening, dialogue, and higher productivity is clear.

Gun Denhart wasn't in her office. The president of Hanna Andersson, the mail-order company that specializes in fashionable 100 percent cotton clothing for children, was supposed to be sharing with me the secret of her company's success. There would be a lot to talk about how the company went from $0 to $40 million in sales in just ten years; why she feels it is important that her company, which sells primarily to women, has women at every level of management; and how her Swedish upbringing affects the way she runs her business.

But she wasn't there. A quick tour of the offices of Hanna Andersson found Denhart huddled with a group of employees who had gathered around the company's chief designer. Everyone was ex-

---

GUN DENHART
Hanna Andersson

TITLE: CEO

EDUCATION: MBA, University of Lund, Sweden

AGE: 49

FAMILY SITUATION: Married; 3 sons

HISTORY: Greatly influenced by her Swedish heritage; started Hanna Andersson with her husband in 1983

HOBBIES: Hiking, yoga

HONORS AND SPECIAL ACCOMPLISHMENTS: *Working Woman* magazine's Harriet Alger Award (1989); Business Enterprise Award (1992); One of the "Best Companies for Working Mothers," *Working Mother Magazine* (1991, 1992, 1993, and 1994); Entrepreneur Achievement Award, Swedish Trade Council (1991)

HEADQUARTERS: Portland, Oregon

BUSINESS: Mail-order marketer of exclusively designed, 100% cotton children's clothes

NUMBER OF EMPLOYEES: 250 (1994)

GROSS REVENUE: $47.5 million (1994)

FACTS: 5% of company profits go to charity; donated over 339,684 items of clothing through 125 charities across the country

---

cited because the woman had just announced that after many months of trying she was finally pregnant.

That news—and the reaction to it—would have troubled many chief executives. First, the mere fact that employees were gathered around the chief designer meant they weren't working. But more important, the pregnancy of a chief designer—a pivotal job at a clothing company—could cause serious management problems. Now that she was pregnant, how long would she be able to work? Once the baby was born, how long would she be on maternity leave? Who would replace her? Would she come back? Would others be lobbying for her position while she was away? And if . . .

Those were all legitimate questions, but Denhart was not thinking about any of them. There was no one happier for the chief designer than Gun Denhart. This response tells you a lot about Denhart, and it also tells you volumes about why her company has grown as quickly—and as profitably—as it has.

The key to Hanna Andersson's success is that Denhart listens, and listens deeply. Not just to customers—most executives are doing that these days—but to everyone—employees, the community, and herself.

Denhart's ability to listen to herself, which brought her into therapy, led her to concentrate more on her family, and ultimately convinced her she should move her company from New York to more tranquil Portland, has enabled her to understand herself at a deeper level. Because she knows who she is, and understands what she has gone through, it is easier for her to understand other people, and see (and hear) their point of view.

If you learn to listen to yourself—your range of moods, feelings, and experiences—you become more self-aware. You get to know your strengths and vulnerabilities. All of this helps you take another person's perspective, because you have gained a broader perspective yourself. By listening to yourself, you learn why you are the way you are, and you can bring that understanding of human behavior to your interactions with others. Denhart knows what it is like to be a working mother, or an executive wrestling with a tough decision. She understands what it is like to be anxious or apprehensive, and she brings this understanding to her interactions with others.

Listening is important because it tells the other person that she matters, that she is important enough to listen to. And Denhart's listening has tangible payoffs, beyond just making the employees feel good. Compared to its competitors, Hanna Andersson has lower employee turnover, fewer employee sick days, and higher sales per employee. That's not surprising. In addition to truly showing employees that she cares, Denhart's listening helps her identify employee frustrations early, before the frustration can affect the company.

Denhart, who has the Swedish equivalent of an MBA, has realized that business is about people and not numbers. As a result, her reaction to the news of the designer's pregnancy was not what we would expect from a traditional CEO, but rather the reaction of someone who truly cared about the designer as a whole person. Denhart understood what the pregnancy, and the desire to have a family, meant to her designer, and she was happy for her.

Situations like this create special moments of opportunity for a leader. Employees want to be treated as human beings, not instruments of production. How you respond in a situation like this one goes a long way toward coloring how you are seen within the organization. People have long memories. Obviously, Denhart created a lasting positive impression, not only on the chief designer, but on the other employees who were there and the ones who later heard about Denhart's reaction to the pregnancy. But in the context of the company Denhart has created with her husband, Tom, her reaction was not surprising. The well-being of employees is a primary concern.

"We constantly tell people that there should be a balance between work and play," Denhart explains. "A lot of people have asked me if I really believe that, and I do. If you are not happy at home, you can't just pour yourself into work and say that's the only thing that exists. I know that if my family life were not happy, I would not be able to do my job."

To ensure that her employees can do their jobs, the company subsidizes a significant portion of day-care expenses, provides flexible work hours, and offers extended maternity leaves. The company gets higher productivity in return. Denhart provides these benefits because she listened to her employees, and herself. She remembers how hard it was to start the company, when her son Christian was small.

But that is not surprising, either. Because it was listening to customers, actually potential customers, that caused Denhart to create her company, which she named after her grandmother.

"Our son was born in 1980, and with him, our business idea," she explains. The Denharts wanted Christian to wear the same kind of high-quality clothing Gun had known when she was growing up in Sweden. But that kind of material was hard to come by in the States, and when the Denharts did find it, the clothes were extremely expensive. The Denharts' friends were also unhappy with the limited choices they had when it came time to dress their children. The clothes, they said, were unattractive and wore out quickly.

The Denharts had no intention of starting a clothing company.

Tom was a creative director at a large New York advertising agency, and Gun was a financial manager. But on a vacation to Sweden in 1983, the Denharts got curious. Was there a way of creating the kind of clothes that they—and their friends—wanted for their children? "Sweden, with its eight million people, only has a handful of manufacturers who make quality knitted children's clothes," Gun recalls. "And I called them all."

She found the perfect manufacturer. Then the question was: Would there be a market for these kinds of clothes in the United States? There was only one way to find out. Gun and Tom produced their first mail-order catalog in fourteen days. To demonstrate the quality of the cotton, they cut one-inch-square swatches of the fabric and glued them into each catalog. It was a tedious process. But one that paid off. The orders started coming in. Within two years, the business was too big for their home. Nine years, two buildings, and 250 employees later, Hanna Andersson was a $46-million-a-year company.

"EVERYTHING IN LIFE IS ONE-ON-ONE."

When a business is growing that fast, it is easy for the leader to lose touch with those being led. Denhart understands that and takes great pains to see that it doesn't happen at Hanna Andersson.

"Everything in life is one-on-one," she says. "Everything boils down to a connection with people."

This belief, she says, probably comes from being brought up in Sweden. "We don't have that many people in Sweden. You don't have a second chance, if you make a fool of yourself. Everyone would remember forever. You have to be much more careful with your relationships. You can't hide. People at work know you from home, or they know someone who knows you. That brings a higher regard for the individual."

Denhart brings that regard to her interactions with employees. Thanks to her listening, she has a deeper understanding of motivation. Denhart understands that people don't want to be viewed as numbers or to be seen as second-class citizens just because they work for someone. They want to be treated as thinking, feeling human beings who want to contribute.

"The old assumption is that money is the only thing that moti-

vates people, but I don't think that is right," she says. "You do have
to feel that you are fairly compensated, and your office surroundings have to be nice. But those are not the things that really motivate you. What motivates you is an interesting job, a challenge, a
feeling that you fit in, and are connected to something that is
growing."

Denhart tries to institutionalize this feeling as much as possible.
For example, there are no secretaries at the company.

"My mother was a secretary, and when I was growing up she kept
telling me, 'Don't be a secretary.' That really influenced me. Secretaries run someone else's errands, and I really don't like that," she
says, underscoring the fact that traditional secretaries don't feel a
deep connection to the company they work for. "We only have one
administrative assistant in the company. People very much carry out
their own things."

Perhaps the biggest thing Denhart does to foster the one-on-one
connection is to spend a lot of time wandering through her company. "It's really important for me to touch people, and not just
send out memos," she says. "That's why I'll walk around the company really slowly, especially after coming back from a long trip. I'll
just stop to talk to whomever I happen to run into in the filing
room, the warehouse, or wherever. That's really how I learn about
what's going on."

As Gun walks the halls, she build relationships through conversations with others. She listens with genuine interest and concern, and
avoids judgments about people's motives. While being intensely
present, she wonders to herself whether she is hearing people properly or whether she is being understood. She asks penetrating questions, allows people to finish their thoughts, and always finds time
for silence in the conversation.

Gun is building dialogue skills inside her company. She knows
that her company's success depends on people's being able to have
open conversations that are deep, honest, and inquisitive. It's an effective strategy. Not only is it a way to remain connected to her employees, it's also an efficient way of learning what her market wants.
After all, who is closer to customers than the front-line employees
who deal with those customers daily?

"Obviously," says Denhart, "the walking around is not the only way I get information. But I can go into a room, and because I'm so sensitive to how people feel I can tell if there's a bad mood there, or a good one. This is better than any report I can read. It gives me a sense of where people are. If the mood in the company is good, then I know the bottom line will be good. It's amazing how that translates. I really think people want to do a good job, and if you'll just give them the right tools and opportunities to do it—things that put them in a good mood—then they are going to do it."

There is a downside to this course of action. Leaders like Denhart need to feel connected to their employees. They find holding the top job to be isolating. Connecting with employees helps eliminate that feeling. However, it creates problems of its own. Denhart can become overly involved in her employees' lives, making it difficult for her to deliver bad news. And because she is so connected to the business, she responds emotionally to its ups and downs. Still, Denhart says her approach is worth it.

The walking around, talking to people, trying to make sure they are inspired and their needs are being met, sound like simple things. And on one level they are. But on another they are the most important actions Denhart, or any other leader, can take. People are influenced more by the simple things they see their leaders do than they are by the grand pronouncements they hear them make.

If Denhart is sincere in her belief that everyone at Hanna Andersson is important, that she appreciates their efforts, that she wants people to feel connected to the workplace—and to her—despite inherent power differentials, then she feels those things must be reflected in her everyday actions. And they are, whether she gets her own cup of coffee, or helps clean up after a working lunch. Meetings serve as another case in point. At most companies, the meeting starts when the leader arrives. Not so at Hanna Andersson.

"We always start meetings on time," she says. "If people, even me, are late, we start the meeting anyhow. I think if we have five people waiting for the sixth we're wasting five people's time."

You can see how this all ties together. Denhart's ability to listen deeply to herself, to understand what is important to her, has allowed her to understand her employees at a deeper level. That in turn has enabled her to listen deeply to her customers' needs, such as their desire for high-quality, durable children's clothing. And that has enabled Denhart to listen to her community's needs. As a result, her company is socially responsible.

Hannadowns is probably the best example of that. The program is simple. If a customer returns a Hanna Andersson product that her child has outgrown, she'll get a credit of 20 percent of the original purchase price to use toward future purchases. The company donates the returned clothes to needy women and children.

On one level, of course, the program is clever marketing. It underscores that Hanna Andersson clothing is so well made that your child is more likely to outgrow it than wear it out. But on another, more important level, it reinforces for everyone what Hanna Andersson is all about: a company that cares. And a company that listens to its customers. They wanted Hanna Andersson to stand for more than well-made clothes, and it does.

What about the money Denhart gives up by offering that 20 percent discount? After all, it's not as if the company isn't philanthropic. In addition to the Hannadowns program, the company donates 5 percent of its pretax profits to charity. Part of this money is earned back through enhanced reputation, and the other part is a cost of being a socially responsible corporate citizen.

"It's a very unfair world that we live in" is the way Denhart responds. "I don't know why, but I do know that I have a need to help. It makes me feel much better to give that money away than for me to put it in my own bank account."

And listening to her feelings—which, of course, takes us full circle—is what makes Hanna Andersson a success.

Denhart's approach is not perfect. Because she concentrates so deeply on making connections with employees, she finds it difficult to fire people, and making speeches can still make her nervous. But she was really taken by surprise when the company started faltering. By the middle of 1993, sales at Hanna Andersson had slowed considerably and the company's double-digit growth rate had begun stagnating. Value-conscious costumers were less willing to buy expensive products, and the mail-order catalog business had attracted many new competitors.

Gun had stopped listening to her customers, and to her own gut feelings. "We became so introspective that we lost sight of what was happening outside the company. It's surprising how fragile it all is. We always thought making money would come to us if we did the right thing. But it's not so automatic."

To her credit, Gun started listening again. She refocused the company on reducing expenses, reevaluated many of the company's business practices, and brought in two seasoned marketing and finance executives. Her greatest insight came when she acknowledged that she did not enjoy, and was not good at, the operations side of the business. In contrast to many entrepreneurs, Gun moved aside and chose someone from inside the company to take over. Today, Gun is responsible for long-range growth and international expansion, her husband has returned to the business, and the company is prospering again.

"The culture here is changing because it has to change to survive and grow. But we are not abandoning our values. We are only modifying them."

Gun Denhart has a special quality of listening and communicating deeply, of connecting with others. She has an intuitive sense of how people feel, and she's learned to trust her gut. Consequently, she understands the fragility of relationships, and how important they are to people. She knows how hard it is to build those relationships, and how easily they can be destroyed. Perhaps most important, she understands how listening to others, and to herself, is the work of leaders.

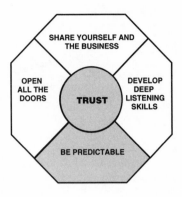

BEING PREDICTABLE

In a complex and chaotic world, a leader who is consistent and predictable helps the people who work for him feel secure. Since they know the ground is not going to shift under their feet, they are open to new ideas. They are willing to take risks.

The converse is also true. If the leader doesn't provide a feeling of security, people find the workaday world a stressful and unpredictable place. People cannot survive under these conditions for too long. They get scared and angry, and unwilling to try much of anything that's new.

This is where a leader can help. Being solid and predictable makes it safe for people to work together, to take risks, and to expose themselves even when the rest of their lives is filled with complexity and chaos.

Douglas G. Myers, the executive director of the San Diego Zoo, believes in the power of predictability. His people prove every day that he's right to believe in it.

There may be no more challenging enterprise to run than the San Diego Zoo. There are the standard business concerns, of course: making money (by charter, the zoo must cover its costs out of admission and concession revenues), labor relations (the zoo is unionized), and dealing with customers (the zoo is open 365 days a year).

But then there are the special problems that make the zoo unique. Most capital improvements are paid for by contributors, who must be courted. A large part of the labor force is comprised of volunteers, who must be made to feel their work is important, other-

DOUGLAS G. MYERS
San Diego Zoo and Wild Animal Park

TITLE: Executive Director

FAMILY SITUATION: Married; 2 children

HISTORY: Employed by Anheuser Busch and Busch Entertainment Corporation for 11 years; General Manager, San Diego Wild Animal Park (1981), Deputy Director (1983), Executive Director (1985)

HONORS AND SPECIAL ACCOMPLISHMENTS: Board member, San Diego Convention and Visitors Bureau; Fellow, American Association of Zoological Parks and Aquariums

HEADQUARTERS: San Diego, CA

BUSINESSES: Preservation of animals; reproduction of species requiring natural surroundings and large territorial domains; conservation outreach

NUMBER OF EMPLOYEES: 1,400 (1993)

BUDGET: $81 million (1993)

FACTS: Has about 4,000 animals from 900 different species

wise they won't contribute their efforts for free. And there is no clear career path for employees. If your job is taking care of the lions, where do you go from there? If you can't offer promotions, and the amount of money you can afford to pay is limited by the fact that you run nonprofit, how do you get employees to stay? What incentives can you offer so they will do their best?

As if these management problems weren't hard enough, there's one more. The zoo is held to an extremely high standard. Its mission is nothing less than "increasing the understanding and appreciation of the inherent worth of all life forms by exhibiting animals and plants in natural settings and applying its efforts and influence to the conservation of the earth's wildlife."

Still, given all this, Myers's organization has been growing rapidly. The Zoological Society of San Diego, which runs both the zoo and the San Diego Wild Animal Park, is now the largest zoo anywhere. Union complaints have dropped by two-thirds since he has been director, and the zoo is consistently recognized as one of the world's best.

Myers says there are many reasons why he has been able to accomplish what he has in the past ten years. He's been able to hire good people who believe in the zoo's mission (the two parks receive a total of between 7,500 and 10,000 employment applications a year), and he listens to employees' ideas. But Myers's biggest contribution, he feels, has been that he is absolutely clear and consistent about what he is trying to accomplish. Whether he is talking to the zoo's board of trustees, who serve as his boss, the manager of Tiger River, or the person picking up trash in Sun Bear Forest, everyone knows exactly what Myers wants the organization to accomplish.

"I had a very consistent childhood. My father, the police officer, was very fair. He expected certain things and taught us to be reliable, responsive, and to listen. I like being predictable," Myers says as he leads a visitor around the wild animal park. "I like to have my people understand what I'm thinking, and where I'm going with it. If they know we are not going to change direction every day, that we are not going to grab every new management philosophy that comes along, it gives them a sense of comfort. It gives them a feeling of security."

By knowing that Myers is going to stress fulfilling the zoo's mission above everything else, employees don't have to be concerned about office politics, or what they are supposed to be doing. "If they understand our purpose, which is our mission, they're going to understand what they need to do in their day-to-day jobs."

With that understanding comes the security that Myers spoke of. Instead of worrying about making mistakes, they can concentrate on how to make the organization better, which presumably is why they became employees of the zoo in the first place.

Predictability is about being the same person in all situations so people can predict how you might react. It's also about clarifying one's intentions and ground rules and setting clear goals and objectives. The more leaders clarify these things, the more people will be able to predict and influence what happens to them.

BEING HONEST AND DIRECT

It is easy to be misunderstood and misperceived in the workplace. Because it is so easy to be misunderstood, perceptions matter. How you communicate is as important as what you say. People will spend a lot of time studying where and how your message is presented. They'll pay attention to your body language and the tone of voice you use. These need to be consistent with your words.

"I get up once a quarter and talk about what's going on," Myers says. "We hold the meetings more frequently if there's really something we need to talk about. During the recession, we were trying to get to display a particular endangered species. It would have meant a lot to this organization, but we didn't get it. Stories about why we didn't were running rampant through the zoo, so I wanted to talk to everyone before it got into the press. So I called an 'emergency communication session.'

"Everybody showed up, but it was clear no one was listening. So right in the middle of talking, I stopped and asked, 'Why are you just staring?' And Mike, one of my favorite gardeners, said, 'When are the layoffs, boss?'

"Well, there weren't going to be any. But what I discovered was you don't call something an emergency communication session during a recession. Ever since, we have called special meetings 'special meetings,' and I make clear ahead of time what they will be about, so people don't start worrying."

By doing that, people know what to expect. Part of knowing what to expect is knowing what is expected of you. And Myers is clear about that, too. He expects a lot.

"Maybe the best example of that is the large glass house for butterflies we built recently," Myers explains. "I'm kind of a stickler for deadlines, and once we decided to go ahead with the project, I told everyone we would open the butterfly house on July 2nd at 9 A.M.

"As the time got closer, I started hearing rumors people were working double shifts. I found out that the buildings and grounds people, the folks who keep things nice around here, were helping the construction workers. We're a union shop, and suddenly there weren't any job classifications. Everybody was doing everybody else's work to get this thing done.

"So July 2nd about 8:30 A.M., I'm heading toward the exhibit, so we can open it up, and I see our head horticulturist, Kerry, digging in the mud. He's probably been there since the sun came up. I said, 'We're getting pretty close, Kerry,' and he turned to me, all covered with mud and sweat and said, 'Yep, getting close, but we're going to make it, boss.'

"Nine o'clock comes, he's all done, and he stood there as proud as could be. He said, 'I'd like you to meet my wife.' And here is this lady just covered with mud. It probably wasn't a good time, but he was just so proud. People had brought their families out to make sure we made the deadline. There really was a sense of 'We can do this.' This is what I want the zoo to be like."

Myers lets people know what is expected of them in order for the organization to accomplish its goals. And because people share those goals, they respond. This is not only symmetrical, it's fair.

"I think being fair is important," Myers says. "Life is not fair, and I can't do anything about that. But I can be consistent as hell, and as honest as I can be. I've said a hundred times to people, There is not a confidential thing in my office, help yourself. I think being open and letting people know all the facts is good for them."

Myers understands it is important for employees to know they'll be heard if they have a comment, suggestion, or criticism. He holds quarterly public forums for anyone who wants to attend and communicates regularly through *Zooview*, the zoo newsletter. In it, employees talk freely about what they like—and dislike— about the Zoological Society. To Myers, all this information belongs to everyone, and each person is the best judge of how it should be used.

But giving employees a say is not the same as letting them decide. Being an open, approachable executive—as Myers is—doesn't mean he abdicates his primary responsibility, which is making sure the organization remains solvent. If an organization isn't viable, by definition it can't be healthy. And ultimately the responsibility for making sure an organization is healthy rests with the chief executive. Myers can do what he has done, create an environment that is open and ensure that employees have a vested interest in the organization's success, but ultimately he alone makes the call.

The decision to move to teams serves as a case in point. Myers thought creating cross-functional, self-governing teams would accomplish two things. First, it would reduce overhead. If the teams governed themselves, the zoo would need fewer managers. Second, a team environment would offer employees a chance to learn new things. Since there is no true upward career path at the zoo, teams were a way to guarantee that employees would remain constantly challenged.

"Moving to teams seemed to be the answer to all the highly intelligent, highly motivated forty-year-old fellows we have who kept coming into my office and wondering what they were going to do with the rest of their working life," Myers says. "We needed to build an organization that allowed that kind of person to do more, to accomplish more."

The problem was that some of the employees, especially those with advanced degrees, saw the change as a threat.

"We had one guy who said he'd rather work by himself, since he worked better that way," Myers recalls. "I said, Okay, Dave. We will be rolling out the idea of team through sections of the park, so we still have places where you can work by yourself. But I don't know how long that will last. Eventually, this entire place is going to run in teams. You're going to have to keep looking over your shoulder, buddy, because the teams are going to keep coming into your area and you are going to run out of places to hide. Eventually you are going to change, or we're going to have to change you, because this is where we're going. It's nonnegotiable.

"I listened to the concerns of people who were scared. They told me they were worried that they would lose their identity as gardeners or whatever. My line to them was 'No, I'm just going to use your skills more productively. You're still a gardener. You're still the expert the team will turn to when it comes to figuring out how to take care of this incredible collection of plants. And they'll be teaching you things about their areas of expertise as well.' "

A few people have left, but most have accepted the idea of teams enthusiastically, once they've gotten used to it.

"It's also been real good for the bottom line," Myers says. "And it does real neat things that people don't see. For example, workmen's compensation problems go away. I have healthier employees so the health benefits are not quite as much. I don't have absenteeism. I don't have bad morale."

The lesson here is straightforward. Myers remained predictable. He never wavered in his commitment to teamwork. He was consistent—and persistent—with his message, while being sensitive to the fears and frustrations of his employees.

There are no surprises with Doug Myers. What you see is what you get: an open, clear leader who calls everyone by his first name and jokes about being boring and hard of hearing. He is not afraid of telling the truth and consistently delivers the same message and lets people know exactly what is expected of them. This predictability enables people to feel safe, and people who don't have to worry about the workplace careering out of control, or which way the boss is leaning, produce better work. Myers believes deeply that people will go the extra mile, if they feel safe. It is hard to argue with the success he's had following that approach.

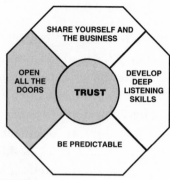

SHARE YOURSELF AND THE BUSINESS

OPEN ALL THE DOORS

DEVELOP DEEP LISTENING SKILLS

TRUST

BE PREDICTABLE

OPENING ALL THE DOORS

Nothing builds trust better in an organization than opening all the doors—top to bottom, bottom to top, and in all directions.

In an open organization, information flows freely through all the arteries. Executives, managers, and "associates" are well informed about what is going on inside the company. How well the company is doing—including all of the company's financials—is readily available to everyone. In return, everyone gives and gets honest feedback, and takes responsibility for telling the truth about the business.

Open communication does not happen by accident. The leader must be honest and accessible. His beliefs and behavior create a sense of trust and commitment that lay the foundation for building an open culture.

It was a bad idea. Everybody in senior management said so. One day, a woman working at the Wal-Mart in Crowley, Louisiana, went to her store manager and said, "You know we're a friendly group of people at Wal-Mart. What if we put someone at the front door to greet customers?"

The store manager agreed his people were friendly. But he wasn't sure he could afford to have a full-time person greeting everyone as they came in. Still, he figured it was worth a shot.

"Lois," he said, "since it was your idea, why don't you become our first people greeter?"

The response was overwhelming. Customers loved the idea of having someone say good morning to them as they walked in. Equally important, they loved being met by a person who could direct them

---

DON SODERQUIST
Wal-Mart Stores, Inc.

TITLE: Vice Chairman and Chief Operating Officer

EDUCATION: B.A., Wheaton College

HISTORY: Ben Franklin Stores (16 years, 6 as President and CEO); joined Wal-Mart as Executive Vice President of Administration (1980); Vice Chairman and COO (1988)

HONORS AND SPECIAL ACCOMPLISHMENTS: Honorary doctor's degree, John Brown University (1993); honorary doctor's degree, Southwest Baptist University (1989); Chairman of the Board of Trustees, John Brown University; Board of Directors, First National Bank, Rogers, Arkansas; Chairman of the Board, International Mass Retail Association; National Advisory Board, MAP International; Board of Governors, Children's Miracle Network Telethon; Board of Directors, Wal-Mart Stores, Inc.

HEADQUARTERS: Bentonville, Arkansas

BUSINESS: Chain of discount stores

NUMBER OF EMPLOYEES: 630,000

NUMBER OF STORES: 2,700

GROSS REVENUE: $82 billion (fiscal 1995)

FACTS: Wal-Mart started with $6,000

---

to the part of the store that had what they needed. A week later, the district manager came in, and was greeted by Lois. He went immediately to the store manager.

"Who was that?" he asked.

"Our people greeter," the store manager said. "She's there all day."

"You can't afford that. Think about the payroll costs."

"But you should hear what the customers say."

The district manager went and listened and discovered that Lois was quickly becoming a major reason for visiting Wal-Mart, and so the people greeter stayed. Not only that, but he established the position in all of his stores.

Then a regional vice president walked into one of the stores and asked, "Who is this?"

"He's our people greeter."

"You can't afford that," the vice president said. "Think about the . . ."

Today there is a people greeter in every one of Wal-Mart's over two thousand stores, Wal-Mart's vice chairman Don Soderquist proudly points out. In the company handbook, the people greeter's responsibilities are described as "handing out shopping carts and smiles."

The people-greeter story is a wonderful example of the way Wal-Mart does business. The idea didn't come from top management, it came from a person on the floor. And while the initial reaction of leaders at every single level of organization was no, they were willing to listen seriously to why the suggestion was made, and changed their minds, once they realized they were wrong.

This is a company where communication is open and flows in all directions. It starts with Soderquist, a man who truly believes that "our people make the difference . . . everyone is important . . . and ordinary people can produce extraordinary results."

Soderquist is an honest, open, and accessible person. Any executive who is willing to dress as Mr. T in front of associates—and be videotaped doing it—is not someone who is ever going to be described as a stuffed shirt. In addition to being open personally, Soderquist is also open with everyone in the company when it comes to sharing facts, numbers, and information about the company's performance. Soderquist believes everyone has a right—and a responsibility—to know what is going on. Throughout Wal-Mart's offices, and in the backrooms of its stores, you see signs that read, "Today's stock price is 27 $\frac{1}{4}$, tomorrow's depends on you."

Not only is sharing information the right thing to do, it is an approach Soderquist feels makes the most financial sense. That's why Wal-Mart has what it calls its store-within-a-store program. Every manager of the thirty-six departments within every Wal-Mart has complete profit-and-loss responsibility. He has access to all the numbers, costs of goods sold, mark-ups, overhead expenses, and profits. As a result, he knows to the penny how well his department is doing, and he runs his department just as he would a small store.

Soderquist believes that sharing information increases trust in the organization. If associates know what is going on, and are listened to, they will contribute more. They'll take more responsibil-

ity for the company's success, going out of their way to delight customers, and will offer ideas about how Wal-Mart can be run more
efficiently. He also believes an open discussion between leaders
and associates will lead to better solutions. He is a trusting and
trustworthy leader.

Wal-Mart had a solid business strategy to begin with. In 1962,
when Sam Walton started his first Wal-Mart store in Rogers, Arkansas, the world was ready for his approach to retailing. The concept then—as now—of selling brand-name merchandise at discount
prices is appealing. And the idea of being committed in some way to
the community it serves—being a good corporate neighbor by
letting the Boy Scouts use your parking lot for a car wash, and providing a college scholarship for a local high school senior each
year—just reinforced the positive feelings people had about shopping at Wal-Mart.

Walton's starting business strategy was sound, but then Wal-Mart
did something else. It invested early on in creating an open culture
characterized by teamwork and "aggressive hospitality."

Adding open communication to a solid business philosophy is like
adding jet fuel to a race car—a good performance becomes better.
How much better? Well, that one store that Sam Walton opened
thirty-three years ago has grown to become an international company with $82 billion in sales, and $2.6 billion in earnings. In the
process, Wal-Mart—which is now comprised of 1,900 Wal-Mart stores,
150 Supercenters, 425 Sam's Clubs, and 225 retail stores in foreign
countries—long ago became the nation's largest retailer. And it is
not only the company that has benefited. Shareholders have as well.
If you had bought 100 shares of Wal-Mart when the company went
public in 1970, you would have paid $1,650. Twenty-four years later,
that investment was worth $2,713,600. That gives you some idea of
the power of combining a good business idea and a healthy organization, one that communicates openly in all directions.

From the beginning Sam Walton understood the importance of
opening all the doors. In 1992, shortly before his death, Walton
wrote: "Sam's Ten Rules for Building a Business." Number four was:

Communicate everything you possibly can to your partners. The
more they know, the more they'll understand. The more they

understand, the more they'll care. Once they care, there is no stopping them.

If you don't trust your associates to know what is going on, they'll know you don't really consider them partners. Information is power, and the gain you get from empowering your associates more than offsets the risk of informing your competitors.

Walton would be happy to know that the concept of open communication would continue after his death. In fact, Walton's funeral was broadcast via the company's satellites to every one of its stores.

PUTTING OPEN COMMUNICATION
INTO PRACTICE

The question for Soderquist was how to put the lofty idea of open communication into practice. The answer? Open communication follows a four-step model. First, you must share the facts, including the most essential facts, the company's financials. Step two occurs when associates begin to apply those facts. Knowledge occurs when facts are put into context. The next level is understanding. It occurs when people truly understand what the data mean, and how their performance can influence the outcome. Only then will people make commitments. It is the associates' commitment to Wal-Mart that makes it so successful.

Soderquist is a strong believer in leading by example. "You can't preach about the importance of people orientation," he says. "You must practice it every day." Soderquist does. He is the person anyone in Wal-Mart can call if they think they have been treated unfairly.

Typically, one of the main obstacles to open communication is that leadership has an inflated opinion of its knowledge. The leaders feel they know what's right for their people. Soderquist works hard to see that this feeling doesn't permeate the ranks of Wal-Mart.

"The premise we operate under is that no small group of people, be they buyers or senior management, have all the answers," Soderquist explains. "I challenge our management people, sometimes, by saying, 'You know, if we did an IQ survey of the more than 600,000 people in this company, and we categorized the results by management and hourly workers, and we compared the results, the difference in IQ scores might not be that much. In fact, the hourly people might score higher.' Management has had a chance at education. We've been at the right place at the right time. We have had great opportunities, but, man, there is a wealth of knowledge in our people who work outside of the home office."

To make sure Wal-Mart continually taps into that wealth of knowledge, Soderquist is constantly out in the field.

"It's too easy for leadership to get insulated from what is happening in the company," Soderquist says. "When that happens, middle management ends up running the company, letting senior management know what they want them to know, instead of what is really going on. As much as we talk about the open door and as much as we try to practice it, there is an innate feeling that if I go around my boss or talk to somebody up the ladder, I'm going to get it. There will be retribution." That's why a lot of work must be done with middle managers.

To prevent that fear, Wal-Mart's fleet of seventeen planes leave Bentonville every Monday with senior executives aboard to visit their national network of stores. Soderquist spends about three days a week in the field, visiting three to five stores a day. The purpose of the visits is not to tell people what to do, he says, but "to ask them how we can help them do their job better," and find out what is really going on.

"I am looking to see if people come out to greet us when we walk through departments, or are they hiding," he says. "I watch to see how they are handling customers. Are the cashiers smiling? Is there interaction between the employees? Within ten minutes, you'll know the atmosphere in the store.

"We'll go out unannounced, and spend fifteen or thirty minutes on the floor of the store and then meet with managers—the people in the store who have responsibility for the hourly people and particular departments, such as women's apparel, hardware, health and beauty—and we'll just have a good old time with them and talk about what is going on in the company and what is going on in their store.

"I'll ask them, What are the problems you are having in the store? How would you rate yourself on customer service, on a scale of one to ten? How would you rate yourself on housekeeping in the store?

Then we have a conversation back and forth, and I share what I saw, and then they tell me what's going on, and we try to figure out the problems together."

In Soderquist's visits there is always a true dialogue.

"I'll ask to see some of the merchandise that's not moving, and ask why," Soderquist says. "Just recently, someone told me that the reason our cotton pants weren't selling was that the mall had the same pants for $1 less, and theirs were wrinkle free. The department managers all know things like that, and they can tell you."

The idea behind all this is to make open communication a two-way process and to make that process commonplace in the way the company does business.

But sometimes two-way communication is not possible, so Soderquist takes to the airways. "Every month we do a video via satellite to all the stores. We'll give them all the numbers. We'll tell them exactly how we performed, what divisions did a good job, and where they need to improve."

Soderquist understands that people need to have access, to be aware of what's going on, to feel trusted, to know where they stand. So he communicates openly about the business. The more things are communicated, the easier and safer it is to give and get honest, direct feedback. Because of the open communication, associates receive a clear assessment of their performance, and are better informed about how the company is doing. In return, they feel free to discuss things openly, rather than behind closed doors, expressing their real concerns and needs. Without this openness, there would be no bottom-up communication. And even if a system was created, the odds are associates wouldn't take advantage of it, since management would have made clear their opinions were not important. As a result, the company would have underinformed associates and inefficient work processes.

But it doesn't, and that is true in large part because of Soderquist. He has made it clear to everyone that Wal-Mart believes in open communication. He reinforces those beliefs in his everyday interactions with associates, and then he works hard to make sure this way of doing business is institutionalized.

Part of open communication is providing direct feedback—both positive and negative. Soderquist is known within the company for giving and getting that feedback. He asks lots of questions, is quick to praise when someone is doing a good job, and is consistent in the message he sends. For example, in his interactions with managers, he is quick to stress the kind of behavior he wants within Wal-Mart. The key, he tells them, is to focus on what associates are doing right.

"I'll be in a store on a Saturday morning, and I'll see one of our associates walking with her little girl, pointing to the end of the aisle, and I'll hear her tell her daughter, 'Mommy set that up this week.' And I've heard associates, walking with their girlfriends past a new layout in the men's clothing department, say, 'My store manager said I did a good job on that,' " Soderquist recalls. "Everybody wants to be somebody. People want to know that their work is valued. Everybody wants to know they're making a contribution.

"Are there lazy people? You bet," he adds. "But you can sort through that pretty fast. The average American wants to do a good job, and the way you motivate them is by letting them know what they're doing right. You also tell them, 'This is good, but we can probably improve it.' "

Soderquist believes that people who know what is expected of them will go well beyond their job descriptions. The extra effort is what gives Wal-Mart its competitive edge.

"I was visiting a store in Wilkesboro, North Carolina, and I was talking to the young lady who met us at the airport and drove us to the store. I asked how the store was. And she said, 'Real good.' She said there was open communication, and a family feeling, and she told me morale could not have been better. I asked her why that was and she said it was because of the store manager. 'She really cares about us, and is always interested in what we have to say, and when we do something good, she tells us. When we do something wrong, she comes and shows us how we could do it better. We don't ever want to let her down.'

"Man, is that powerful? 'We don't ever want to let her down.' Motivated people go above and beyond what they're asked to do. This isn't brain surgery."

But for open communication to work, associates have a responsibility as well. They must know the answer to the following five questions:

- What do you expect of me?
- How am I doing?

- What do I have to do to get ahead?
- Where do I get justice?
- Is what I'm doing important?

It is incumbent on associates to discover the answers to these questions. At Wal-Mart, associates are expected to speak up, not only about ways of improving their working conditions but about what will make their store better. If the company is going to be open about its financial performance, as it is, not only do associates have to keep that information confidential, they must work to make those numbers better. And if the company is going to communicate openly, making it possible to push decision-making authority down to the lowest level, then associates must take the responsibility that comes with having that authority. In a company where there is open communication, everyone knows what is expected of him or her.

There's also another benefit. There is a direct relationship between communication and commitment. The best way to create commitment among the more than half a million people who work for Wal-Mart, Don Soderquist believes, is to start with open communication.

The people at Wal-Mart are committed to the company's success. The numbers prove what you intuitively sense once you go in one of their stores.

"Hi, welcome to Wal-Mart."

PARTICIPATION

All of your power is in your people. Your job is enabling everybody to contribute to their fullest.

ALAN R. MULALLY, SENIOR VICE PRESIDENT,
AIRPLANE DEVELOPMENT, BOEING

If vision provides the direction, and trust creates the safe foundation, then participation is the fuel that drives the organization forward. This power is found lying dormant in the hearts and imaginations of the people inside the company. The leader's challenge is to unleash that power and focus it on achieving the organization's goals.

Why is participation so important today? Primarily because the competitive environment most organizations find themselves in now requires them to do more work, in less time, with fewer resources. If they can, they will gain a competitive edge.

To achieve that edge means expanding the capacity, and increasing the commitment, of each and every person in the organization. People must work faster, smarter, and more effectively. They must produce higher quality and better service, and do it with a greater sense of urgency than ever before. Customers are now more demanding, and only the people closest to the work can give them what they want, when they want it.

But those individuals must want to do it. Organizations need people who will take initiative, be accountable for results, and support the organization's goals. And there is something beyond mere economics driving this. Employees want a voice, to have some control over their work, and to feel they have a sense of ownership in the organization. They want to believe in themselves and feel like winners. They have a longing to invest in something that matters.

For human as well as economic reasons creating a participative culture is critical for business success. The most effective leaders understand this. They know their success depends on unleashing the power lying dormant inside their organizations—inside the members of their team—and to lead effectively, they must learn how to tap into it.

The best leaders have a deep understanding of power and participation. They realize their influence does not come with their title, but rather is earned through hard work and the respect of others. They know power increases as they share it and give it away, and that each person can make a real difference. To them, power built on fear is an expression of impotence, not leadership. Fear and ego are no substitutes for strength and character.

The best way to tap into that power is by abandoning the old baggage of dominance, control, and self-centeredness, and empowering others instead. Leaders must be willing to surrender authority, share power, trust people's judgments, and let others share ownership and the limelight. Some days they do a better job of this than others, and if they fall back on controlling ways, they self-correct. But participation is always their goal.

By sharing power, and sharing all the tools that go along with it—information, skills, responsibility, and rewards—effective leaders are able to create full participation and an environment where workers contribute freely and to the best of their ability. When leaders succeed in creating a participative culture, employees act as mature business partners. They take initiative, are literate on business issues, provide competent feedback, and accept responsibility. In short, they act as if they own the company.

With no psychological ownership, one's work, and its consequences, become irrelevant. When there is no emotional connection, people put in their hours and then go home. They feel indifferent, even hostile or destructive. There is no concern if a job goes unfinished, a product is shoddy, a customer walks out, or money is wasted. But when there is a feeling of ownership, and commitment is high, everything matters.

This participation process is circular. Greater participation leads to higher commitment, which leads to people doing better jobs. Since they do better jobs, processes become more efficient and the company turns out a better product. More desirable products sell better, which means jobs at the company become more secure and higher paying. That leads to even more trust and commitment, which leads to greater participation, and the entire process feeds on itself, eventually becoming institutionalized within the company. The results are a company committed to continuous improvement with great organizational pride.

The five leaders in this chapter illustrate the principles of participation. The process begins with unleashing people's potential. As Michele Hunt, the head of the federal agency charged with helping to reinvent government, knows, there is potential inside each of us that is waiting to be explored. Once the leader unleashes that potential, it is time for everyone in the organization to join together. Adult partnerships, such as the ones being forged in the Wixom, Michigan, plant of the Ford Motor Company, are the building blocks for creating a successful company. Without them, caution, fear, and adversarial relationships will poison the company's best efforts.

Helping build those relationships is a key part of the leader's job. He must be a team leader, sharing power, creating leaders at all levels of the organization, and trusting people's competence and judgment. Alan Mulally did each of these things as he led the team that created a new generation of aircraft at Boeing.

This team environment will only develop if people feel and act as if they own the company. Employee owners are more committed and productive at work. Russell Maier has created just such a workforce at Republic Steel.

Successful leaders know how to capitalize on the environment they have helped create. They make sure it continues by creating a winning attitude that pervades the organization. Creating this environment is a key reason that Barry Alvarez was able to turn around the losing football program at the University of Wisconsin and lead the team to victory in the Rose Bowl.

UNLEASH
PEOPLE'S
POTENTIAL

CREATE A
WINNING
ATTITUDE **PARTICIPATION**

BUILD
PARTNER-
SHIPS

PROMOTE
EMPLOYEE
OWNERSHIP

NURTURE A
TEAM
ENVIRONMENT

UNLEASHING PEOPLE'S
POTENTIAL

Many organizations smother the potential of their employees under layer upon layer of control and bureaucracy. As a result, our human resources are painfully underutilized, not only in business but in nonprofit organizations and government as well.

What is being underutilized is what might be called people's "discretionary effort," performance above and beyond the expected minimum. It is their initiative, creativity, motivation, and loyalty. This discretionary effort is the part of a person's performance that is liberated or shut down by the way they are treated by their leaders, and the quality of their work environment.

It is the leader's job to strike a match, to light the employees' potential. To do that requires the leader to undo any structures and systems that might snuff it out. If she can, people will be able to work up to their full potential, and amazing things can happen.

Michele Hunt has two simple questions: If there are 2.9 million people employed by the federal government, why is it that government doesn't work very well? Why aren't those 2.9 million people doing more to improve the daily life of the average American?

If Hunt were just a typical citizen, these questions could be dismissed as the complaining of a taxpayer who doesn't feel she is getting her money's worth out of Washington. But Hunt is the executive director of the Federal Quality Institute. And those questions go to the very heart of her job as the person responsible for carrying out the changes recommended by the National

---

MICHELE HUNT
Federal Quality Institute

TITLE: Director

AGE: 45

FAMILY SITUATION: Teenage daughter

EDUCATION: B.A., Eastern Michigan University; M.A., University of Detroit

HISTORY: Michigan Department of Corrections (1971–80), first female Treatment Director; Herman Miller, Inc., global responsibilities in quality leadership, human resources, government, communications, and media relations (1980–88); Vice President for Quality and People Development (1988–93); Clinton government transition team (1993)

HONORS AND SPECIAL ACCOMPLISHMENTS: Board of Directors, Service-Master Company; Advisory Team on Research Projects, MacArthur Foundation; Board, Jesse Owens Scholarship Fund

HEADQUARTERS: Washington, D.C.

BUSINESS: Fostering quality improvement in U.S. government

NUMBER OF EMPLOYEES: 33

Performance Review, the organization charged with reinventing government.

If government is to be run more efficiently—and effectively— then the people who work for it will have to do a better job. Most of them certainly intend to, Hunt says.

"The majority of federal workers are baby boomers," Hunt says as she sits in her Washington, D.C., office. "They came here after the Kennedy era. They didn't come here to make a whole tubful of money, they came to make a difference."

So why aren't they doing that? Hunt thinks the answer is as simple as the question: It's not the people working for the government who are the problem, it's the government—particularly the way the government has been structured—that is causing the problem.

"These civil servants are adults who have been underutilized, if not demeaned," she says. "My thirteen-year-old has more freedom, and is treated with more dignity and respect, than they are. She has more opportunities to make judgments than a federal worker. You tell me, does anyone want to live like that?"

It is not surprising that Hunt, the former Vice President for Quality and People Development at furniture maker Herman Miller, draws analogies to her daughter when she talks about heading the Federal Quality Institute. She believes that there are needless boundaries between the way people act at home and the way they are at work. She brought her daughter with her when she worked on President Clinton's transition team, and her daughter—who now has a government i.d. card—frequently appears at her mother's office after school. It may be a symbolic act, but it shows there is no reason a federal employee has to shut down part of her life when she goes to work.

Indeed, Hunt was molded by her family's values. Her parents established an environment where all their children were encouraged to be the best they possibly could be, and to take responsibility for their own actions. Starting at age fourteen, Hunt decided what time to go to bed, and how late she could stay out on a school night.

Her father, who worked with the Air Force setting up entertainment shows, constantly created informal communities of all the kids in the neighborhood—rich, poor, black, white—every time he was transferred to a new base. Hunt's father's reaching out was not always reciprocated. "I can remember when we were stationed at Fort Campbell, Kentucky, and I had been playing with Madelyn all this time. One day her mother came home, and told me to get out, 'I don't want my daughter playing with little nigger kids.' " In response to this, and other humiliations, Hunt's father—who once had been thrown into the stockade for protesting segregation on the base—constantly preached to his family never to hate and always to love.

The lessons took. At Herman Miller, and before when she worked as a probation officer for the Michigan Department of Corrections, Hunt was constantly looking for the "beauty inside a person." These experiences taught her that "what you think and feel is probably what each and every person thinks and feels; the only differences are the conditions that distinguish us."

Hunt brought all of this background with her when she was named head of the Federal Quality Institute. She needed that kind of grounding because she faced a daunting challenge: How do you get federal workers who have traditionally been seen, often accurately, as passive, dependent, and lethargic, to become excited, to take initiative, and to become energized about their work?

She began with the employees themselves. Her premise was that they had come to Washington to do a good job. "Everyone has that capacity," she says, "but it has been shut down."

And it is easy to see how that happens. At virtually every turn, federal employees are reminded of their powerlessness. Mid-level managers, who are responsible for deciding who will receive multimillion-dollar grants, for example, must sign in before they can use the copier and then must provide a written explanation of what those copies will be used for. We trust them to give away millions of taxpayer dollars, but then worry they may be making a copy of their child's baseball schedule on company time.

"At every corner there's a no. At every corner there's a can't, and a did-you-check-with-the-ethics-folks. It's an incredible environment to try to live and operate in. For me it is personally abusive."

If this is how a woman who meets regularly with federal agency directors feels, what about the mid-level government worker? "They've got layers upon layers of baggage around the pilot light that is their potential," Hunt says, and eventually, that light, which represents the discretionary effort employees could exert if only they wanted to, goes out.

Discretionary effort is the part of an employee's performance that is heavily dependent on how people respond to the work environment. Are they excited and energized to do their work? How satisfied and committed are they? Do they like their boss? Does the organization encourage and support people to take risks and push up against the system? Does the environment tap into their creativity, or shut it down? Although people control their discretionary effort, their willingness to spend or conserve it can be—and is—influenced by their organization's actions.

The question is, How do you get people to use their imagination, creativity, enthusiasm, and intimate knowledge of their jobs for the benefit of the organization? How do you get people to think about outcomes and care about customers? Hunt decided the most effective way to do this was by relighting the pilot flame inside federal employees. She would provide the spark.

"I don't consider myself a leader," she says. "I consider myself a cat-alyst. I don't provide a vision for people, because I don't believe you can change them. My goal is for people to catch the vision on their own and become part of a common momentum."

Where does that vision come from? From the federal employees themselves. It's inside them. "We're here to unleash the potential of the people to participate in the system," she says. "What I do, whether we are meeting with employee groups, or with senior agency leader-ship teams, is to ask a lot of questions that are designed to get people to talk about the problems we are facing, and the frustration we all are having doing our jobs. I'll start by sharing my hurts, my disappoint-ments, and my frustration. Then, I try to get them to share theirs."

By sharing her personal struggles and asking a lot of questions, Hunt helps people shed some of the baggage that is smothering them. When she senses the light has been uncovered, "then I'll ask them what it was that brought them into public service. And all of a sudden the pilot lights just go whoosh. People start bouncing off the walls. Everyone has a story. 'It was just after the riots, and I thought . . .' or 'I was part of helping to rebuild cities and it was exciting, and we be-lieved we could make a difference' . . . everyone has a story."

By reminding them of what it was that got them interested in public service in the first place, Hunt is able to spark off the initial enthusiasm. To keep it going means removing the layers of bureau-cracy that tend to snuff it out.

"The government as it grew mirrored big corporations in that it became internally focused, huge, and into processing data for the sake of processing," Hunt says. "As a result, it became this bureau-cracy that just moves stuff around. The government has not been in the business of managing. It's been in the business of regulating, and doing compliance. No one thought about how the organization should be run. They have literally separated policy from operations. The bureaucrats have tried to do the best they can from within their individual stovepipes, but it just became a mess."

Hunt believes that each person has special gifts, including the abil-ity to do productive work. The talent and energy necessary to do that work were lying dormant in Washington. Her job was to help the agencies dismantle the bureaucracy in such a way as to let them out.

"Our role is to help liberate the federal workforce, to undo outdated, top-heavy rules, regulations, and structures, and build a government that enables people to work better and spend less in providing quality services to the American public," Hunt says.

Many people say that the private sector has everything to teach the public sector, and the reverse is not the case. How could government teach us anything about running a business, these people argue. After all, government has constraints that industry does not, such as the Congress, and the fact that its employees are civil servants. Yet the public sector, particularly government, has much to teach the private sector in the areas that it does well, such as serving the larger good, balancing political power, and treating people equally. And, as the Federal Quality Institute is proving, government has some new successes when it comes to refocusing an organization's attention from looking inward to looking outward toward serving a customer and concentrating on outcome thinking.

"The compelling reasons for change aren't as evident in government," Hunt says. "You don't see your profits drop in one quarter, or you don't have a customer call up and say, 'I'm canceling a $10 million order.' But in fact that's exactly what is happening. We are losing market share. The trust of the American public, our customers, in government is the lowest in recorded history."

Hunt and her institute are working with federal agencies to get them to focus on performance and customer service. The questions she asks when she goes into a federal agency are always the same: What is your mission? What are your vision and values? How do we bring about systemic change? How do we create an environment that supports empowered federal employees working in teams throughout the government to serve their customers?

One of the most successful groups she worked with was the U.S. Customs Service. The goal of the Customs reorganization project—dubbed People, Processes, and Partnerships—was to develop a new vision of the agency, one that would make the service "efficient, effective, and adaptive, with high employee involvement." Specifically, the agency wanted to streamline procedures, create a better partnership with its union, and place an increased emphasis on using technology to increase productivity.

Inspired by the National Performance Review, a team of twenty people, represented by all parts of the organization, worked full time for six months to develop a plan of action. They looked at everything—culture, values, mission, operations, management, and organizational structure.

"I haven't seen a group work more diligently and be more open in saying, 'We're really going to rethink the way we do business,' " Hunt explains. "They had not looked at their mandate since 1789. When they did, they started organizing horizontally around serving the customer, instead of vertically around enforcement and regulation." Instead of focusing exclusively on making sure that it captured every tax dollar owed, the agency realized that a large part of its customer base was law-abiding U.S. citizens who found the customs forms they had to fill out confusing and long lines frustrating. So the forms were simplified, and staffing patterns changed. And because Customs works closely with the Immigration Department, as well as the IRS, interagency task forces were created to eliminate duplication of effort and staffing. Information gathered by one agency is now communicated to all three, instead of requiring the separate agencies to each ask the same questions.

"The only way you are going to get lean is to get creative, and liberate people to do things quicker, and better," Hunt says. "You can't trick people into doing that, or order them to; they are going to have to want to do it."

That desire can be a long time coming, when people have spent years, or maybe even decades, working inside an environment that thwarted their creativity at every turn. But if you turn to employees and ask for their help, you will undoubtedly find people who want to have a voice, to make a difference, to believe in their own worth, and to do something of value.

The kind of change Hunt is preaching is difficult to achieve, but the effort is worth it. She uses a metaphor to show what the payoff can be.

"A barnacle swims throughout the sea looking for a home, and then finds it, be it at the bottom of a rock, or vessel, or something else," Hunt says. "He cements his head to his home and stays there the rest of his life. And that's how most of us think our lives should be. We graduate from high school. Graduate from college. Find a job, get married, and then when we become unhappy we ask 'Is that all there is?'

"But I always say I would rather be a butterfly than a barnacle, despite what it has to go through to get there. A caterpiller goes through a whole lot of pain becoming a butterfly, and if you look in on it when it's going through the transformation process, it's ugly, it's messy, it looks near fatal, and you'd be wondering why in hell somebody would subject themselves to that. But the end result—becoming a butterfly—is worth it. And a butterfly is only a caterpillar that learned to let go."

Hunt is trying to help federal employees let go, by freeing them of the restraints imposed by the bureaucracy.

There are promising signs that Hunt's work is beginning to pay off. In a recent study of how well the federal government is run, *Financial World* magazine concluded that the Clinton administration is making "real progress when it comes to improving government financial controls, contract oversight, strategic planning, training, procurement, and a host of other seemingly mundane administrative procedures, which ultimately determine the success or failure of any federal program." Before coming to that conclusion, *Financial World*'s team of reporters went back and revisited ten agencies they had examined two years before. Their conclusion? Seven out of the ten had shown dramatic improvement in the intervening twenty-four months. This improvement is in part a direct result of the work that Hunt and her task force are doing.

Michele Hunt makes her approach to management sound appealing, but there is a danger. If you do what she has done, people will begin to discover their true potential and their real power. They will start challenging you and questioning your authority. But if you are truly ready for such heartfelt participation, you can tap into the most powerful energy that lies dormant inside people.

UNLEASH
PEOPLE'S
POTENTIAL

CREATE A
WINNING
ATTITUDE PARTICIPATION

BUILD
PARTNER-
SHIPS

PROMOTE
EMPLOYEE
OWNERSHIP

NURTURE A
TEAM
ENVIRONMENT

BUILDING PARTNERSHIPS

Partnerships are the building blocks for creating a successful company. You need everyone working together to create a world-class product. Unless everyone is involved, caution, fear, and adversarial relationships will eventually poison a company's best efforts.

Successful leaders build partnerships with all their stakeholders—employees, unions, and suppliers. Each stakeholder is responsible for living the company's mission and values. Everyone has a voice, and everyone must take responsibility for his performance and for the company's success.

History is filled with countless instances where partnerships between labor and management have broken down, or have never been created at all. But when they work, both sides are committed to the principles of participation and cooperation.

It was a life-threatening crisis that got labor and management to change their ways at Ford Motor Company's Wixom Plant. The catalyst for change was Ford's truly disastrous performance in the early 1980s. In less than sixty months, the company lost more than $3 billion, laid off half its workforce, and was on the brink of bankruptcy. The oil shocks and rise of global competition were two of the factors that led to this decline.

But there were internal reasons that contributed to the crisis as well. Ford was producing an inferior product. There were no clear corporate values, and there were intensely adversarial labor relations built on a history of mistrust.

Plant closings in the early 1980s became commonplace. Indeed, it

PAUL NOLAN AND RICHARD GREENFIELD
Wixom Assembly Plant, Ford Motor Company

Paul Nolan

TITLE: Plant Manager

AGE: 54

FAMILY SITUATION: Married;
3 children

EDUCATION: B.A. in Management, Dyke College

HISTORY: Hourly employee at
Ford assembly plant in Lorain,
Ohio (1958–66); numerous
supervisory and management
positions at Lorain (1966–79);
Assistant Manager at Ford
assembly plants in New Jersey
and Kansas City (1979–81);
Manager, Kansas City Assembly
Plant (1981–85); Wixom
Assembly Plant (1985–present)

HOBBIES: Skiing and sailing

Richard Greenfield

President and Chairman
Local UAW

35

Married; 2 children

Oakland Community College
UAW Leadership & Training
Courses

Hourly employee at Wixom
Assembly Plant (1977–85);
full-time union leadership
(1985–present)

Softball and Wallyball

HONORS AND SPECIAL ACCOMPLISHMENTS:
Member, Board of Regents,
Rockhurst College; Government
Labor Management Council,
State of Missouri; Board,
Oakland Community College;
Chairman, United Way,
Major Gifts Division

President, Wayne Ford Civic
League; Member, Westland JCs
Special Olympics Volunteer

HEADQUARTERS: Wixom, Michigan

BUSINESS: Luxury-car production

NUMBER OF EMPLOYEES: 3,700 (Wixom Plant)

GROSS REVENUE: $107.1 billion (Ford Motor Company), 1995

FACTS: According to *Industry Week*, one of the best manufacturing
facilities in the country.

was the experience of closing plants that convinced Paul Nolan, who as manager of Ford facilities had to tell loyal employees that they were suddenly out of a job, and Richard Greenfield, who was out of work for three and a half years as the result of a plant closing, that traditional labor-management relations would have to change.

"Coming up, I was the personification of the old-style Ford manager, the toughest guy on the block," Nolan said, "and I enjoyed being it. I followed that style for twenty years, and then over the course of eighteen months I had to close one plant, and I saw how devastating that could be. People suddenly saw their entire lives uprooted. People—including me—didn't realize how temporary these jobs really are.

"I think the closing of all those plants [eleven in all, nationwide] shook us to the bedrock on both sides," Nolan continues. "It definitely changed the climate and the culture on both sides. It made us realize that we couldn't continue as two warring parties, à la our history. If you're going to battle all day, it isn't going to be good for the leader, for the person on the line, for the person sitting up in the office. It just isn't going to be good for anybody. We would have to learn to work together, in order for us to survive."

Greenfield agrees, adding that because of Ford's financial crisis "we came to realize what's best for everybody is building a quality product, and it takes both sides to do that."

Today, Paul Nolan is in charge of the Wixom Plant, in Wixom, Michigan, the facility that manufactures all of the company's luxury cars—the Mark VIII, Town Car, and Continental. It's a huge facility. Under one roof are more than one hundred acres of assembly lines and machine shops that during two ten-hour shifts produce a total of 1,040 cars every day, five days a week, and have since the first new Lincoln rolled off the line in August 1957.

Richard Greenfield now heads the United Auto Workers (UAW) union local at the constantly busy 320-acre plant site in the Detroit suburbs, where his members unload more than 200 trailers and 21 rail cars each day to get the more than 5,200 parts, from 630 suppliers, used to feed the assembly process.

It has taken Nolan and Greenfield more than just saying they want change for it all to happen. It has taken a level of mutual trust. Nolan has to take Greenfield at his word when he says that the union is going to try to do what is best for producing a world-class product, and in return Greenfield has to believe that Nolan will try to understand the needs of the 3,000 people who work at the plant.

"It's important that I believe Paul cares about us," Greenfield says. "Because if I feel he is not going to help me do my job, then it's going to make my job tougher. And if he makes my job tougher, then I'm going to want to make his job tougher, and then we are right back to the way things were ten years ago."

What helped Nolan and Greenfield start establishing mutual trust was a new mission statement that Ford adopted in the midst of its financial crisis. In talking about corporate values, Ford's senior executives began stressing the importance of the commitment, capacity, and competence of their employees. They wrote:

Our people are the source of our strength. They provide our corporate intelligence and determine our reputation and vitality. Involvement and teamwork are our core values.

- Quality comes first.
- Customers are the focus of everything we do.
- Continuous improvement is essential to our success.
- Dealers and suppliers are our partners.
- Employee involvement is our way of life. We are a team. We must treat each other with trust and respect.

At the core of the new mission statement was the assumption that Ford wanted to build an open, participative culture, where employee commitment and participation at all levels would be essential.

"We used the mission statement as a road map to creating a new partnership," Nolan says.

The road map showed two interconnected paths: management would have to be willing to empower employees, and employees would, in Greenfield's words, "be willing to step up to the pump," and take responsibility for helping to improve things at the plant. Both paths would have to be followed, if there was to be a true partnership.

The new business strategy got institutionalized by putting the guiding principles into practice. Instead of merely talking about what the company wanted to accomplish, Ford would show the world what its new words meant. It would produce "world-class cars."

Both Nolan and Greenfield knew that the secrets of success lay within the people at the plant. It is the people on the line who know how to improve the work processes and produce a quality product. To get those people involved meant Nolan would need to be committed to have participation at all levels of the plant. That meant power in the workplace would have to be shared. Managers would have to motivate, inspire, and partner with workers, not just control and direct them. And the union would have to change as well. They would have to volunteer ideas, act responsibly, and take initiative. They would have to go beyond doing just the minimum called for in the contract.

Greenfield said his membership would be willing to "step up to the pump," providing that it would be safe to take a risk, and that they sincerely believed their contribution would be valued.

"You can't say, 'Okay, we're going have employee involvement,' and then hold a meeting where an employee offers a great idea and then not empower him to carry it out. If you take that approach, you never are going to have employees involved."

So not only did Nolan have to trust that employees would be willing to contribute ideas for how the line could be run better, or defects could be reduced, but he also had to believe that they would—if empowered—carry out those ideas. Employees were also expected to walk away as mature adults when they didn't get what they wanted. This new way of working meant that he would have to trust employees to police themselves, and take responsibility for acting in a way that would allow the plant to be run efficiently. Greenfield gives a simple example that makes the point.

"I think in the past management was much too quick to discipline," he says. "One of the first things Paul did was to instill a policy that said if there is a problem then we—members of the union—will talk to an employee to find out what the problem is, before someone is disciplined.

"A couple of weeks ago we had a guy come in with a radio that he knew was too loud for his area, but the supervisor didn't have to get involved. A few of the people he worked with went to him and said,

'We don't mind you bringing in your radio, but we don't want to hear it.' Still, he kept it kind of loud.

"Nobody said anything else to him, but all of a sudden when it was time for lunch he found no one would sit with him," Greenfield continues. No one wants to be the lone bird, and eventually the guy got the message, and turned the volume on his radio way down. This could have escalated to something where the union was involved and eventually the plant manger would have had to say, 'No more radios,' but it worked out pretty well."

If you focus on the good people, the small number of bad ones will stand out, and peer influence will help to manage them. As part of the "stepping up to the pump" process the union has decided to deal with difficult people on its own.

Life in the factory is tough. The assembly line is constantly moving and people have little down time. In a pressure-packed situation, small things can escalate into big problems in a hurry. (That's why both Nolan and Greenfield believe in the importance of being role models and must be more mature and engage in active problem solving.) Greenfield stresses that you can't tell people what they want to hear, you must tell the truth, or you'll get caught in your own lies. Nolan constantly reminds everyone of the need for patience, as both sides go about building a labor-management partnership.

LESSONS LEARNED

In many ways, what is going on under the huge roof in Wixom, Michigan, is a model for the way future labor-management relations may work. We are seeing a new kind of labor leader emerge in Wixom, one who is mature and accountable and understands the business. And we are seeing a new kind of plant manager as well. He now is accessible and empowers and treats people with respect. And not only have these two jobs changed, so has the role of the worker. He now acts responsibly, communicates, and tries to solve problems.

It is important to stress what everyone has learned, when forging the new partnership.

- **We all have to work at this.** Labor and management leaders have to accept the day-to-day operating responsibility for the partnership. The concepts governing the new partnership—fairness, honesty, open communication, and taking responsibility—are easy to understand. The execution is difficult. Both sides must channel time, money, and people resources into getting the job done. Everyone in the organization must be made to see that cooperation is in the best interests of all.

- **We must model the behavior we want.** Labor-management partnerships must be relationship intensive, if they are going to work well. Both sides must continually demonstrate the right attitudes and actions, especially in the presence of others. And both must trust that the other will do the right thing. Without that trust, the partnership will fail. And the trust that is required to make the partnership work will require continual nurturing.

- **The partnership will be constantly evolving.** People must be willing to make running changes in their efforts and relationships, as the needs and the priorities of the company change. It requires everyone to be willing to run some risks. What is happening at Wixom is an ongoing organizational renewal process. Both sides are discovering that a company can change, adults can learn, and creating a common future is a much more compelling vision than constant bickering between union and management.

- **We can build on our successes.** Initiatives at Wixom have evolved over time from fairly simple applications of labor-management cooperation to those that are comprehensive and need to be integrated to create and sustain a large-scale organization transformation. The secret is to start small, achieve a success, and use that success as a stepping-stone toward undertaking a larger project.

Nolan and Greenfield created a climate of trust, shared values, and common purpose. At Wixom they replaced caution and compliance with initiative and independence. They knew that participation was not an end in itself, but a means of producing a better car—the best way they both could ensure that the Wixom plant would remain up and running.

They also understood that people needed to learn how to participate as partners, needed to be recognized for their contribution, and needed to learn how to deal with conflict and shared planning. Everybody in the plant is responsible for living out the values and guiding principles of the new corporate mission statement. Everyone has a voice in deciding how the work gets done. This is vital. Each person must discover his voice, take responsibility for his behavior, and make commitments to others. That is the only true way a partnership can be built.

The new approach to producing a car has paid off. The Wixom plant was the first one to receive Ford's Q1 Award, which recognizes plants or departments that are living up to the company's goal of producing the highest quality possible. And the plant was cited by *Industry Week* as one of the ten best manufacturing facilities in the country.

Indeed, it was this new approach to management-labor relations that helped Ford gain recognition for having the most productive plants in the world, led to an increased market share, and perhaps most important helped turn Ford back into being a successful, profitable company. It has allowed Ford to move rapidly toward its goal of being best in class management, best in class products, best in class service, best in class processes, best in class values, and best in class people.

"The bottom line comes down to this: There's an old way of doing business and a new way," Greenfield says. "I don't know if the new one's going to make us successful as a union or not—or whether it is going to make Ford successful—but I can tell you the old way definitely was not."

In the end, both company and union must succeed. In order to be successful, there must be greater interdependence, cooperation, and focus on common goals. Nolan and Greenfield have set the stage for making that happen.

UNLEASH PEOPLE'S POTENTIAL

CREATE A WINNING ATTITUDE

PARTICIPATION

BUILD PARTNER-SHIPS

PROMOTE EMPLOYEE OWNERSHIP

NURTURE A TEAM ENVIRONMENT

NURTURING A TEAM ENVIRONMENT

Two minds are better than one. Many minds are best. Collective wisdom is simply greater than individual insight. Leaders can tap into this collective wisdom by nurturing a team environment.

The leader starts by inspiring his people with a meaningful mission and a clear business plan. He communicates his plan with simple messages and sets clear goals. Then the leader gets out of the way. In a fast, flexible organization, the leader inspires others to take responsibility and make commitments. He shares power, trusts people's competence and judgment, and creates leaders at all levels of the organization. He is both facilitator and follower.

To be successful, the leader must understand that his power is outside himself. It rests with the people he is responsible for. To tap into that power, the leader must abandon the old baggage of dominance, control, and self-centeredness. This does not mean an abdication of responsibility. While inspiring others, the leader must retain not only his vision but accountability for the project.

On June 12, 1994, more than a thousand people from around the world stood alongside a runway at Paine Field in Everett, Washington. A plane about to soar into the air is always a dramatic sight. But for the people gathered outside the Boeing plant, the flight on this particular rainy spring day had added significance. They were watching the maiden voyage of the Boeing 777, a plane that soon will become the new backbone for airline fleets around the globe.

Some 7,000 people, in over a dozen countries, working in 238 separate design teams, spent four years and $4 billion to create the 777.

ALAN MULALLY
Boeing Commercial Airplane Group

TITLE: Senior Vice President, Airplane Development and Definition

AGE: 49

FAMILY SITUATION: Married; 5 children

EDUCATION: B.S. and M.S., University of Kansas; Master in Management, Massachusetts Institute of Technology

HISTORY: Boeing Commercial Airplane Group: Senior Vice President, Airplane Development and Definition (1994); Vice President and General Manager, 777 Division (1992–94), Vice President, 777 Engineering (1989–92)

HONORS AND SPECIAL ACCOMPLISHMENTS: Alfred P. Sloan Fellow; Associate Fellow, American Institute of Aeronautics and Astronautics; Fellow, England's Royal Aeronautical Society; Advisory Board Member: National Aeronautics and Space Administration, University of Washington, University of Kansas, and the Air Force Scientific Advisory Board; Boeing's Engineering Employee of the Year (1978); American Institute of Aeronautics and Astronautics Technical Management Award; *Space Technology* magazine's "Laurels" recognition

HEADQUARTERS: Seattle, Washington

BUSINESS: Largest aerospace firm, leading manufacturer of commercial jet transports, and the nation's largest exporter.

NUMBER OF EMPLOYEES: 125,000

GROSS REVENUE: $25.4 billion

The plane, which will be in the fleets of over two dozen airlines around the world by 1998, has 3 million parts, from 1,500 suppliers located in 62 countries worldwide.

Managing this project was as tricky as machining all the pieces together, and yet Alan R. Mulally, vice president and general manager of Boeing's 777 division, says he deserves virtually no credit. "Our team did it," he says. "I just don't have enough hours in the day to say thank you for everything they do. It's the most special thing I've ever seen. What we can do together is unbelievable."

To build a team that turns in this kind of performance, Mulally began by looking inside himself. "It is important to me that I am associated with something meaningful," Mulally says. "Making a new airplane that can bring people together, and communicate around the world, is a very compelling vision for me. The only way I would be able to make the contribution I wanted to make would be by getting everybody involved in the project together and enable them to contribute."

Team leaders believe that each individual is essential and can make a difference to the overall success of the enterprise. So what Mulally did, in order to accomplish something important to him, was change the mental model of what a leader is. Leaders in traditional, hierarchical, formal, compliance-driven organizations are domineering and controlling. Their task is to recreate themselves inside the organization. As a result, they value individual performance. Mulally, as a new kind of leader, understands the power of working together, and he believes in collective wisdom.

"I am not arrogant. I don't know whether humble is the right word, but I do know that I know relatively very little," he says. "When I talk to a lot of people, I get the feeling that they are trying to tell me how much they know. Well, we all know only what we know, so why don't we just work together, and stop all the inhibitors of trying to tell each other what we know.

"Now if you really believe that, then all your power is outside of you. All of your power is in everybody trying to figure out how to accomplish your plan, to accomplish your goal. The rest of your job is enabling everybody to contribute, to feel appreciated for great work with a thank you."

This means that Mulally is comfortable playing the role of the leader (by challenging, participating, and clarifying) as well as the follower (by listening, taking advice, and supporting).

The way Mulally runs things, a leader is a resource person, has great interpersonal skills, and is supportive. This requires being secure in his position as the team leader. "I have to be self-confident to act this way," he says. "If I worried that people were going to talk behind my back, or tell something to my boss, I could never operate this way."

He sees his primary job as establishing an enabling environment. That means "everybody knows what is going on, and everybody knows what needs to be done. That's my biggest contribution: I help set the goal, help establish the plan, make sure everybody knows where we are, and then I carry water.

"I have a fiduciary responsibility in my leadership position to bring all of our thoughts together in a plan, to satisfy the customer and keep us in business. I can't escape that. But it is the team that makes us a success."

Mulally uses these insights to create a team environment. There are over two hundred work teams at Boeing 777. At the top of the pyramid is a team of five who oversee the project. Mulally is their team leader.

One of Mulally's greatest strengths is his ability to promote the idea of "working together." In fact, "Working Together" was the name given to the 777 project; it was the phrase emblazoned on the first plane, and it is the internal, international philosophy of collaboration that governed the entire project.

There is a sense of interdependency within the Boeing 777 team. The work is about having a shared mission, a shared plan, shared involvement, and shared responsibility.

Step 1. Shared Mission

"We wanted to create a shared destiny for our team," Mulally says. "It starts with everybody wanting to support the mission. We want everyone to feel, 'Boy, building a brand-new airplane would be worth contributing to.' The mission has to be bigger than any one of us, and it has to feel good. Making a new generation of airplane feels like a really good thing. It's meaningful. So that became our mission: building the best new airplane we possibly could in our customers' eyes."

Step 2. Shared Plans

Once we have everyone united around a mission, we need a plan to make our goal a reality.

"We all have to use our collective knowledge to achieve what we have decided we are going to devote our lives to," Mulally says. "The plan tells us how we are going to get there."

An implicit part of the plan calls for using all the skills of everyone involved. Drawing on everyone's creativity and resources, Mulally says, is fundamental.

"If you are going to do a project that involves so many people around the world—all of the manufacturers, all of the airlines—you are going to need every skill imaginable: program management, finances, designers, analysts. And if you're going to make the best plane in the world, which was our mission, then you must include everybody's knowledge." That's why from the very beginning Mulally had his customers, representatives from the major airlines, sitting in with his teams. He was looking to bring as much knowledge as possible to the project.

But that knowledge must be applied to where it is needed. People must not only buy into the plan but know where they fit in. And letting them know is the next step Mulally takes in creating his high-performance team environment: everyone knows exactly what he is supposed to do.

"The work can change over time," he says. "We will grow and develop more skills and do different jobs. But we don't want any ambiguity about what our contribution is. Everybody needs to know our business reality, because this is our business. Everybody needs to know what our customers want and need. Everybody needs to know what our plan is to exceed our customers' expectations."

And the plan needs to be *simple*. In complex projects such as this one, which involved not only extensive computer modeling but also people from different cultures around the world working together, the *simpler* you can keep things the better. And simplicity can be achieved by communicating with clear messages and accessible goals.

In a memo, he offered some easy rules to help make the plan a reality:

- Know our business realities.
- Know our plan to exceed customers' expectations.
- No secrets.
- Respect each other.
- Answer notes quickly.
- Keep everyone informed about your progress.
- Expect the unexpected; expect to deal with it.
- Ask for feedback regularly.
- Ask for help.
- Enjoy the journey and each other.

"The world is very complicated," Mulally says. "So if we want to engage a large number of people to accomplish a meaningful mission, everyone must be able to understand everything quickly and easily."

Mulally was able to reduce his plan to a simple equation that everyone instantly understood:

Our 777 Business Plan = Customer Satisfaction + Continuous Quality Improvement + Working Together.

"We have three goals that were chosen by the customer. We wanted to produce a better plane. We wanted to produce a plane that was going to be completely ready to go into service when we said it would. We wanted to produce a plane that was better value in our customers' eyes.

"These goals were broad enough to enable anyone to make a contribution. They don't tell you how to do your job. The goals were also different enough from the way business was being done to create a picture of a new way of working. It was enabling."

CATIA, the new Computer Aided Three-Dimensional Interactive Application design program, is a tangible example of how this new approach to leadership played out in practice. Up until the 777, the creation of an airplane was linear. Designers would have a conversation with the boss and maybe some customers, and a mock-up would be created. Individually or by function (engineering, maintenance, etc.), people would examine the mock-up and suggest what needed to be changed. A new mock-up would be created, and the process would start all over again. Mulally had the mock-ups done through CATIA, a computer system to which just about everyone had access. Gathered in a room lined with computer screens, everyone involved in the project sat before a terminal that showed the current configuration of the plane. Everyone could suggest changes.

"This way an electrical person could talk directly to a structure person and they could both talk to the mechanics," Mulally says. And each time a suggestion was made, it would be typed into the CATIA system, so that people could see the changes in real time. "Everyone was in constant communication with everyone else, so that we could make a better plane."

Sharing is the key to Mulally's management approach. He shares information, letting people involved in the project know exactly what is going on at all times, and he shares decision making. The team, not Mulally, used CATIA to design the new plane.

Step 3. Shared Involvement

Mulally's way of leading was different from the traditional model, in which the boss controls all the information and tells people what to do. A few examples tell the story:

- In the old model, Boeing built the plane the way it thought best, and then delivered it to customers. In the new model, customers were part of the design process from the beginning.
- In the old model, engineers were part of the design process from the beginning. In the new model, engineers, mechanics, and others worked together on the design.
- In the old model, maintenance manuals were written by engineers and delivered to the maintenance department after the plane was built. In the new model, mechanics and technicians helped write the manual, and the manuals were in place long before the plane arrived.

"One of the most important things I try to do is create an organization that enables everybody to contribute to their fullest," he says. "To me this ties back to having a meaningful mission, a goal, and a plan to get there. The more that plan tells you what we are trying to achieve, and the less it tells you how to achieve it, the better it is. It's almost the antithesis of delegating. This approach allows each of us to use our creativity to figure out how to make the plan happen. My job is to ensure that this process happens."

Step 4. Shared Responsibility

Team leaders believe that a sense of ownership and responsibility must be strongly felt at every level of the organization. The way to do that is to create teams organized around the customer. This breeds a desire to be accountable within the people closest to the work, and ultimately improves quality, cycle time, adaptability, and customer service.

In the initial design for the 777, for example, the toilet seats closed with what focus groups called "a big bang." This certainly wasn't a safety problem. And there was nothing wrong with the lid itself. It fit exactly as it should. But the sound of its slamming was annoying, and potential passengers didn't like it.

"So the airlines said, 'We'd like to have the sound go away,' " Mulally recalls. "You can imagine the hours that the team working on it spent trying to understand the problem, not only what caused it, but exactly what passengers were objecting to. What do you mean by 'big bang'? What kind of sound, if any, would be acceptable?"

Not only did the team come up with a way to eliminate the problem, it added another feature. Now, as the top goes down, it attaches to the bottom, and they both go down *quietly* together. There is now no way to leave the toilet seat up. The team felt this would delight the passengers. Says Mulally: "The message the team was trying to send was, 'Look at this, wow, the people who designed this thing are really being thoughtful. They are trying to be customer oriented. They're really trying to make a meaningful contribution.' " It only takes thoughtfulness like this to inspire customer loyalty.

Mulally spends almost as much time caring about what is going on inside of him as he does about what is going on inside the organization. He wants to ensure he has what he calls "emotional resiliency." What he means is that it is very important that the leader take care of himself, be able to deal with change and uncertainty, and control his reactions to situations.

"What I have the most influence over is my own response. I think I can be most effective and help everyone else by staying on an even keel. If there are things that you feel bad about one minute and good the next, you won't be able to deal with everything as well as you could if you were balanced."

The way to do this, he feels, is to "look at things the way they really are. They are not good or bad. They just are the way they are. And then we can decide together, develop a plan, and move forward from where we are to where we want to be. You aren't encumbered by judgment calls. Just look at the data. Emotional resilience means not getting too tired, not getting stressed out, not getting too happy or too sad." It's all about attitude—attitude about yourself and the world around you.

Alan Mulally creates leadership at every level of the organization. He still maintains the leadership roles of vision, initiative, and accountability. But he has abandoned the old baggage of believing that power should be centralized in the hands of one person. Mulally inspires and enables people to take responsibility and ownership. He is available and visible to his team, modeling the behavior he wants others to emulate. He is a source of inspiration and support.

For Mulally, different business problems require different kinds of teams. Some people are natural team players, others prefer to work alone. The challenge is to create the right team, with the right people, for the right job.

It is also hard to let go of the past and adapt to new ways. Many senior managers at Boeing have chosen to leave, instead of change. Mulally understands that team leadership requires a whole new set of skills, and that the best solutions come from the collective wisdom of individual insight. It works. It is rewarding. And it is fun.

PROMOTING
EMPLOYEE OWNERSHIP

The dream of every leader is to build a workforce of people who act as if they own the company. Employee-owners are responsible and resourceful. They see the whole picture, are literate on business issues, take initiative, experiment with new ideas, and solve problems on their own. The results of their efforts are higher productivity and commitment, continuous improvement, and organizational pride.

Successful leaders know that creating an "employee-owned" culture requires both psychological and financial ownership. Psychological ownership results from true participation. When people see that their efforts can make a difference, that they are an integral part of the process, they give more of themselves. To reach full participation, people must also own the financial risks, and rewards, of the business.

In November 1989, led by Russ Maier, the 5,000 employees put up $4,000 each and bought the steel bar division of LTV Steel for $280 million—$260 million of it borrowed. They named the company Republic Engineered Steels.

The first lessons Maier brought to Republic were those he had learned in the final frustrating months at LTV Steel, trying to help his company cope with the fact that the steel market was going to hell. He had helped arrange the merger of Republic Steel, where he was chief operating officer, with J & L Steel, in the hopes that the two companies would be able to operate more efficiently together,

---

RUSSELL W. MAIER
Republic Engineered Steels, Inc.

TITLE: Chairman and Chief Executive Officer

AGE: 57

FAMILY SITUATION: Married; 3 sons

EDUCATION: B.S. in Industrial Management, Purdue University

HISTORY: Joined Republic Steel in 1960 as industrial engineer; positions of increasing responsibility for nonsteel subsidiaries; Executive Vice President and Chief Operating Officer (1983); Executive Vice President of LTV Steel when Republic merged with J & L Steel (1984); led employee purchase of LTV Steel's Bar Division, which became Republic Engineered Steels (1989)

HOBBIES: Active in youth work, particularly boys and girls clubs and Boy Scouts

HONORS AND SPECIAL ACCOMPLISHMENTS: Board, Aultman Hospital, United National Bank & Trust Company, Republic Storage Systems, and American Iron and Steel Institute

HEADQUARTERS: Massillon, Ohio

BUSINESS: Production of high quality bar and specialty steels

NUMBER OF EMPLOYEES: 5,000 employee owners

SALES REVENUES: $805 million

---

but it hadn't helped. The combined company kept lopping off costs, divisions, and even Maier's friends, but nothing would stanch the flow of red ink.

"I can't overemphasize how difficult this period was, because we didn't see any other alternatives," Maier recalls. "It was like the patient has cancer, and you keep operating, thinking if you take off the arm it will stop the cancer from spreading. So you do that and say, 'There's another ten thousand people we have to fire, but at least we'll save eighty thousand jobs.' But it didn't work. So you go back the next year and take out another twenty thousand jobs, and say, 'Now this will do it.' But it didn't. It was a very frustrating period, because nothing we tried worked because we had too many forces against us."

And what was even more frustrating for Maier, who by then was running LTV Steel's Bar Division, was the uncertainty of the future of the Division. Because of LTV's bankruptcy filing, many aspects of the future were difficult to define.

"LTV had gone into bankruptcy by this point, and all they would say was they were going to exit bankruptcy without the Bar Division. We didn't know if they were going to sell it or shut it down. People would ask me what was going to happen, and I would have to tell them I didn't know."

This experience, more than any other in his professional career, brought home to Maier exactly what the people who were working for him felt.

"At the end of the day, what they want is exactly what you want," Maier says. "They want to feel like they are being treated fairly. They—and you—want to have at least some input, and if possible some part of the decision-making process that affects their workplace. You don't want to come and be told what to do, and feel like you have no control over your life."

This insight led to another. "Our managers always felt if there was just a way to get all the people as dedicated to the business as we are, we could be successful," Maier says. "We never understood that to do that we had to give something away. What we wanted was for our employees to feel the way we did, and we thought we could get them there with money, or with a great pension plan, or with incentives. The fact is, you need to do all those things, but I found you need to do more, thanks to the experience I went through with the way I was treated. People are willing to share the pain with you, but what they want in exchange is a voice in how they go forward. If you give them that, they're hooked."

With Republic Engineered Steels, Maier was committed to leading differently than had been his experience in the past. He would tell the truth, share pain as well as information, and always give people hope about the future. He was convinced that this was the best way to inspire an organization and draw the best out of people.

Maier knew that, in order to get employees to contribute fully, he would need to teach people how to be independent, responsible, accountable employee-owners. The best way to do that, he believed, would be by putting information, resources, and power in the hands of people closest to the work—and closest to the customer. He was convinced that if he could get every person to feel responsible for the performance of the company, everything from morale to product quality would improve. "It makes sense," he says, "that you would get better steel if it were made by the owner."

"Our objective was to build a company that provides our customers with world-class quality products and services which fully meet their needs," Maier says. "Only by meeting those objectives would we, as employee-owners, make our jobs more secure and increase the value of our company."

To do this, Maier knew, would require Republic to enter a new era of employee involvement and cooperation, if the company was going to survive in a steel industry that was facing foreign competition, as well as the rise of specialty mills that were skimming off the high-margin products. To be successful, Maier said, "we would have to develop a new management system that provided the opportunity for every employee to fully contribute to the success of the company."

The composition of Republic Steels' board of directors reflects Maier's philosophy. Four of the directors are union designees, three are from management, including one salaried employee, as well as Maier.

Yet it wasn't all easy for Maier getting his employees to think they should take responsibility for the successes and failures of Republic Steels. The employees may have become owners, by virtue of putting down their money and owning stock, but they had no idea what that meant. Worse, many employees said they wanted more responsibility and more participation, but they wouldn't take their share of the responsibility. They were conflicted about being an independent adult and being a dependent child.

Many of us have an inherent desire, at some level, to be taken care of, to have others protect us and keep us safe from the cruel competitive world. In return for this protection, we are willing to be compliant, dependent, loyal, and give up control. So even when employees said they wanted more responsibility, and wanted to participate in decisions that would affect the company's future, they weren't always willing to follow through on their promises, because they were either afraid of failure or afraid of the unknown. And so they would hang back. Maier understood this.

"We are all creatures of our environment," Maier says. "If you spent thirty years in an environment where everything was done one way, and now someone came along and said everything's changed, you would be confused too. You'd say things like 'Even though I am an owner, you expect me to come to work forty hours a week? You mean I still have my same job and same pay? So what do you mean I'm an owner? All of the owners I have ever seen ran into the liquor store for a quart of beer or took off whenever they wanted.' "

So Maier had to teach his employees what it meant to be an owner, to get their thinking to go from "Well, that's their problem" to "I am the company, so I better go deal with that."

To help employees make that transition, Maier began holding classes designed to explain what stock ownership was all about. He began by drawing analogies to one of Republic's biggest customers, General Motors.

"You can go out and buy stock in General Motors, and you'll be one of the owners of GM," Maier began. "As you receive stock here, you are an owner of Republic Steels. Just like at General Motors, we have a board of directors and the board hires the management and is responsible for providing the leadership of the company. The biggest difference is that you, as a shareholder of General Motors, really can't affect what happens at GM. Here, you can, by doing your job better. You can be a problem solver. You can directly contribute to the success of the company. At GM, someone else has control."

Republic's workers now wear two hats, one as employee and the other as owner, and each role enhances the other, although each is different.

"This was the beginning of teaching people how to be responsible, accountable, employee-owner adults in this new workplace," Maier says. "Everything else grew out of that."

Employees began to want a wider perspective of how the business worked. Maier helped by offering information on Employee Stock Ownership Plans (ESOPs), and taught everyone how to read a balance sheet and an income statement.

The overarching goal behind all his actions was to get employees to feel and act like owners. He wanted them to internalize a sense of responsibility for the business, and have them do all they could to achieve Republic's business objectives. But to get the behavior he wanted required Maier to share information about the entire business—everything from the company's business plans to its quarterly performance. People want to know where they stand, and how they can contribute. Employees must have access to information, knowledge, power, and rewards at every level of the company; otherwise they won't care to put forth the discretionary effort necessary to optimize their performance.

"I remember a woman, one of our hourly workers, coming up to me in one of our Gary plants, after I went out there to give one of my updates about how we were doing," Maier recalls. "She said, 'You know, Mr. Maier, what you are doing is good. You're the first manager who ever came out when we were making money. In the past, management only came out to talk to us when they were in trouble, and they wanted something from us.' This is when trust started to develop, when we told them the bad news and the good, when there was good."

There are two parts of an employee-owned culture. One is the psychological aspect, the other is financial. Pay is very symbolic in our lives. We measure our self-worth and personal security, in large part, by how much we get paid. Most of our current pay systems reward executives in a disproportionately high manner compared to the rest of the employees. That sends the very clear message that there are different rules for executives and the rest of the workforce. There is another problem with the way we pay people. Our pay systems are aimed at rewarding individual behavior, not team or companywide performance.

At some point, when employees are asked for their opinions or ways to save money, they are going to ask, "What's in it for me?" If employees are going to share in the bad times, they also want to share in the good.

We need new pay systems that are fair, that value teamwork and interdependence and are based on outcomes. If we want to create a workforce of employee-owners, then we need to redistribute the pieces of the pie and create wealth at every level of the organization. Russ Maier understood the psychology and business concepts behind this principle. He knew that until there was psychological and financial ownership people would not trust enough to participate fully.

"Our pay for the next several years is all based on cost savings and profits," Maier says. "As employees reduce costs, based on a predetermining formula, Republic essentially shares one half of those savings with employees in the form of increased pay. The program is called 'Target 60' and the salary and hourly employees' pay increases are both linked to achieving target levels. When the 'Target 60' goal has been reached, profit sharing begins for all employees. So now the driver for more pay is the same whether you are hourly, salaried, union or non-union. To me this makes sense."

In other words, everyone in the company now shares the risk (after all everyone is an owner), and everyone shares the rewards. Making changes of this kind was not easy at any level of the organization, including the top. The new approach to employee participation required Maier to change as a leader. (He would have to share power, trust people's competence and judgment, and share ownership and the limelight.) This, to be kind, is not the way things are traditionally done in a steel mill.

Equally hard, Maier had to be patient. There was so much pain and mistrust built up inside the company that it would take a while for people to believe they could truly make a difference. He chose not to protect them from the stresses and challenges of running the business. And he would not put a Band-Aid on their cynicism. Instead, he acknowledged it was there, and asked employees to join him in partnership. It took a constant dialogue about common purpose, ownership, and responsibility until employees were ready— and willing—to be true partners.

Maier needed that patience with his managers, as well. Many of them had never shared power, which just compounded the problems of converting to employee ownership. The first line of supervision, 80 percent of whom had originally started as members of the union, were not comfortable with their new roles. Instead of ordering people about, they now had to engage them, guide them and their work, and spend more time on people issues. And they were concerned about sharing too much information.

"I told them I understood, but I also told them the risk of not sharing was greater than the risk of doing it," Maier says. "You can't give people selected information. You've got to give them all the information, the good and the bad. Everything. And you have to teach them how to understand it, and they have to be responsible for it. They have to suffer the consequences of their own actions. If they don't understand what their actions are doing to them, that's not fair. If that happens, you haven't done your job."

There was one other major fact Maier had to deal with. As hard as it was, he had to recognize that some of his people would never go along with the changed environment, no matter how much power he was willing to give away, or how participative he wanted the culture to become.

"We want to create a culture in which anyone who wishes to help this company be successful can find a mechanism to do it," Maier says. "I can't make you do it. I can only create the environment that will allow it to happen. We have had seventy years of 'we-they' in the plants. And I'm willing to bet it will probably take seven to ten years to fully institutionalize this new way of doing business. And even when we get it done, there will be ten or fifteen percent of the people—managers too—who just won't buy in. They won't give a damn if we are successful or not. There is nothing you can do about that. You have to accept that there always will be background noise, and some people who won't want to become part of the program, and so you just have to let them go. They have to understand we are trying to align the economic motivators, the intellectual motivators, and the emotional motivators, so that all our people can create success in the enterprise."

Are those objectives in alignment? Look at the results.

Union and management are working well together. There has been a significant drop in grievances. Problem-solving and continuous-improvement teams are interspersed within the company. Employees now have the responsibility for selecting peers, helping design new work systems in factories, and picking suppliers. Continuous improvement has become everyone's job. On the shop floor, workers and supervisors sit on production-management committees, looking for ways to improve quality and cut costs—and are finding them.

Employee suggestions for revising the way work is done generated $65 million in cost savings in just eighteen months. In one case, the company saved $3.6 million just by separating different types of scrap. (Mixing types of scrap results in steel of uneven quality, frequently requiring rework.) In addition, more than one hundred continuous-improvement projects are producing savings in excess of $2 million a year.

In an era when many American steel producers are cutting back and some even shutting their doors, unable to compete with nonunion mini-mills, Republic Engineered Steels is expanding. It recently invested in a $165 million state-of-the-art continuous caster-direct billet mill, purchased two competitors' plants, and paid off half the $260 million in debt it took on to fund the leveraged buy-out. The company has received three General Motors Mark of Excellence awards, four Ford Q-1 awards and a Honda Production Support award, as well as an award from the U.S. Department of Labor.

"I would say we have improved our productivity by 20 percent since the buyout, with no real capital investment," Maier says. "There's tremendous power if you use the mind of every employee."

CREATING A
WINNING ATTITUDE

Successful leaders create successful people, people who know how to win. They do that by caring deeply about their people. They recognize that the people who work for them want to feel good about who they are and what they are doing.

Successful leaders know how important dreams are for creating a winning tomorrow, and how to instill a team with the right principles to both inspire it and glue it together.

Successful leaders also know how to nurture a winning environment, by creating a winning attitude that builds people's confidence one day at a time.

These leaders teach others how to win, how to lose, and how to play by the rules. This ability—and the skill to make it happen—grows out of a deep understanding of people's needs and aspirations. It also comes directly from blending two sides of the leader's personality—the tough, competitive side that demands winning performances and loves to win, and the softer, compassionate side that is caring and understanding of others.

It all came down to this. With fifteen seconds left, UCLA, trailing by five, faced a fourth down on the University of Wisconsin's eighteen yard line. A touchdown would win the game. Anything less, and Wisconsin would take home its first Rose Bowl.

UCLA quarterback Wayne Cook took the snap, faded back to pass, and saw all his receivers were covered. As the Wisconsin defense drew ever closer, he waited, and waited for someone to break free. Finally—in desperation—Cook took off for the goal line. Three-

---

BARRY ALVAREZ
University of Wisconsin Football Team

TITLE: Head Coach

AGE: 48

FAMILY SITUATION: Married; 3 children

EDUCATION: B.S. and M.A., University of Nebraska

HISTORY: High school coach (1971–78); Assistant Coach, University of Iowa (1979–86) and Notre Dame (1987–89)

HONORS AND SPECIAL ACCOMPLISHMENTS: 1993 National Coach of the Year, selected by American Football Coaches Association, Bobby Dodd Foundation, and *College and Football Newsweekly*

HEADQUARTERS: Madison, Wisconsin

BUSINESS: College football

NUMBER OF EMPLOYEES: 20

GROSS REVENUE: $7 million

---

quarters of the crowd—an estimated 75,000 Wisconsin fans, who had traveled two thousand miles for the game—went nuts. Something that they never thought would occur in their lifetime had just happened. The University of Wisconsin had won the Rose Bowl.

Even more impressive than the victory was the fact that Wisconsin was there at all. For decades, the Badgers were a joke in the Big Ten conference. In fact, they were a joke in all of college football. The university may have been known as one of the country's better state schools, but the football team was known as everyone's doormat. They were expected to lose.

Barry Alvarez, who took over as head football coach in 1990, changed all that. Alvarez has been a winner his whole life, beginning back when he played "midget" football. The teams he played on won in high school. He played in three college-bowl games, as a linebacker for the University of Nebraska, and he was a member of the coaching staffs at Iowa and Notre Dame that produced championship teams.

While the match between Alvarez and Wisconsin was perfect, the situation he inherited was anything but. Game attendance was poor. The school couldn't recruit the best high school players, because they didn't want to play for a college with a losing football program, and the expectation everyone—both on campus and off—had when the Badgers played on Saturday was that the game would end with their team on the wrong end of the score.

Alvarez began his tenure by changing attitudes off the field. Immediately after taking over, he had the worn carpets torn out of the Camp Randall Stadium locker room, had all the training facilities painted, and he instructed the secretarial and support staff on how to dress, act, and answer the phone. If the University of Wisconsin football team was to become winners, they would be surrounded by winners and a championship environment.

Then he went on to his coaching staff—the people who would interact with his potential players. The change he made was small but symbolic—it was all in a ring.

"When you go out recruiting, the kids all look at your ring," says Alvarez, who, when he took over at Wisconsin, was still wearing the ring he received for being the assistant head coach when Notre Dame won the national championship. "Well, I'm sitting in a staff meeting, right after I came here, and there are three guys who are wearing Illinois Rose Bowl rings, and two of us wearing Notre Dame national championship rings, and somebody else had one from Iowa. We were selling other schools. We weren't promoting the University of Wisconsin. We needed to have a symbol that we were moving forward. So in my first year here I had rings made for us. They are a little bit bigger than all the others that were out there. They're bigger than the national championship ring and all the bowl rings. We have the nicest ring."

The coaching staff's larger ring symbolized success, made people feel special, important, and part of a first-class program. Especially when you're combatting years of a losing attitude, pride and self-esteem are critical. Alvarez learned about both from his Spanish grandmother, who lived with him when he was growing up. So proud was she of her Spanish heritage she never learned English. She managed to transfer some of her pride to her grandson.

But while important, pride and self-esteem are not sufficient. People need to believe in their leaders, their own abilities, and also need to receive constant positive feedback from the community around them.

Alvarez's approach is to win one day at a time. "There are no short-cuts," he says. Growing up in a blue-collar household in a small mining town, he learned that you have to work hard every day to accomplish what you want. That learning has stuck with him. You hear it as he talks about how he goes about building a successful team. "Instead of talking about winning the Rose Bowl every damn day, you focus on having a great practice today, and a great game on Saturday."

He starts with actions that are within his players' control and are tangible and easy to accomplish. Setting relatively easy goals at first minimizes the cost of trying, and reduces the risk of failure. It also builds people's confidence and reinforces their natural desire to succeed. As they got used to succeeding, Alvarez raised the bar a little each day, understanding that small successes breed larger ones.

This process works because players believe in their coach, a man who is comfortable with himself. Alvarez allows his leadership style to reflect his principles and his personality. He has the courage to be who he is, a self-described "people person." Alvarez is always patting his players on the back, has a fully stocked candy dish prominently displayed on his desk, as an additional inducement to get people on his team to stop by to discuss whatever is on their mind, and in general treats his players as he would his own son.

And Alvarez is not afraid to ask for a lot. "I've asked my guys for some ridiculous things," he says. "When we went to [play a bowl game in] Japan, I had them kick back their body clock an hour and a half a day, in the week leading up to the trip. The day before we went, we practiced from eleven at night until one-thirty in the morning, then we jumped on a bus, drove to Chicago, and I told them they couldn't sleep either on the bus or the plane—and it was a fifteen-hour plane ride—because it was going to be midnight when we landed. If they don't trust me, things like this aren't going to work. But they do trust me, because they know I am trying to give them an edge. That's why I can ask them to do anything."

In thinking about the upcoming season, a student athlete might expect that the coach would have him run extra laps around the field after practice, or maybe even stay up all night to reset his body clock for a bowl game to be held overseas. Nobody would expect that players would have to write letters home explaining to their parents how they feel about them.

"We teach and encourage our players to get close to one another," says Alvarez, explaining how the letter came about. "I'm an emotional person, but I think it's hard for most people to express how they feel. So the first day the freshmen come in, I hand them a piece of paper and pencil and tell them to write their parents, and tell them they love them. They have probably never done that, express love. Then I'll ask one of the players who has been here for a while to talk about who they respect most in the room. He may pick out a kid who is not even on scholarship and say, 'I respect so-and-so because he's been here five years and he's busted his tail all the time, and he has never complained.' "

The idea behind these exercises is simple. Alvarez is trying to create a team in the truest sense of the word. Alvarez understands the principle of winning. He knows that winners need to feel good about themselves, to be proud of their performance, to work together with others to create a common goal, and to believe that the success of one is linked to the success of all. Creating a true team makes it easy to win.

To build that team, Alvarez has developed four principles. "I have found that these principles are important not only to winning football games but to any kind of relationship.

"The first one is love for one another," he says. "If you don't truly care about your teammates, you can't win.

"The second is trust. Then comes commitment to what we are trying to do. And finally comes belief. These are the four principles that are the glue that keep us together," he says.

These are principles that are bound to work. Without trust, no one can feel safe to take risks. Without the entire team's commitment to the goal of the organization, resentment and weak links can develop. And without a belief that you can do it, victory cannot be achieved.

Alvarez understands the value of teamwork. He knows a good team builds self-esteem, group cohesiveness, and stronger bonds; promotes sharing and mutual learning; and creates a healthier atmosphere. The result of all this is a higher degree of self-confidence and self-worth, which translates into more wins.

His own needs and experiences with getting close to people (his closest friends are members of his coaching staff) have taught him how important it is to build strong bonds with the people you work with. To make sure that is possible, he chooses coaches who reflect his values and are people oriented, and he recruits players who are overachievers.

Alvarez knows that if he can select the right kind of people to work with, and can get his team to live by these principles through day-to-day leadership, it will become dramatically easier to win. What further reinforces these principles is the university community's belief in the team. Alvarez sees the leader's job to be to nurture both the institution and the individuals affected by the institution.

"I try to get the community involved, for a number of reasons," he says. "First, I like to be the big show in town. I have coaches assigned to fraternity houses and dorms, to get them to talk to the students and get them involved with the team. I have a coach take out each of the deans of the separate colleges, to try to get them involved. We try to draw the whole campus together, including the alumni." Alvarez has gone all around the country explaining to Wisconsin graduates how he is going about creating a team that will be as good athletically as the University of Wisconsin is academically.

All this requires a continuous effort. "You've got to sell your program, and make it a happening." He did just that; all the jokes about the football team stopped; and the stadium started getting filled on Saturday afternoons. But in addition to getting the community to believe in the players, and players to believe in the coach and themselves, Alvarez did something else that was vitally important. He taught his players how to handle a loss.

"I talk to my kids about adversity," he says. "The first thing I tell them is that it is going to happen, whether it is a game that we're supposed to win and we don't, or the fact that someone gets injured. Now, there are different ways you can deal with it. We've got to deal in a positive manner and get stronger.

"Anybody who has been successful has been knocked down. They've lost games. They've gone bankrupt. Regardless of what it is, you have to bounce back. Everybody has to deal with adversity. If you don't, then you have set your goals too low."

In football, as in life, setbacks are inevitable. Alvarez understands that it is not good enough just to survive a loss. You must rebound stronger than before. That is what resilience is all about. Developing this skill is what distinguishes winners from losers.

Alvarez helps his people do this by staying positive, making sure they know that, despite the loss, success is possible. That the loss is just a setback on the road to achieving their goal. He helps them stay focused on the task at hand, be it the next practice or the next game. He models the behavior he wants them to follow, by being flexible when he is blocked and figuring out new ways for them to succeed.

But just because Alvarez meets problems head on doesn't mean that dealing with them is easy. "I have to be a sonofabitch sometimes," he says. "I've sat here and ripped guys and suspended them. I've booted kids off the team, I have fired three different assistant coaches. As the head guy, bad as things get, you can't flinch. If we lose to Minnesota on Saturday, and I walk in on Monday in the tank, the kids are going to be in the tank. They are going to read me like a book."

So Alvarez stays positive. That doesn't mean he's afraid of the reality of life or telling the truth, or facing problems as they arise.

Not surprisingly, Alvarez has developed a way of dealing with them. "I always try to break the problem down to its simplest form," he says. "Once you do that, it is probably not as difficult as it appears. And I won't have a confrontation with someone unless it's worth creating an enemy over. I'll try to resolve it, but unless it's worth making an issue about, I'll move on."

Leadership is all about blending the tough side and soft side of our personalities. Leaders must feel empathy, yet be demanding and competitive. In a profession in which rough-and-tumble is a way of life, Alvarez talks as proudly about his soft side that cares about, and values, people as he does his won-lost record. He has an uncanny ability to blend compassion with competition. He has developed his tough, competitive side and his soft, compassionate side, enabling him to be demanding and caring at the same time. He is compassionate inside the walls of the Camp Randall Stadium locker room, and demanding and competitive outside it, with that competitive drive being directed against the team that the Badgers are playing.

The results have been impressive. Freshmen applications climbed more than 15 percent after the football team's Rose Bowl victory. The alumni are now more involved, and donations are up. And Alvarez and his coaches are finding it much easier to recruit the best high school players. The university community has benefited as well, thanks to the biggest year-to-year increase in home attendance of any team in NCAA history.

And, oh yes. The University of Wisconsin is now consistently rated among the top twenty-five teams in the country.

All this is what happens when you create a winning attitude.

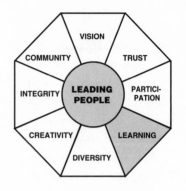

*L*EARNING

I'm one of those people who doesn't pretend to have all the answers.

CARLA GORRELL, FOUNDER, FOOD & FRIENDS

You learn from everything you are exposed to.

TOM JOHNSON, PRESIDENT, CABLE NEWS NETWORK

On the surface, there is not much that Carla Gorrell and Tom Johnson have in common. Gorrell, a minister, built a nonprofit organization that provides food to people infected with the AIDS virus. Johnson, a Harvard MBA, who served as a special assistant to the President of the United States, runs the world's largest news-gathering organization. And yet they—like every other leader in this book—are united in their belief that leaders, and the organizations they run, must continuously learn.

What matters most today is how leaders deal with the intellectual assets inside their organizations. The knowledge, insights, and skills of their workforce will determine whether these organizations will succeed or fail. The leader's challenge is to figure out how to leverage these assets, in order to improve performance. Learning is what's behind real change and development within every successful organization.

Why is learning important? The bottom line is we need a smarter, faster, more productive workforce, and the only way we are going to create it is by developing lifelong learners and learning organizations. Learning organizations are those that constantly encourage and nurture employee development, that see learning as an investment designed to increase the capacity and success of the enterprise, and ones that create an environment that is conducive to learning and development.

Organizational learning enables companies to solve their own problems, expand their capacities to create new ideas, and determine their own future. But this will only happen if leaders establish a work culture that nurtures the learning of everyone in their organization—including themselves.

Leaders must have a deep understanding of themselves—who they are, and who they are not—in order to be successful in business. They need this self-knowledge, because they will be setting the organization's tone and agenda. Without these insights, leaders are vulnerable to tripping over themselves, and casting shadows on their organizations.

But self-knowledge is only one part of the learning process. In a world where change is coming faster than ever before, leaders must develop the ability to adapt and renew themselves, as the environment around them changes. They must reinvent their leadership every day. The best leaders do that by constantly questioning the assumptions about themselves and their business, always looking for new perspectives to increase their capacity and that of their organization. They also learn from others—both from healthy and unhealthy people—and they integrate that learning into their thinking and relationships.

Learning is also a two-way street. In addition to their own learning, leaders must also enable others to learn. Just like their leaders, people in successful organizations need to adapt and grow in a dynamic and changing world. This will only work if people take on their reciprocal responsibilities. They must commit themselves to continuous growth and development. Leaders and followers, together, will increase the capacity within the company, making it easier for it to grow.

Capacity will increase only if the relationships and environment within the company allow people to learn and develop. An efficient way to do that is to develop learning communities, organizations that are open and safe for people to try new ideas and allow employees to expand their knowledge and skills. In a learning community, people learn collaboratively, openly and across boundaries. The structures and systems support the learning process. And there is little fear and defensiveness about learning. Ultimately, inside a true learning organization there is a feeling of hope, enthusiasm, and possibility.

The profiles of leaders in the following pages reveal people who are experts at creating that kind of environment. In each case, the learning environment starts with the leader, a person like Carla Gorrell of Food & Friends, who is constantly reinventing herself as she journeys through the opportunities and travails of life.

A key part of that learning comes from mentors. Tom Johnson of CNN has made the most of his mentors. He has been able to incorporate their lessons throughout his career in politics, newspapers, and television. As the leaders learn from others, they learn about themselves. They learn what their strengths are, and where they have shortcomings. This is not an easy process, but one that has definite payoffs, as Anita and Gordon Roddick, the couple who founded and run The Body Shops, have learned.

Once they have knowledge, it is incumbent upon the leader to share it. Kermit Campbell, CEO of Herman Miller, has discovered an effective strategy for doing that. He brings out the latent talents of his people by creating an environment that not only makes it easy to learn, but celebrates the learning that takes place. This all comes together if a learning community is created and a commitment is made to continuous growth and renewal. Tim Cuneo is building just such a community at the Oak Grove School District in San Jose.

All these leaders know that to adapt successfully to rapidly changing economic, technological, and social trends, their organizations must support the development of the highest capacities of people at all levels. By doing that, the organization stays ahead of the learning curve, and ultimately ahead of the competition.

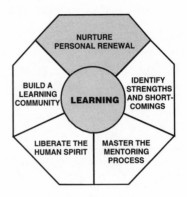

NURTURING
PERSONAL RENEWAL

"The only constant is change." Leaders have said that for as long as there have been leaders. But the changes are coming faster now.

While economic changes are hard enough, they're just the beginning. It seems technology changes daily. So does the nature of the workforce. And society. And . . .

Given this, leaders need the ability to adapt and constantly renew themselves. They need the ability to bounce back from crisis. They need to learn and grow on the job.

A true leader has the capacity to shed old baggage, to reinvent herself and to develop new skin, always in the context of searching for creative ways to express herself fully and making herself and her organization stronger. Her entire life is a study in continuous renewal.

What strikes you most about Carla Gorrell is her resiliency. At several points in her life, she could have just given up. Certainly being married and becoming a parent at age sixteen could have caused her to quit. Our welfare rolls are filled with people who did. When her job as a makeup artist at CBS ended, her commitment to developing herself could have ended as well. But it didn't. When her three-year search for a congregation to lead, following her ordination, failed to yield a single job offer, she could have turned her back on the idea of helping people. But she didn't.

Gorrell constantly turns obstacles, mishaps, and rejections into learning opportunities. She embraces adversity as a challenge, instead of seeing it as a threat. As a result, she has a tremendous ca-

CARLA GORRELL
Food & Friends

TITLE: Founding Executive Director

AGE: 50

FAMILY SITUATION: Divorced; 3 children, 1 grandchild

EDUCATION: Undergraduate degree in Pastoral Counseling; Divinity

HISTORY: Began as a housewife; freelance work for CBS; church volunteer pastor; opened Food & Friends at Westminister Church in Washington, D.C. (1988)

HOBBIES: Reading, learning computer skills from her youngest son, Brian

HEADQUARTERS: Washington, D.C.

BUSINESSES: Nonprofit organization that prepares and delivers nourishing meals to individuals homebound with HIV/AIDS in Washington, Northern Virginia, and Maryland

NUMBER OF EMPLOYEES: 20 staff; 800+ volunteers

BUDGET: $2 million

FACTS: Served 4,800 meals in 1989; 106,997 in 1994

pacity to grow, renew herself, and continue to learn. How she started Food & Friends is an example. "I couldn't find a job as a clergywoman," she says. "I kept looking further and further away from Washington, where I live, but I couldn't find a job. About that time, the church I belonged to started talking about creating a program to provide food to people with HIV or AIDS. Given all the rejection letters, I volunteered to develop the program."

There is a tendency among managers of for-profit companies to dismiss nonprofits, because their success is not measured by return on capital, or earnings per share. But to do that is to forgo an opportunity, because as a rule, nonprofits have a stronger sense of mission and community and have better people-management skills. They need to, since many of their workers are volunteers.

The organization Gorrell created serves as a case in point. It is true that when she started Food & Friends she had never run anything. She had no experience in delivering food, or in raising funds. But while she didn't know about these things, she did know she wanted to operate an urban ministry. And if she couldn't do it the traditional way—by running a church—she would find another. She would create a healing community of volunteers who would deliver love, support, and most importantly food to people who were sick. When Food & Friends started in 1988, no one in the Washington area was providing food to the rapidly growing number of people who were contracting either AIDS or the virus that causes it.

But as clear as the need was, Gorrell met frequent rejection as she tried to get under way. From the beginning, Gorrell knew that the need would outstrip whatever resources she could put together at first. So at the outset, she turned to existing organizations for help.

"We tried to contact Meals on Wheels," she recalls. "We discovered twelve people that we just couldn't get food to, and we were hoping they could help us. When I called them, this very unsympathetic woman answered. When I told her that there were a dozen people who needed help, she all but hung up.

" 'We would have to add a whole new route to reach them,' she told me.

" 'Yes. That's what I am trying to do, but in the meantime I was hoping you . . .' "

They never did anything, Gorrell says. The lack of support just spurred her on. Other leaders would have retreated, scaling back their organizations to a point where the risk of rejection would be less. Many people get stuck in the face of adversity. Maybe their egos won't let them deal with the problem confronting them. The adversity could depress them, or perhaps the pain of rejection makes them unable to react. No matter what the cause, they become powerless. Events can either knock you out or make you stronger, if you have the courage to lean into the challenge. When it comes to dealing with challenges, Gorrell is nothing if not courageous.

After realizing that she was unlikely to get help from other organizations—to be candid, most nonprofits, as well as their volunteers, find dealing with AIDS patients unsettling—she decided to do more on her own. To grow faster, she began applying for grants. Today, her organization has over $2 million in annual operating income, all

from grants and donations, but back when it started, it was a different story. There was virtually no money.

"I learned to do fund-raising initially by getting my grant propos-
als constantly turned down and finding out why they were rejected,"
she says. "I learned from that what I had to do."

That learning is a constant in her life. Gorrell has learned from
her rejections, of course, by being turned down by churches and
Meals on Wheels, and for grants. But it goes well beyond that. Gorrell learns aggressively, and from every possible source. She learned
about death and dying from a sister who became fatally ill with
leukemia. She learned about business not only from reading but by
talking to business leaders, such as T. Boone Pickens, whom she had
applied makeup to while she was at CBS. And she learned to offset
her organizational weakness by hiring a deputy director, Michael
Morris, who could help compensate for her deficiencies.

Every time Gorrell is confronted with a new situation—especially
one that does not go well at first—she learns from it. From her early
days, when money for Food & Friends was difficult to come by, she
learned that she shouldn't let a single day go by without making at
least one phone call to try to raise funds. And initial lack of organization skills taught her the need to hire people with those skills.
Each new experience represents another chance to understand
something about business, or people, or both. Her experience with
Food & Friends' first board of directors serves as a case in point.

"For our first board, we asked five people, who had been showing
up to help out, to be our directors," Gorrell recalls. "It turned out
two of those people wanted my job.

"It took me a while to figure that out. I started going to board
meetings, and those two were very critical of me. They found the
smallest things to pick on, in order to point out to the other board
members how bad I was, and to frustrate me. I'd go home and cry,
because I felt like I had been beaten up and abused. Finally, we got a
consultant in, and she wrote a scathing report about what was going
on, and the two people who were causing the problems left.

"But I learned from that," Gorrell continues. "We were more careful with whom we picked as replacements, and I have gotten better
at dealing with the board. I'm much better now at picking up the
phone and having one-to-one conversations with directors before

our meetings. I make sure I have the support of the board ahead of
time, and I make sure they understand the issue, if I think it is going
to be controversial. I do a lot more preparing now."

To many executives, what Gorrell has learned is just Business 101.
They would never have thought to go to a board meeting without extensive preparation. But while those executives might have been better at office politics, it is unlikely they could have handled any better
the adversity Gorrell has faced.

FLEXIBILITY FOLLOWS, IF YOU'RE OPEN TO NEW IDEAS

The result of Gorrell's constant learning is flexibility. And her flexibility allows her to learn. It is a nurturing circle. By having been constantly confronted with problems and new situations—and having
constantly learned from them—Gorrell has become almost infinitely
adaptable. She has been that way all her adult life.

"When you've raised three kids, you know that sometimes you
may want to be on the phone, but there's a little crisis that you have
to take care of," she says. "Or when you're making dinner there is always a phone call you have to take."

Most people segregate what they learn at home from the workplace. Not Gorrell. She brought her learning about flexibility to her
job. In the business world, her need to be flexible could come from
managing a volunteer staff (you can't demand as much of them as
you can from employees you pay), from her clients (the health of
people who suffer from AIDS or HIV is far from predictable), or it
simply could come from the weather.

"I was out running errands when I heard a weather report saying
there was a chance for a really big snowstorm," she recalls. "I don't
know why, but I really believed it would happen. By the time I came
into the office, it was about eleven o'clock and we had just finished
getting out the meals for the day. I told everyone about the storm,
and said if there's any way to get tomorrow's meals out today, we are
going to do it.

"The people who were just winding down from the intense labor
of getting out today's meals just looked at me and said, No way. But I
said we had to do it. These people depend on us. Our chef modified
the menu to eliminate items like bread, which would take hours to

bake, and we rounded up as many volunteers as we could find, and we got the meals out," she says. "I delivered the last ones myself, as the snow started falling.

Gorrell says the reason Food & Friends didn't let them down, and could do two days' work in one was because "the more organized you are, the more flexible you become." The systems she had put in place to handle day-to-day challenges had enough flexibility to allow it to respond to a crisis.

Many employees want their leaders to be right, to be tough. They don't want them to acknowledge vulnerabilities, or to shift in midstream. And leaders pressure themselves to be omniscient. The result is an environment that makes it difficult for leaders to grow and change. Quite often when that happens, the organization stops growing as well, especially during a crisis when it needs to adapt the most. Gorrell has gotten around the problem by acknowledging—indeed celebrating—the fact that she, like all of us, is imperfect by nature. She knows she will makes mistakes. That does not worry her. She learns from them. As Gorrell puts it: "I'm one of those people who doesn't pretend to have all the answers. I'm still a learner."

As a result of being open about this, which is nothing more than acknowledging the reality of living, Gorrell has created an organization that is as open and human as she is. She has done this in a number of ways:

- By allowing people to be people at work—pictures of friends and family cover employees' desks and walls.
- By acknowledging what the organization does for a living— an honor roll of clients who have died from AIDS is prominently displayed in the office.
- By being honest about her feelings. Gorrell openly cried the day Mike Morris, her deputy, died, and she took the time to explain to her organization, through a letter, what Michael not only meant to Food & Friends, but to her personally.

[In the beginning] Mike and I worked side by side in the small office next to the kitchen. There was one phone, two desks, and no computers. We were full partners in every program area, which means we both packed and delivered meals, did client intakes and follow-ups, and worked with volunteers.

The only division of labor was Mike managed the financial accounting, while I did the fund-raising. In those two areas we took opposite, yet complementary roles. Mike was Mr. Gloom and Doom ("There's barely enough money in the bank to cover expenses"), while I drove him crazy with optimism ("Don't worry, we'll make it"). We didn't always agree, but honesty, mutual respect, and a good sense of humor made us the best of friends.

If I had to choose one word to describe Mike's gift to Food & Friends it would be strength. For over two years Mike lent us his strength of character, intellect, purpose, and moral courage. Mike (was) my mainstay, the embodiment of supportive strength.

Gorrell, in short, balances the duties of a leader with the feelings of a friend. By publishing this letter Gorrell openly acknowledged the depth of her friendship with Morris and offered a way for everyone to celebrate his life and grieve his loss. As a result of taking this approach to leadership, her organization is more forgiving of her and has allowed her to grow.

It is now time for Carla Gorrell to move on. Food & Friends and Gorrell have outgrown each other. The organization recently launched a major capital campaign and signed a ten-year lease for a larger facility. "The job was getting too administrative, and my heart was not there. It was with the people in the community," says Gorrell. "My board and I came to this mutual realization. We needed a person with more organizational and fund-raising experience." But transitions are never easy. And Gorrell is no exception. "I had a hard time letting go and was resistant to leaving so soon. There's a lot of grief and loss when you give six years of your life."

But once again Gorrell shows us how to turn adversity into advantages. She turned to her friends and her inner resources for help. "I meet weekly with a group of professional women for lunch and we support each other. I was able to discuss my concerns there. I also went back to a quote inside my desk at home that gives me inspiration. It reads: 'We are given two lives. The life we learn with and the life we live after that.' Maybe I'll use my gifts working with foundations next time, or maybe even corporate America."

Gorrell sees herself as imperfectly human. She recognizes everyone has strengths and vulnerabilities, and that the phrase "dysfunctional families" is simply redundant. We all had problems growing up. We all have skeletons in the closet. The most successful among us acknowledge this and move on. Gorrell has a deeper understanding of who she is and where she comes from. She not only accepts that, but embraces it. Carla Gorrell is comfortable with the unknown, curious about it, and most important, willing to grow and adapt, based on what she learns.

It is these qualities that prepare a leader for the pressures of a rapidly changing word.

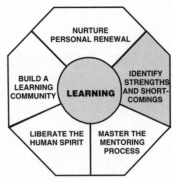

IDENTIFYING STRENGTHS AND SHORTCOMINGS

We hold our leaders to such high standards. To be successful, they would almost have to maintain the status of saints. If they falter or stumble, we view them as hypocritical or incompetent. This is not only unrealistic, it's bad business. We must allow our leaders to be real people.

Leaders must bear some of this responsibility. They must have a deeper understanding of themselves—who they are and who they are not. They must know their strengths and weaknesses, the areas they excel in, and the places where they have shortcomings. They also must know what they stand for, the principles that are fundamental to their personalities and the blind spots in their characters.

Leaders cannot do this alone. We must give them the freedom to grow.

What link Gordon and Anita Roddick together—both personally and in business—are shared beliefs and common values. They are what attracted them to one another twenty-three years ago, and what have kept them together through the travails of marriage, children, and running their business.

They are also the foundation of their company's success. Gordon is the Chairman and Anita is the CEO of the The Body Shop International, a worldwide chain of retail stores that sell skin and hair products. But just as important as what the company sells is what it believes, beliefs that stem directly from the Roddicks, principle-driven entrepreneurs who want to improve the world around them. Their goal for The Body Shop is nothing less than having them become a "symbol of business consciousness."

ANITA AND GORDON RODDICK
The Body Shop

TITLES: Founder and Chief Executive (Anita); Chairman (Gordon)

FAMILY SITUATION: Married; two daughters

HISTORY: Anita trained and worked as an English and History teacher. She worked in the department of women's rights at the International Labor Organization, based at the UN in Geneva, before traveling to Polynesia, New Caledonia, Australia, and Africa. Gordon trained as a farmer; traveled extensively, including tin mining in Africa and sailing down the Amazon in a canoe. They married in 1971, opened the first branch of The Body Shop in 1976. The first franchise shop opened in 1977.

HONORS AND SPECIAL ACCOMPLISHMENTS: (Anita) Veuve Clicquot Business Woman of the Year (1984); Order of the British Empire (1988); Retailer of the Year (1988); Communicator of the Year (1988); International Banksia Environmental Award, Mexican Environmental Achiever and Audubon Medal (1993); Woman in Leadership Award, NFWBO (1994). Author, *Body and Soul* by Anita Roddick

HEADQUARTERS: Watersmead, Littlehampton, England

BUSINESS: The Body Shop is a manufacturer and retailer of toiletries and cosmetics.

NUMBER OF EMPLOYEES: Approximately 8,000 worldwide, of which about 3,000 are employed directly by the company

GROSS REVENUE: $795 million (1994)

FACTS: The Body Shop runs over 600 community projects worldwide.

To try to make that happen, they start with a quality product and build their values—which center around the interconnectedness of people, business, and the environment—into the company that surrounds it. There is a definite business logic to this approach.

"If a product is harmful to the environment, or if indigenous people are exploited by its production, then a customer won't want to buy it," Gordon says. "And if I am a salesperson, I certainly won't want to tell you about those things."

And it is exactly those things—caused by corporate greed and individuals' abandoning their personal values when they go to work in the morning—that the Roddicks say is what is wrong with business. Measuring success exclusively in terms of return on assets and net margins, they add, inevitably leads to wastefulness and the destruction of the environment.

"Our products are the opposite of all that," Gordon says. "They are inspired by traditionally used natural ingredients, and are never tested on animals, so naturally our people want to tell you about them. We're reinventing the role of business, really, putting it in harmony with the environment and with people."

These values are reflected in The Body Shop's Trading Charter and Mission Statement. It talks of humanizing the business community, showing that success and profits can go hand in hand with ideals and values, and bringing meaning and pleasure to the workplace. And these ideas are represented in the products. Wherever possible their ingredients are drawn from areas of the world—Africa and parts of South America—where the local economy will benefit substantially

---

THE BODY SHOP'S MISSION STATEMENT
OUR REASON FOR BEING

To dedicate our business to the pursuit of social and environmental change.

To *creatively* balance the financial and human needs of our stakeholders: employees, customers, franchisees, suppliers, and shareholders.

To *courageously* ensure our business is ecologically sustainable, meeting the needs of the present without compromising the future.

To *meaningfully* contribute to local, national, and international communities in which we trade, by adopting a code of conduct which ensures care, honesty, fairness and respect.

To *passionately* campaign for the protection of the environment and human and civil rights, and against animal testing within the cosmetics and toiletries industry.

To *tirelessly* work to narrow the gap between principle and practice, while making fun, passion, and care part of our daily lives.

from trading with The Body Shop. And when The Body Shop opens a store in a depressed area, such as Harlem in New York City, a substantial portion of the profits is given back to the community.

This, the Roddicks say, is the right way to do business. Success, they argue, is not having the world's highest return on assets. Instead, success is building a socially responsible company, preserving the environment, creating a good place to work, developing young people, providing economic opportunities to indigent populations, and making money.

"I think big corporations that regard our ideas as being flaky, or greeny, or whatever, would do well to study *their* companies to see how social and environmental values could be applied to enhance *their* businesses," Gordon says. "We view out ideas as just plain old common sense. All the talk about social responsibility being odd, or quirky, is just rubbish. It is practical to engage people in a larger purpose."

There is an obvious potential problem with taking this approach to business. As Anita says: "Organizations who stand out, or up, or on the edge of bravery automatically wear bull's-eyes on their backs. They're measured against the status of angels, so anytime you fall down, or stumble, you are seen as hypocritical."

The Roddicks learned about the dangers firsthand in 1994, when an investigative journalist did a piece in *Business Ethics* magazine that claimed The Body Shop was not all that it was cracked up to be, citing examples of contaminated shampoos and writing that the company had misrepresented some of its socially responsible programs.

"My first reaction was almost like a lion protecting her cubs. I wanted to attack the article immediately," Anita says. "I mean how do you feel when your character is being assassinated? Here we have our kids ringing up asking, What's going on? Why are they saying these things? I was very angry about being constrained and controlled by the lawyers, who say you've got to be measured."

Anita's response is not surprising. Most entrepreneurs are extremely connected to their companies. Who they are as people and who they are as a company are often one and the same. This is particularly true for socially responsible companies in which the principles of the owner are so intertwined with the politics and practices of the company. It's not surprising that when something bad happens to the company the owner-entrepreneur takes it very personally.

The problem, of course, is that leaders are almost always subject to attacks—whether justified or not. One way to bring down our leaders is to charge them with hypocrisy, to discover places where they fall short of their idealized standards.

The Roddicks were being charged with not living up to their social-responsibility standards. Any hint of inconsistency between ideals and reality was brought to the forefront of the article. Often when criticisms are leveled, there is some truth in them. The question is how much truth, and what do you do with the information?

We, as a society, are quick to dismiss the accomplishments of leaders, particularly leaders who live on the edge and challenge the status quo as the Roddicks do. But it is important to remember that inconsistencies between aspiration and reality are not necessarily signs of deceit or immorality.

That said, the Roddicks have a responsibility to learn continuously and renew themselves, as they stand up so strongly for what they believe. "Anita and I are very protective of the business," says Gordon, "but we probably have been oversensitive and overdefensive to criticism at times." But the Roddicks are in the process of changing that right now, in the aftermath of the attack. They are examining corporate procedures, making sure that all ingredients and manufacturing processes live up to the high standards they have set, and they are communicating with employees and franchises about what is going on, and what they believe.

Through it all, the Roddicks are drawing on one another to compensate for their individual weaknesses.

WHO WE ARE. WHO WE ARE NOT.

A major reason the Roddicks' partnership works so well is that they both are committed to knowing their strengths and weaknesses. This insight is critical. The leader must be able to answer—objectively and honestly—"What am I good at? Where am I not so strong? And how can I compensate for my shortcomings?"

The first step in compensating for weakness is to know that the weakness exists. And that requires self-knowledge. For example, Gordon understands the roots of his personality. He knows why he is strongly independent. It comes, he explains, from being sent off to boarding school at age six, rarely to return home.

"The instant I completed my education, I just jumped on a boat to Australia, and I was there for four years," he says. "I worked on a sheep ranch, cleaned railways, and served as a petrol pump attendant. As a result of these experiences, I realized that there wasn't any such an animal as insecurity. You could always work. You could always eat. You did not need to have huge resources to enjoy yourself. The people I admired the most were always the explorers and the risk takers."

These experiences have helped Gordon become a self-confident, methodical leader. He leads through gentle persuasion, and by setting compelling business strategy. It was he who mapped out the company's international-expansion plans. Based in the U.K., The Body Shop now has over 1,200 stores in 45 countries. After expanding throughout the U.K., the Roddicks opened stores in Canada, Australia, and Europe. The Body Shop was in 33 countries before the Roddicks opened their first store in the U.S. For the Roddicks, the U.S. was the last major frontier.

But Gordon's real gift is managing people. He does that by clearly defining the mission, listening to what his employees have to say, and constantly pointing out why their job is so important to The Body Shop's success.

Anita's strengths are her unlimited creativity, energy, and drive. She is the heart of the company, and leads by inspiration and example. Every single day, whether she is at a protest rally—either as a speaker, or merely there to lend support—or heading a fund-raiser to save the rain forest, she is making a difference.

Managing, Anita knows, is not one of her strengths. She is sometimes seen as controlling, strident in her passion on issues, and autocratic. Anita excites and incites people, both antagonizing them and moving them to action. But people know her shortcomings stem from her quest for social justice.

"Leadership to me is having values that lead in some direction," she says. So Anita sets the tone and direction for The Body Shop, leaving the managing and the details to Gordon.

How Can Your Strengths Compensate
for My Weaknesses?

Knowing who they are and who they are not becomes the starting point for an honest partnership, one in which each can tap into the other's strengths to compensate for his or her own weaknesses. The Roddicks actively work on this.

"It is important for us to teach each other about life," Gordon Roddick says in talking about his relationship with his wife and business partner of twenty-three years. For example, Anita teaches Gordon about being sociable, about the need to question the status quo constantly, and why it is important to push limits.

"I'm basically a reserved individual," Gordon explains. "She drags me into all those situations and introduces me to people I ought to be talking to. And Anita has this ability to go to the absolute heart of the problem, to listen to all the details and say, 'But what I actually hear you saying is this.' It's a rare thing to be able to do. One of my guys was laughing with me the other day and said, 'You know you can always rely on Anita to ask the one question we do not want to answer.' "

Gordon teaches Anita about balancing life—he has been known to take off and ride horses through the wilds of Africa months at a time. But when he is at work, work gets his complete attention. That has shown Anita the need to follow through on any project she starts.

"He has taught me tenacity," Anita says. "I am very fast in making decisions, but I do not always want to follow through. Gordon has shown me the huge value in moving at a more measured pace, and that there can be huge value in taking the minutiae of a project and loving those minutiae." In addition he is constantly pushing—quietly—to file down some of Anita's rough edges. There is a gentle, caring quality to Gordon.

How Do We Blend Our Strengths
so the Business Benefits?

Gordon realizes he needs to be more outgoing, but if he falls short upon occasion, he knows that Anita—who is the public face of the company, attending to store openings, dealing with reporters, and making a speech to one group or another somewhere in the world just about once a week—will take up the slack.

Should Anita appear scattered, or a bit eccentric, it is not a problem. She knows Gordon will "clear away the dross," and make it easier for her to translate her ideas into reality. And if Anita is not as patient as she should be in dealing with employees, or doesn't pay quite as much attention to a problem as she might, it is not the end of the world. She will try harder, but she knows that employees will seek Gordon out on these matters. Indeed, over time their differences have become institutionalized.

Employees are extremely good at picking up on their leaders' strengths and weaknesses. As Gordon says, after a while they expect you to act in a certain way. "I have a reputation as a good listener, someone who can come up with solutions. So people now automatically come to me when they have a problem, whether it is true that I have these skills or not."

It's good, of course, that employees help institutionalize their leaders' strengths, and know their vulnerabilities, but there is a danger in having others define who you are. "It's easy to become other people's property," Gordon says.

"And it's easy to develop an over-sense of responsibility, and to believe your own public relations," adds Anita. "There are pressures in living up to others' expectations."

Knowing their partner will celebrate their strengths and offset their weaknesses, the Roddicks can concentrate on growing their business. They do this by dividing management functions. Not surprisingly, Anita's focus is on the creative side: she oversees the design of everything from product packaging to the company newsletter, and she is constantly seeking new ingredients for The Body Shop's lotions, soaps, and shampoos. Gordon concentrates on financial matters and on making sure the organization is running smoothly.

"We always have worked together in a complementary way," Gordon says. "I am useless in the arenas in which Anita is strongly involved. It's not that I have no interest in the designing, creating new ideas, and doing interviews. I do. I just would be no good at doing them.

"Doing what we both do would be a torturous job for one person, because there would always be an area of huge weakness for that one person," he adds. "Whereas with the two of us, we complement one another."

And they do so both professionally and personally. Their adventuresome, buck-the-system attitude is a quality that is deep-seated in both Anita and Gordon. They know who they are, and know what they believe is important. Their commitment to their values has enabled them to create a company that reflects their beliefs, both internally and externally.

Inside the company, the Roddicks hire people who completely share the company's mission, people "who want to make a mark, and a difference in the world." To help them achieve their goals, the company encourages employees to take off six days a year, with pay, to work on community projects. "Almost every one of our stores has a community project it is working on," says Gordon.

"When employees see that business can help the common good, and when they get a chance to make a contribution as well, they get inspired," adds Anita. "You can't tell people what to do, you can only show them a route."

These internal beliefs spill over into the company's dealing with customers. The Roddicks have the courage to have their company communicate directly to the public what it—and they—stand for. Since the Roddicks humanize the company—through Anita's public talks, in-store literature that promotes causes such as saving the environment and AIDS prevention, in addition to explaining the ingredients in each product and why and how they came to be created—customers feel they are buying from a company that they know and understand. That creates a tremendous loyalty to The Body Shop brand. Not only do the customers buy, but they tell their friends about what they have bought and the store they have discovered. The result is that The Body Shop is able to expand without spending on advertising.

The honest relationship that the Roddicks have with each other extends to the connections they have with their customers. In each case, the connections are centered around shared beliefs and common values. The Roddicks' complementary personalities and skills are common in healthier companies. The best leaders surround themselves with people who help them compensate for their shortcomings. Too often, we don't reveal our shortcomings because we are taught early to remain in control, to suppress negative feelings, to avoid vulnerability, and to appear competent—especially in the workplace—at all costs. But living in such a cocoon limits our development as people, and doesn't allow others to help compensate for our weakness.

The Roddicks are constantly learning. Their partnership works because they know their strengths and shortcomings. They celebrate their partners' strength, help compensate for their weakness, and allow each other room to grow.

MASTERING THE
MENTORING PROCESS

*We are reflections of our experience. That experience includes whom
we know and how we make use of those contacts.*

*Because of our diverse backgrounds, all of us are inspired by dif-
ferent kinds of people at different points in our lives. Some have had
great relationships with their fathers, or mothers, or both, and they
keep their parents' "voice of reason" inside their heads throughout
their careers. Others seek out teachers, ministers, coaches, even
bosses who exhibit the same qualities.*

*There are others leaders, who have had dysfunctional, un-
healthy, or unrewarding early experiences, who consciously seek out
mentors to rectify these negative interactions. Some leaders get
hooked up with the wrong mentors—people who are manipulative,
narcissistic, or have the wrong values. Consequently they learn, and
have reinforced, the wrong behavior.*

*Whatever the case, we each use the mentoring experience as part
of our own leadership development. And as most successful leaders
have realized, there are lessons to be learned from positive and negative people.*

It was Tom Johnson's moment. In fact, it was the moment every
newsman dreams of—especially if he works in television. War had
broken out, and Johnson's organization was the only one able to ob-
tain pictures, interviews, and reliable information.

When other networks wanted to show the bombs dropping on
Iraq, during the Gulf War, they had to credit the Cable News Network. When asked for comment, White House officials invariably be-

TOM JOHNSON
Cable News Network

TITLE: President

AGE: 53

FAMILY SITUATION: Married; 2 children

EDUCATION: ABJ, University of Georgia School of Journalism (1963);
MBA, Harvard University Graduate School of Business (1965)

HISTORY: *Los Angeles Times,* Publisher and CEO (1980–89), President
and COO (1977–80); *The Dallas Times Herald,* Publisher (1975–77),
Editor (1973–75); Texas Broadcasting Corporation, Executive Vice
President (1971–73); Executive Assistant to Former President Lyn-
don B. Johnson (1969–71); White House Fellow to be press aide to
Bill Moyers (1965)

HONORS AND SPECIAL ACCOMPLISHMENTS: Chairman, Board of Directors, Lyndon B. Johnson Foundation; chairman, John S. Knight Professional Journalism Fellowships Board, Stanford University; Board of
Directors, High Museum of Art, Woodruff Arts Center, and The Atlanta Chamber of Commerce; Board of Trustees: The Knight Foundation, The Southern Center for International Studies, and The Mayo
Foundation

HEADQUARTERS: Atlanta, Georgia

BUSINESS: Produces and airs 24-hour television news broadcasts

NUMBER OF EMPLOYEES: 2,500

GROSS REVENUE: $667 million (1994)

NUMBER OF VIEWERS: 142 million worldwide (1994)

gan their answers with "Well, CNN is reporting . . ." And even President Bush, in responding to a question at a press conference in the
midst of the war, said, "I saw on CNN where . . ."

And what was Johnson doing during all of this? As might be expected, he spent part of his time congratulating his staff on redefin-
ing how warfare should be covered. But the rest of his days were
spent working the phones. It went beyond getting President Bush,
General Colin Powell, and Middle East leaders to appear exclusively
on CNN. The calls accomplished that, but that was not their sole in-

tent. Johnson's conversations with the key participants were also about trading information. It was clear, as the war progressed and CNN remained the authority about what was going on, that Johnson was in the loop.

Why was he uniquely positioned to help provide the world with information about the most pivotal news story of 1990? Part of it was native ability. Johnson is a smart, experienced newsman. After earning an MBA at Harvard, he went on to run *The Dallas Times Herald* and *The Los Angeles Times*, where he ended up as publisher and CEO.

But that is not the whole explanation. The Johnson we see today running CNN—a driven man with a strong sense of public service, who works hard at building the morale of his people—is an amalgam of his past. In large part Johnson's success stems from what he learned from five very different men he worked with. Each distinctively contributed to his success.

THE EARLY YEARS: PEYTON ANDERSON

It is important, Tom Johnson says, to know that he had a very difficult relationship with his father. Johnson grew up in Macon, Georgia, where his mother worked in a grocery store, and his father, among other things, sold watermelons off the back of a truck.

"He and I had a very complex relationship," Johnson says. "I was very disappointed in my father; at times, I was embarrassed by him. I felt at times humiliated. I see him differently today. But at the time I saw a sort of happy-go-lucky person, who enjoyed his life and did basically whatever it was he wanted to do. During most of my life, he held no regular job. He was involved in odd jobs, ranging from selling produce to selling wood. We were of fairly modest financial means, and I really wanted to make something more of myself than I felt my father had made of himself."

Given the difficult relationship with his father, Johnson has spent his life searching for mentors who would help him develop in a positive way. He found his first one in Peyton Anderson, publisher of *The Macon Telegraph*. Johnson started working as a copy boy at the paper when he was fourteen, and quickly came to the attention of Anderson, who had no son. Anderson supported him financially when Johnson attended the University of Georgia, and later the Harvard Business School. The time he spent with Anderson helped form Johnson's love of the news business, as well as showing him the need to help others.

"I learned the importance of reaching out to other young people, to give them an opportunity much as I've had," Johnson explains. "Peyton was very supportive financially, and he was supportive emotionally."

The White House: Bill Moyers and LBJ

Following graduation from business school, Johnson was selected—thanks in part to Peyton Anderson—to be part of the first class of White House fellows, recent college and business-school graduates who would assist the President's staff. "LBJ took an instant liking to this young Georgia boy who had to make his way in the world," recalls Lady Bird Johnson. When Tom Johnson arrived at the White House, his first job was as a press aide to Bill Moyers, who was then press secretary to President Lyndon B. Johnson and later his special assistant.

"From Bill I learned the importance of excellence in everything you do. Bill taught me never to release an assignment until you feel that you've done it the very best you can," Johnson recalls. "I used to see Bill work until he would almost drop, no matter what the assignment was."

When Moyers left the White House, Tom Johnson took his place, and he stayed with President Johnson (no relation) after the President left office. Johnson moved to Texas to run the President's radio and television stations and learned a great deal from the President's quite different style.

"LBJ wanted every assignment completed today," Johnson recalls. "He wanted every phone call completed today, every letter answered today. He was incredibly demanding, but he never demanded more of his staff than he demanded of himself. He worked long hours, but he got the job done, and he got it done today. He probably did more to stretch me and push me, because he had come to Washington as a young man who received many opportunities early in his career.

"He expected us to deal thoughtfully with people of every station in life from the most poor person, who was writing him a letter—a person with no power, no authority, no connections—to a cabinet member. He insisted that they all were treated exactly the same."

The other skill that President Johnson taught him, a skill that would serve him well in the business world, was the need to be politically aware—sensitive to the needs, wants, and desires of others. That is not to say that Tom Johnson would become a politician. Rather, he would work hard at being an authentic leader, one who truly cared about the people who worked for him. "I think it is very important to be politically sensitive, but it is extremely dangerous to be a politician," Johnson says. "Too many people rise to positions of authority and power, and wear titles like company president, and forget that they are, after all, just as human and just as flawed as all the people around them."

THE LOS ANGELES TIMES: OTIS CHANDLER

After running President Johnson's media interests, Johnson moved to *The Dallas Times Herald*, where he was editor at age thirty-three, and then on to *The Los Angeles Times*, first as editor, then publisher. In Los Angeles, he came under the wing of Otis Chandler, a member of the family that had founded the paper. Johnson's competitiveness was reinforced by the time he spent with Chandler.

"Otis always wanted to finish in the winner's circle in anything he undertook," Johnson recalls. "Whether he was racing cars, climbing mountains, or surfing, he wanted to win. He wanted to build *The Los Angeles Times* into the finest newspaper in the United States. That was his goal. He really wanted uncommon excellence journalistically, operationally, and financially."

During Johnson's nine years as publisher, *The Los Angeles Times* won six Pulitzer prizes, increased revenues from $300 million to more than $1 billion, and grew circulation at a rapid rate. By the time he left in 1990, the *Times* had become the largest metropolitan newspaper in the country.

"I have been really fortunate to have worked around people who care deeply about people, and about their products," Johnson says. "All of them had a real desire to excel, which showed up in different ways."

All of Johnson's mentoring experiences up to this point in his life had taught him the value of "repotting" himself from time to time to put himself in a position to experience new responsibilities and new people, every five to ten years. In mentoring relationships, it is quite common for people to outgrow their mentors and the experiences they provide. Hidden conflicts emerge. Jealousy and competition can arise and spoil the relationship; sameness and lack of creativity can set in. When that starts to happen, it is important to pull up roots, and replant yourself in fresh soil with new nutrients. It's the only way to keep growing.

CABLE NEWS NETWORK: TED TURNER

Ted Turner came along at a pivotal point for both CNN and Tom Johnson. Johnson was unhappy after the reorganization of the Times and after Otis Chandler retired. Through mutual friends, he met Turner. Turner, in turn, was looking for someone to head CNN. Turner took Johnson to dinner and spoke passionately about how he wanted to turn the Cable News Network into the world's finest news-gathering organization. Turner was a persuasive sales-man with a history of accomplishing what he set out to do. He had taken the small outdoor advertising firm his father had left him and turned it into a diversified entertainment conglomerate that owned all sorts of things from basketball's Atlanta Hawks and baseball's Atlanta Braves to the MGM film library.

Johnson was intrigued by the man and by the idea of running CNN. "I liked his extraordinary sense of vision and his overpowering commitment to see that vision realized." But before he took the job, he wanted to know what would be expected from his new boss. "Turner said, 'I want CNN to be the best news network in the world.' "

"I said 'What else?' "

"And he said, 'That's it, pal. That's it.' "

That one conversation excited Johnson enough to take the next step in his career. He would take all his mentoring experiences with him and run CNN.

The Cable News Network was at a crossroads. Chairman and founder Ted Turner had proved skeptics wrong and had created the world's first twenty-four-hour news network. By the time Johnson arrived at CNN in 1990, the network was well on its way to reaching 80 million households in 130 countries worldwide. That was the good news. The bad news was that CNN, based in Atlanta, still was an organization, in which the primary motto was "Do it cheap," and its young staff took great pride in the fact that they were snubbed by the traditional news organizations.

Analysts told Ted CNN needed to be more professionally run, without giving up its strengths—primarily its ability to go on the air live at any time, for any length of time. It also needed to resolve its internal problems. The organization was politically divided. There were four different executives, each with his own group of followers, who thought they should have had the job Johnson had just received. In addition, the organization was extremely insular. It was CNN against the world, which made dealing with the rest of the Turner organization difficult at best.

Sparks occur when learning from the past confronts challenges of the present. Those sparks produce opportunities for the future, and it was, to say the least, a combustible situation when Johnson appeared for his first day at work as president of CNN.

On the surface, it was a perfect match. After all, it would be the next phase of evolution for both parties. CNN was primed to be professionally managed and also primed to take advantage of its burgeoning ability to cover any story, anywhere, at any time. And Johnson was eager to apply what he had learned not only from his mentors but in his previous jobs. But while they were both poised to move on, there was a huge hurdle that Johnson would first have to vault.

In the early days of CNN, Ted Turner had promised he would never bring in a president who had spent his working life in newspapers. Yet he had done just that with the appointment of Johnson. Rose petals were not exactly lining CNN's walkways when Johnson arrived. But Turner was smart in recognizing that Johnson was the right man for the job. Johnson is people oriented and a consensus builder. He began building consensus at CNN by stressing something that Turner, he, and the entire CNN organization believed: the most important thing is to get the story right, and get it on the air fast.

"Whether at the Dallas paper, or *The Los Angeles Times*, or CNN, it is imperative that we be accurate," Johnson explains. "The millions of people who, domestically or internationally, turn to this network for news must be assured that we're getting it right. This is a very competitive world, and there are great audience pressures, there are great advertising pressures, and there are many commercial pressures, but all of us must resist the temptation to go for it just for the sake of being first.

"For example, we came very close to prematurely announcing the death of President George Bush. This was the time he took ill in Japan and he was taken to a government guest house. We got a report that he had died, and it turned out—after we checked and double-checked—to be a hoax. It never got on the air. But it was a close call.

"Our number-one priority is getting the story right" is what he told the people at CNN.

Johnson approached this assignment as he had every assignment that came before. He made certain that people knew exactly what was expected of them. His approach is to empower his executives and give them the authority and autonomy they need to do their jobs, but they are also held accountable. "It may sound simple, but I want the very best of you in everything you do," he told his staff.

Johnson will not put up with internal politics. "I told everyone I would not tolerate pointing the guns inside the fort, at each other. The competition is someplace else. The enemy is someplace else. I also said that anybody who isn't really happy working here should look for some other place to work. I believe in having people who enjoy coming to work each day, who are very highly motivated, and who are giving it their very best. And one of our senior people did leave, because he was unhappy with the choice of me as president."

Navigating through this organizational land mine was not easy. But Johnson had learned that people need to be listened to, understood, encouraged, and "stroked." He came to this conclusion by knowing himself well.

The kind of support Johnson gives his people is exactly the sort of support he freely admits he needs. "I need recognition," he says. "I am not talking about publicity. I need recognition for doing a good job. I need it almost more than money, and maybe even more.

"To be sure, there are days that I go home and say, 'I really had a great day today.' But there are others that I go home and I'm frustrated and unhappy. My moods go very much with a sense of accomplishment, or lack of accomplishment. What you see with me is what you get. If we've had a great day, I feel fine. If we haven't, I don't. I get depressed if I can't win every day.

"The dark side of me is burnout and depression to some extent," Johnson continues. "I am a workaholic. I know that. I have never found outside pursuits that mean as much to me as my work. I live and breathe my work. I define myself too much by my work. I am driven. I have a very low tolerance for mediocrity in others or myself. I have incredibly high expectations of myself, and I must be very careful not to work sixteen hours a day, seven days a week."

At CNN, you can see all the things Johnson has learned—both about himself and from his mentors—coming into play, and contributing to CNN's success. Since Johnson's arrival, CNN has grown remarkably. CNN now broadcasts to 208 countries around the world, and as *The Guardian* in London puts it, "CNN is watched in the White House and in the Kremlin, as well as most of the world's capitals."

In large part, Johnson drives his team toward excellence in every area. He embraces change, new people, and new experiences. While he still is in the news business, he now must worry about the availability of satellite time, not ink, and he now talks in terms of stories running a minute and forty-five seconds, not two columns. Still, as Johnson is quick to point out, despite all the technology, "it all comes down to people. Technology is a fabulous enabler, but we are a human enterprise. It's people touching people every day. It's the people and the technology linked."

But while you can see Johnson applying at CNN all he has learned through his career, you can also see something else: the mentoring Johnson has received has come full circle. He's determined to give something back, because he's so appreciative of what has been given him. Establishing and funding the Peyton Anderson scholarship at the University of Georgia is one way he has done this. And trying to institutionalize his beliefs about mentoring is another.

Mentoring is a way of passing down the values, culture, history, and politics of an organization from person to person. Johnson has done that by writing down what he has learned, and sharing it with others. In his "lessons" you'll hear the echoes of what he was taught by his mentors.

"You learn from everything you are exposed to," Johnson says. "I learned the importance of giving back from Peyton, and the importance of excellence from Bill and LBJ, as well as the need to make the most out of every single day. And from Otis and Ted I learned that winning can be achieved with the highest standards—that you don't have to cheat, you can become great with very high-quality standards."

Johnson's mentors have taught him principles, judgment, skills, perspective, acceptance of his own strengths and weaknesses, and how to adapt to business realities. The leader that Johnson has become is in large part a direct result of the interactions he has had with his mentors.

Tom Johnson is a true lifelong learner. As far back as he can remember, he wanted to learn more and develop himself further. He appreciates the talents of others and actively seeks out their knowledge. It is his curious, flexible mind that allows Johnson to benefit from these relationships, and his wisdom in knowing when to ask for help.

TOM JOHNSON'S 21 COMMONSENSE LESSONS FOR TODAY'S YOUNG EXECUTIVE

1. **Decide early on what you want to do.** Go for it. If it doesn't work out, go on to another choice.
2. **Attach yourself to a rising star** (profession/leader/company), not a falling star.
3. **Be the best you can be at all you do.** Your last job is your next reference check.
4. **Have fun.** Pursue pleasures outside your office. Do not define your self-worth solely by your job.
5. **Do right.** When in doubt, ask yourself, "Is this right? How will my actions look if published on the front page of the newspaper?"
6. **Don't knock. Build.** Never build yourself up by cutting down your competition.
7. **Life is 99 rounds.** You'll get knocked down. Get up and go on.
8. **Don't forget the customer.** What the customer wants matters, but don't pander to it.
9. **Be loyal.** But not blindly loyal.
10. **Measure your *psychic* income.** It often brings more happiness than financial income.
11. **Be a friend.** You will need them.
12. **Have a dog.** It, and only it, will provide unqualified love.
13. **Treat people the way you want to be treated.**
14. **Only you are responsible for yourself.** Don't blame others.
15. **Never give up on what you want to do.** A person with a vision is more powerful than anyone else.
16. **Make a list of things you want to do before you check out.** Put it in your wallet. Examine it regularly (river raft trip, balloon ride, visit to pyramids, etc.).
17. **Don't select the wrong spouse.** It's tough enough living with the right one.
18. **Take care of yourself.**
19. **Don't neglect the spiritual side of your life.**
20. **The best gift you can give another is a good memory.**
21. **What often makes the difference in life is attitude**—about life, love, business, and athletics.

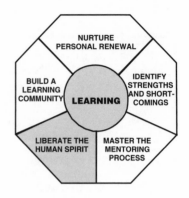

LIBERATING THE HUMAN SPIRIT

Just like their leaders, successful organizations need to adapt and grow in a dynamic, changing world.

In order for the organization to evolve, the leader must liberate the talents and spirits of his employees. That will increase the capacity within the firm, making it easier for it to grow.

But capacity will only increase if the relationships and environment within the company allow people to learn, develop, and contribute.

To sustain such growth, people must be willing to grow and renew themselves at all times. And the organization must always be seeking better ideas and better results.

What impresses you most about Kermit Campbell, the president of office furniture maker Herman Miller, is his insatiable thirst for growth. "I must understand more today than I did yesterday, and I must be better equipped to do something today than I was yesterday. I have always been that way."

His management philosophy flows directly out of this insatiable thirst. "I encourage people to step out from where they are, to expose themselves to growth opportunities," he says. That is good for employees, and good for business. In a firm like Herman Miller, which faces global competition and shrinking markets, the company must be creative in the way it decides to grow the business. Campbell has decided to grow from within, and tap the talent that is lying dormant inside his company.

J. KERMIT CAMPBELL
Herman Miller, Inc.

TITLE: President and Chief Executive Officer

AGE: 56

FAMILY SITUATION: Married, 2 children

EDUCATION: University of Kansas; Massachusetts Institute of Technology

HISTORY: Herman Miller, Inc., President and CEO (1992); Dow Corning Corporation (1960–92), Group Vice President (1987–92)

HOBBIES AND OTHER ACTIVITIES: Volunteer: United Way, Midland Symphony Orchestra, Opera Grand Rapids, and Impressions 5 Museum; enjoys singing, viticulture, tennis, golf, and water sports

HONORS AND SPECIAL ACCOMPLISHMENTS: American Architectural Foundation, Board of Regents; Hope College, Board of Trustees; Chair, State of Michigan Partnerships in Education Task Force; Chair, Michigan Cities in Schools; Co-Chair, Michigan First; Henry Ford Museum, Board of Trustees; Awarded Northwood University's Outstanding Business Leader, February 1995

HEADQUARTERS: Zeeland, Michigan

BUSINESS: Manufacturing and selling furniture systems, products, and related services for offices, health-care facilities, and other uses

NUMBER OF EMPLOYEES: 6,453

NET SALES: $953,200,000 (1994)

COMPANY HONORS: *Fortune*'s Most Admired U.S. Corporations (1986–1994); *Business Ethics'* excellence in Ethics Award (1989); White House Presidential citation for environment management (1991); The National Wildlife Federation presented Herman Miller with its 1993 Environmental Achievement Award.

That decision is consistent with the company's past. Founded in Zeeland, Michigan, in 1923, the Herman Miller company has a worldwide reputation for modern furniture design, and innovative management. Chairman Max DePree brought the company into the limelight in the 1980s with his book *Leadership Is an Art*, which for many has become a management bible. Given this, it would take a special person to succeed DePree, and the company found him in

Campbell, who knew that if he was going to increase the organization's capability he would have to minimize the fear of failure.

"We talk constantly about how it's okay to take a risk, and how, in
fact, it is necessary to take a risk, if both the individual and the company are to grow."

Campbell used his beliefs as the foundation for the organization
he is building. That organization in turn institutionalizes his beliefs
in the way it behaves. It is clear that Campbell understands, based on
his own experience, people's desire to learn and contribute at the
maximum level possible. And indeed in all his interactions with employees he talks to people's strengths, to their natural desire to grow
and develop.

But there is no guarantee that employees will learn just because
you tell them that's what you want. Leaders must create an environment that allows this development to take place. At its most basic,
that means eliminating an employee's fear of making a mistake,
since fear is the major obstacle to learning. Saying you are going to
eliminate fear is easy. Accomplishing it is another matter.

"Because of a lifetime in top-down, order-and-obey workplaces,
employees are unaccustomed to freedom, and therefore are afraid of
it," Campbell says. "They fear that they will stumble under responsibility's weight, and that if they do, they will be humiliated, or fired."

The best way for a leader to deal with fear is to meet it head on.
"When I came to Herman Miller [from Dow Corning, where he was
a group vice president], I set out to meet all 5,500 of our employees
worldwide, and in the first three months I visited just about every
work station in the company. That sent a message that I was open.
We have meetings where people sometimes ask me things that I
can't answer, and I think that is good. The best way to overcome an
employee's fear is to demonstrate that as a leader you are open, that
you don't have all the answers, and you are willing to join with employees in taking risks."

By accepting—and sharing—his imperfections, Campbell showed
he was not afraid to look weak or uninformed in front of others. It
was a conscious decision and one that paid off immediately. Campbell's admission that he doesn't know everything frees other people
at Herman Miller to admit that they don't have all the answers
either. That opens them up to learning. An inability to admit weak-

ness or ignorance gets in the way of taking risks, making commitments, and growing on the job.

But it is not just the leader who has to be open. Every manager in the company must be. They all need to want employees to grow and learn.

"You must remove any purveyors of fear. You must remove any manager who is limiting your people instead of liberating them," Campbell says. He refers to this as "liberating the human spirit" at Herman Miller.

"I believe there is a direct correlation between liberating the human spirit and performance," Campbell adds. "There is a direct payoff for the company in letting people capitalize on the innate, inbred skills they don't even know they have. They don't know they have them because they have never been able to let them out of the box. I want those skills to start popping out."

Campbell believes that Herman Miller's success will depend on innovations made by people at every level of the organization. Those improvements—be they major breakthroughs, or incremental ones—will require full participation of everyone at the company. To achieve that goal, Campbell has a vision of the company that is always becoming, always seeking better ideas, better ways of doing things, and better results. This kind of company will be staffed with people who embrace learning and renewal.

Kerm Campbell is trying to institutionalize his ideas inside Herman Miller. To do that, Campbell is helping people learn how to learn. He is creating a team of "learning coaches," within the company. The coaches' full-time jobs are to help Herman Miller's business units learn while they work. Specifically, the coaches work with the leader and his team to help them reach consensus, think deeply about the problems they face, and keep them from going off on tangents. They learn the art of dialogue—to suspend judgment, advocate positions, and take risks with each other. The results are decisions that are stronger, more systemic, and more sustainable over time.

Campbell believes it is the responsibility of a leader to challenge, liberate, and nurture employee development. When employees are given the right tools, environment, and opportunity—in addition to being given the confidence of their leaders—they will reach, stretch, and grow. To make that happen, Campbell feels it is vital that the leader be open and accessible.

"I just read something that said the Latin root of the word 'educate' is to lead, and the root of the word 'instruct' is to pile on, and I think that says it all. If I'm going to lead, if I'm going to educate, then I have to open myself up so dialogue can occur," says Campbell. "I believe that only when employees can get inside my head do they start seeing how what I am thinking applies to their head. This way a dialogue can result. I can grow as part of the dialogue, and they can too."

In his beliefs, Campbell's vision of his employees is often greater than their vision of themselves.

"We had a meeting about a week before Christmas where I brought our thirty top operating managers together so we could talk about what we would be doing next," Campbell recalls. "I used the half-day that we had together to get people to open up, and talk about what, from their point of view, we were trying to accomplish, and what they didn't quite understand about what I was trying to do. The participation was very intense, and it kept feeding on itself, and by the time the half-day was complete, we had, as a group, gone up to a much higher level than we had ever achieved before. That is what I should be doing as CEO, taking each of our employees to a higher plane, not just in terms of potential, but in helping to build greater capacities."

Believing that people can rise to new heights is a great gift, analogous to parenting. Campbell understands that organizations need to create within their people a feeling of security and self-confidence, if they want them to express themselves, grow, and learn. This growth is good not only for the employees but for the leader, as well as the company.

Trust Your People to Save You

"Have you ever stood in a swimming pool and caught a leaping four-year-old?" Campbell asks. "The first time you see the hesitation, fear, and excitement on the child's face. After the first leap, you can't stop the youngster from climbing out and leaping in again and again.

"That, in a nutshell, is my idea of leadership. But it may surprise you that the leader in my metaphor isn't the adult. It's the child. Managers today are leaping into waters of risk, constant change, and increasingly tougher competition—and it's scary.

"So who's the grown-up on the scene? Who's there to catch the leader when he leaps into the uncertainty of business conditions? The answer is the people in our organizations. What will save us is the creativity and commitment of our employees, the skills and knowledge of a diverse organization. What we leaders have to do is, like the child on the edge of the pool, trust our people.

"The swimming-pool metaphor isn't perfect," Campbell continues. "For the child on the edge of the pool, trust means taking the leap into the outstretched arms of the adult. For managers standing on the edge of the future, trust means doing one crucial thing before taking that leap: untying our employees' hands so that they can, in fact, catch us when we jump.

"In most companies, employees wear shackles—not on their hands, but on their minds and spirits. They are not allowed to innovate or create. They can only do what they are told. We are devoted to hands-on management. But we ought to be keeping our hands off. It has been my experience that managers achieve the best results when they use their own hands only to untie those of their employees."

Campbell tries to live those words in his interactions with employees. He understands that every interaction is a learning interaction. It is a chance to potentially liberate the human spirit, or shut it down. Which way the interaction goes depends in very large part on the leader.

True, employees have a reciprocal responsibility to try to grow, to initiate training and seek out learning opportunities, but the odds of that happening are substantially reduced if the leader doesn't work to create an environment that enables growth—both personal and corporate—to happen. Campbell gives an example.

"A long-time employee was talking to me recently," Campbell recalls. "He asked me what my position was on a certain issue. I told him that my position was his position. He is the leader on this issue. He has the responsibility and the accountability. He has to act, based on his knowledge and the advice of others with knowledge on the subject. I can facilitate, but I shouldn't decide an issue others are held accountable for."

What Campbell feels he should do is metaphorically untie employees' hands so that they can decide. And once their hands are untied, profitability—and a healthier company—follows.

What results from liberating the human spirit, says Campbell, is "a relational, adaptive organization. I compare the adaptable organization to a living organism, because I don't want our imaginations to be constrained by what an organizational chart tells us. All is possible. Part of adaptability is the ability to constantly form new teams. This is where the merger between adaptable and relational starts.

"Adaptable, relational organizations will not only survive but will thrive in today's world," says Campbell.

To thrive is the key. An organization can't survive long term without making money.

"I think our approach to management probably has a more profound effect on the top line than the bottom, at least at first," says Campbell. "By that I mean the company will grow faster, and will have new ideas for growth, if it liberates the human spirit of its employees. As a result of liberating the human spirit, we will have a bigger stockpile of ideas to choose from, and we will choose the most profitable ones, and that will make the bottom line grow."

What is clear from his description is that Campbell understands deeply the value of human investment as a business strategy. He knows that the growth of an organization depends on the growth of its employees. If his company, or any company, is going to succeed, then the leader must unleash the talent lying dormant in its people.

Liberating the human spirit leads to more-inspired workers, workers who are confident in their skills, and the value they add. That leads to healthy, more-productive relationships and a willingness to take risks. So the payoff to this investment in employees is not only people who grow but a company that grows as well. This is not easy to achieve. For one thing, a leader who fosters a learning environment can often end up learning and hearing things he would rather not.

"A lot of leaders say that when they open up communication, they get bombarded with criticism and negatives. Well, you have to expect that," Campbell says simply. "There is often a lot of pent-up frustration. I remember meetings at which employees asked very hostile questions. If I had responded in kind, they would have retreated into their fear, and the door to communication would have slammed shut. So, I would bite my lip and say, 'Tell me more about that,' or 'Let's look a little deeper at the situation.' That way they could let off steam.

"If they came up with a good suggestion, I'd empower them on the spot to implement it. If they made a suggestion that I thought was off base, I'd address that politely but candidly, saying something like 'I understand your concerns, but my first impression is that, if we did that, it might cause a negative reaction over here.' "

The way Campbell said no to the idea showed he had a genuine, honest commitment to his employees, and wanted to create a partnership with them. But it also did something else. It showed that Campbell believes deeply in the need to balance a caring environment with good business acumen. If you don't have a good product, a receptive market, and control of your finances, a corporate environment that fosters learning and growth won't mean much.

Indeed, that was one of the problems at Herman Miller before Campbell arrived. "The company had been wonderful on the philosophical side of the fulcrum," he says, "but not as sharp as it needed to be on the business side."

"The caring alone doesn't guarantee success," says Campbell. "All your business systems have to be world class. But when you have all those business things in place, then the caring environment makes all the difference in the world. It becomes the strategic advantage.

"If we can take the caring qualities and balance them with good business action, then it becomes a kind of perpetual-motion thing, and we will continue to do well. Good leadership is balanced leadership. It's a balance of all things that are necessary to ensure success. It's the balance of caring, business vision, and direction."

Figuring out a way of balancing all those competing needs can create tension. Only a commitment to achieving balance, coupled with the fact that Campbell is comfortable with the uncertainty that the need for balance can cause, has allowed him to deal with this tension successfully.

At least up to a point. On July 12, 1995, Kerm Campbell "resigned" from his job as Chairman and CEO of Herman Miller. The reasons for his resignation were clear. Profits at Herman Miller were lagging and the office furniture business had become more competitive than ever. Campbell needed to shake things up to improve the situation. He started by slicing operating expenses, closed down plants in Texas and New Jersey, and laid off several key senior staff, something that simply doesn't happen at this Midwest company. These moves were simply too much for Herman Miller.

As Kerm Campbell reflects on these events, he believes there are several lessons to be learned from his experience. "At a company as large as Herman Miller, balancing the needs of the board, the shareholders, our customers, and employees is not as simple as it seems. All of these key stakeholders must be in sync and they must buy into the transformation together. If they are out of sync, something must give. In the process of cutting costs, I must have alienated the board. I clearly did not spend enough time developing relationships with them. So when confidence was lost the leader must step aside and part ways. Maybe next time I will be less patient with those in management who were uncooperative or incapable of making the changes fast enough. I guess we are all vulnerable."

From his insatiable thirst for growth to his belief about people's capacities for learning, and the need to liberate the human spirit, the organizational strategy that Kerm Campbell created revolves around building an adaptive, relational organization. And if it's not at Herman Miller, Campbell says, he will take his message elsewhere.

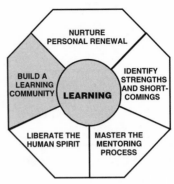

BUILDING A
LEARNING COMMUNITY

Organizations that learn the fastest will be the ones on the cutting edge. But learning communities are not built overnight. Like people, they require a long-term commitment to continuous improvement. The leader's job is to create the conditions that allow the organization—and its members—to grow and shape the future.

Building a learning community starts with a curious, imaginative leader, who is willing to lay out a vision and start a dialogue about the gap between his vision and the current reality.

The next step is to create an environment that promotes learning, one that is open and safe for people to try new ideas, and one that expands their knowledge and skills.

Learning organizations are not bashful about borrowing the best ideas of others. They are also not shy about having honest conversations about their successes and failures. People are given time to reflect, and to solve their own problems. Working in teams offers people opportunities to learn from each other, while allowing conversations to move easily across the boundaries of the organization.

The leader is the steward of the learning process, changing attitudes, behaviors, and work processes along the way.

If you want to see how much schools have changed, pick up one of those "Dick and Jane" readers that were commonplace thirty years ago. It is not only the style of artwork and the typeface that makes them seem hopelessly outdated, it is also how people are depicted. Only father works outside the home. Mother's sole job is to take care of house and hearth, and everyone is white. The idea of stepchil-

---

TIM CUNEO
Oak Grove School District

TITLE: Superintendent

AGE: 53

FAMILY SITUATION: Married; 2 children; 2 grandchildren

EDUCATION: M.A., University of Santa Clara (1975); B.A., Chico State University (1966)

HISTORY: Superintendent of Schools, Whisman School District (1987–92); Assistant Superintendent, Instructional Services, Pajaro Valley Unified School District (1984–87); Principal, Aptos High School (1979–83); Dean of Curriculum and Instruction, Fremond Union High School District (1977–79)

HONORS AND SPECIAL ACCOMPLISHMENTS: President, Association of California School Administrators (ACSA); The Tech Museum of Innovation, Board of Directors; Institute for Effective School Leadership, Packard Foundation Board Member; California Air and Space Center Advisory Board; Chair, Mountain View Chamber of Commerce Business/Education Committee; State Legislation Committee, ACSA; and Chair, Schools of Choice Position Paper Task Force; Member, XEROX K–12 National Educational Advisory Board, Joint Venture Silicon Valley and Smart Valley Education Initiatives

HEADQUARTERS: San Jose, California

BUSINESS: Public school system, serving grades K–8

NUMBER OF EMPLOYEES: 1,200

BUDGET: $55 million

---

dren, single-parent homes, minorities, households where both parents work, or any other of the situations that occur frequently today just don't appear in the pages of what was for many of us our first reader.

Tim Cuneo understands how far we are from 1965. Cuneo is the superintendent of the Oak Grove School District in San Jose. Oak Grove is an urban district, serving some 12,100 students in kindergarten through eighth grade. It is also a school district undergoing considerable change. You can see that in the ethnicity of its students. Some 16 percent are Asian, 24 percent Hispanic, 6 percent black, 2 percent Filipino, and 50 percent white. That makeup is typical of the California school system, and unfortunately so too are these facts. Compared to other school districts nationwide, California students are:

- Less likely to be immunized.
- Less likely to go to college.
- Less likely to receive child-support payments.
- More likely to grow up poor.
- More likely to have babies as teenagers.
- More likely to be victims of homicide.

So much for Dick and Jane.

"Today's public schools are educating the most culturally, economically, and educationally diverse student population in the history of the world," Cuneo says. "At no time has the place 'school' been more crucial to the future of society than it is today. We will be judged as a society by the choices we make that relate to children and their future."

Today's children are tomorrow's adults. In the twenty-first century, we will need adults who know how to learn, listen, and convey information. We will need workers who can solve problems in innovative ways, have good negotiation skills, are business literate, and who can assume responsibility and motivate others. To make sure tomorrow's workers will have all these skills requires no less than a major transformation of the educational system, changing what a school is, what it looks like, and what it means if we say it is doing its job.

Cuneo set out to do that—on a small scale. He would change just one part of the educational system—his district. The goal? To improve the lives of the 12,100 students he was responsible for.

Cuneo is a curious, imaginative leader, who was willing to lay out a vision of what he wanted the school district to look like. He envisions a day when public schools will have to compete for students— and he wants Oak Grove to be the place where students choose to go. To make that happen, he is "trying to break out of the present paradigm of very structured and very specific job descriptions," he says. "We need to create a world-class school district with world-class students."

The most effective way of doing that, Cuneo thought, was to change the schools into learning centers, places where students could, in large part, teach themselves, using the resources available. Their teachers serve as facilitators. And those teachers—and professionals such as the school psychologist—work together to create an instructional program. In fact, even the district's painter, the person who is responsible for painting the inside and outside of the schools, is involved. He is called upon to teach the unit on color and design.

In the school system Cuneo envisions, parents are more involved. They work with the principal and staff to make decisions on what should be taught. In addition to covering the basics, they make sure the curriculum includes instruction about the history and development of the communities that make up the Oak Grove district. Says Cuneo: "We are trying to build bridges to the community so they better understand us, and, in turn, we better understand their culture."

In addition, the business community also is involved. It contributes time and resources, and would let the school system know what kinds of job skills students will need to successfully compete in the workplace and society, by the time they finish their education.

Cuneo's decision to create learning centers started a cultural change process in the school district that would dramatically alter the learning environment for students, teachers, and the community. As a result of his changes, teachers now work in teams, not alone, and the entire curriculum is becoming integrated. "Today you have fifty minutes on mathematics and then go on to language," Cuneo says. "What I would like to see instead is that when sixth graders are doing a unit on China everything is tied together. They learn Chinese history, language, art, what the sciences were about at the time. We want them to see the connection between all the different disciplines."

The goal behind every change Cuneo proposes is to make it easier for everyone to grow. "I'm trying to develop a community of learners. The whole idea is that if we're in a learning organization, and that's what we are all about, we, too, should be learning," he says. And if teachers are constantly learning, that, in turn, guarantees continuous improvement in the schools.

It is obvious that schools should be leading the pack in building learning organizations, yet that is not the case. Schools tend to be closed, insular environments. Their primary customers—students—constantly graduate and move on. Residents of the community tend not to pay much attention to the schools, unless they have kids attending, and often it seems that teachers' attention is on achieving tenure and protecting what they have, more than anything else.

To fulfill his vision, Cuneo is committed to changing all this.

To do it, Cuneo started talking to everyone involved, trying to gain their support. The focus of the dialogue was clear: Where are we now? Where do we want to go? And how do we fill the gap in between?

The next step in the learning process was perhaps the most vital. Cuneo reached out to the entire learning community—teachers, administrators, parents, and business—and said in essence, "I need you." They would evaluate the district's needs and ability to change, and create the future together. Cuneo knew this would not be easy. It would require a new way of operating, one that would be open to diversity, conflict, and reflection, and would also value the participation of all employees, empowering them to make the changes Cuneo envisions. A key decision Cuneo made early in the process was that there was no reason to "reinvent the wheel." Other companies and schools had successfully grappled with the issue of creating learning communities, and the Oak Grove district would benchmark what they did.

The move had two benefits. The obvious one was that Cuneo learned how nearby companies and school districts set up their programs. That allowed him to develop his own that much faster. But equally important, by reaching out to the community he gained another resource to draw on.

"I don't believe educators can teach children by themselves," he says. "I think it takes an entire community to do that, so we are building partnerships with all kinds of companies and parents."

Those partnerships can be as simple as creating an electronic network that goes into the homes within the district and offers instruction in parenting skills. "We want to show parents how to add to their child's development, to understand what is happening here, and help them with their child's homework," Cuneo says.

Or the partnership could be as complex as setting up a school-industry council. San Jose is in the heart of Silicon Valley, and the companies that are members of the council are—with the support and guidance from parents and teachers—helping the districts develop a core math-science curriculum that will serve the district well into the next century. In addition, they are donating computers and software to be used in the classrooms.

Ensuring that the learning community became a reality required that Cuneo create an environment that promoted learning. Given the way the school system was set up, that meant Cuneo had to create new ways of learning, working, and governing. Along the way he would have to manage the tension between his vision of the future and the current state of the school district.

Cuneo's first challenge was to reengineer how the school operated, changing the district from one that offered traditional instruction to one that provided active, participative learning.

Reengineering, when stripped of the buzzwords, means looking for ways to do work more efficiently. Cuneo has reinvented the way schoolwork is done. He now has teams of teachers teaching students and teachers teaching teachers how to create a learning organization. Cuneo is moving from functional departments to having people work in core processes. He is breaking down organizational boundaries, and is creating dialogue in all directions. This requires educating teachers about new ways of learning.

"One of the ways we are doing this is by establishing professional development schools for teachers," he explains. "Some 25 percent of the professional development school teachers will be permanent, while 75 percent will come for one year. People who are there full time won't have assignments one day a week so they will have time—indeed it will be their responsibility—to coach and teach the other teachers. At the end of the year, the 'visiting teachers' will return to their schools with the knowledge and skills ready to apply what they have learned, and a new staff of teachers will come in. This way I can rotate the experience. They have to come in pairs, because I want them to return to their schools with partners that they can communicate with the following year.

"One thing we learned from the business community is to be outcome oriented," he adds. "Everyone involved has to be able to answer, 'What are we trying to accomplish?' before a project gets under way.

In this system, administrative hurdles are knocked over, and just about any approach to education will be considered."

Cuneo is attempting to stimulate entrepreneurial behavior among teachers. And he is trying to get them to take responsibility for their own learning, in addition to taking responsibility for creating learning communities.

"Right now I have two sixth-grade teachers who want to build a community of third through sixth grades," Cuneo says, giving an example of how the new system is beginning to pay off. "One of them is very right brain, and the other is very left. They both are very well aware of each other's strengths and weaknesses, and they complement each other. Together they are building a whole new curriculum."

But if educators are going to become entrepreneurial, then their roles must also change. Cuneo had to flatten the organization, and teachers and administrators are having to learn new ways to work together. "The biggest challenge is dealing with old behaviors," Cuneo says. "We must move from bossing and managing to leading. Part of our process is teaching each of us how to become a leader. There has been resistance, because people don't have the skills yet. But they will. We must learn to lead by influencing others to achieve mutually agreed upon goals for the district."

It has to be that way, Cuneo adds. "Our job as administrators should be to make sure that nothing gets in the way of learning. The job is not only to help the teachers ensure that what they want to accomplish happens, but that we set the highest standards for our students and ourselves. We should be saying to teachers—and the entire learning community: You tell us what is important, and we will work with you to make sure it happens."

All of this is governed by a learning cabinet comprised of teachers, parents, and members of the business community.

THE NEED FOR LIFELONG LEARNING

Obviously, the same principles that Cuneo is applying within the Oak Grove district will work elsewhere with other employees. A research and development lab at a pharmaceutical company has to learn new work processes, develop multifaceted teams, and establish ongoing conversations with manufacturers, physicians, and patients. Retail food-distribution businesses need to learn from other companies how to ask difficult questions about serving customers, and they need to develop more efficient work processes. And so it goes in every industry.

What is unique about Cuneo's work is that he is building a learning organization by involving the entire community. First, he is creating a learning community for students, preparing them to be healthy, creative, productive adults. Second, he is creating a learning community for teachers, where people are continually expanding their capabilities to shape the future. And finally he is creating a learning community for outside stakeholders (parents, businesses, and the community) who have a vested interest in the success of the education of our young people.

For this to work, all the stakeholders—those inside and outside the school system—must make a contribution. They need to take responsibility for their own learning. They must continually expand their skills, test new ideas, seek out new learning experiences, question others, and think deeply about the root causes of problems. This means they will have to work productively with other people from other disciplines and have honest conversations about what is and what is not working.

Why are lifelong learners so important to business success? In a global environment, where technology continuously speeds up both the rate at which tasks are accomplished and the speed at which competitive situations change, organizations need people who can adapt and grow in their work. Lifelong learners become better problem solvers, who can think more creatively and work faster. They will have the flexibility companies need in order to compete.

The sad fact is most of us don't spend very much time trying to learn new skills, once we leave school. If the upheaval in our economy over the past decade has proved anything, it is that people—and the organizations they work for—need to learn continuously. Tim Cuneo understands that. He carefully cultivated a change in attitudes, behaviors, and new management processes that fostered a school environment that was conducive to continuous learning and improvement. The result, as the Oak Grove School District is proving, is an organization that is constantly getting better.

"The conversation in the district used to be about the great old days, how thirteen years ago everything was wonderful," Cuneo says. "How ten years ago they were pretty good, and how the last two years were the pits. I don't have those conversations anymore. The discussions now are about where we are going and how fast we can get there. Can we do this? Can we try that?"

Diversity

We are all different. There was a time when we checked those differences at the office door, but those days are gone. Today, valuing differences is critical to business success.

This fact is unsettling to unhealthy leaders. They harbor strong biases and resentments. Generally arrogant, they feel superior to others, and believe that people are born different and unequal. Not surprisingly, they tend to be dogmatic, unable to take another's perspective, and typically demand conformity in the workplace. The fact that employees want to be themselves, and no longer automatically bend to the will of their leaders, is a source of constant irritation and strife at work.

In contrast, the best leaders have a deep appreciation for what makes people unique. They believe people are created equal and different, and that each person has a special contribution to make. To them, we are all extensions of everyone we know, and we have a right to be accepted for who we are. These differences don't threaten healthy leaders. In fact, they love it when employees bring their special talents and perspectives to work. How to manage and make use of those differences is a business challenge they enjoy.

Diversity is a business issue. Companies need a diverse workforce to serve a demanding customer base in a global marketplace, and those that attract and maintain such a workforce serve customers better and develop new markets for their products. How does a leader go about creating this kind of diverse workforce? He starts by looking inside himself, examining his own prejudices and the breadth of his personality. The best leaders understand how their own prejudices influence the way they lead. They make sure their biases are not getting in the way of running the organization.

These leaders also take pains to cultivate their entire self—both their male, competitive side and their female collaborative one. Understanding and tapping into their own diversity makes it easier for them to deal with the diversity within their organizations.

They can do this because healthy leaders think differently. They start with the assumption that each of us is on a journey—as an individual, as a member of a group, and as a citizen of the world. Collectively, we all have a fundamental need to feel respected. We want to feel at home in the workplace, and have the freedom to be ourselves. We want to be safe from discrimination. When we feel this way, we are willing to take risks and make commitments to the organization.

These philosophies are put into practice in the leader's day-to-day actions. She confronts and censures intolerance. She assures equality of employment and opportunity. And she pays special attention to people outside the mainstream culture, knowing that they can easily feel isolated. In such a culture, people are hired, promoted, and fired independently of their color or gender or lifestyle. And management makes sure this happens by attracting diverse candidates, offering diversity education, creating minority networks, and celebrating diverse holidays. But the best leaders don't stop there. They go beyond just tolerating human differences and build a culture of respect, one that views differences as the fuel for creative energy and insight.

This can work only if diversity is everyone's responsibility. Each person must bring his unique talents to work; he must value the differences of others; and he must support the company's way of doing business.

The four people you are about to meet represent the four stages leaders go through in creating a diversity-sensitive organization.

As Kenneth Brecher points out from his experiences running museums and foundations, step one is for the leader to confront and resolve the prejudices within himself. Part of that resolution will involve confronting the leader's own diversity, what makes her unique and what makes her similar to everyone else. Joan Claybrook has learned to draw on her full personality in running one of the country's most effective public interest advocacy organizations, Public Citizen.

Only when the leader is comfortable with his own diversity will he be able to deal successfully with the diversity inside his organization. Caesar Odio, Miami's city manager, understands that diversity goes beyond ethnicity and gender and extends to the way people think and feel.

How do you know when you are dealing with the issue of diversity effectively? Elliot Hoffman, president of Just Desserts, has the answer: You'll know when you are not only accepting but *respecting* the diversity within your organization.

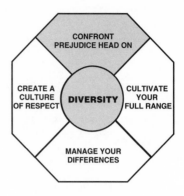

CONFRONTING
PREJUDICE HEAD ON

Let's face it. We are all recovering sexists and racists. Some of us just heal faster than others.

Why we are in recovery is easy to understand. Many of us live isolated lives. We attended cloistered schools, socialize with like-minded friends, and live in protected neighborhoods filled with people basically like us. As a result, we are often blind to the diversity around us, and cautious with those who are different. Stereotypes develop easily, and, if they are left unchecked, turn quickly into prejudice and discrimination.

Successful leaders understand the roots of their own prejudice and are aware of their personal blind spots. They realize the power of diversity, and the poison of discrimination. And they know well that people will not give their best, most creative work unless they are free to be who they really are and free to express themselves fully within the organization.

Confronting prejudice head on—inside oneself and inside of others—is the first step toward tapping the rich diversity within your organization.

Kenneth Brecher's entire career is a study in diversity. He has been an anthropologist based at Oxford, traveling the world examining different cultures; a theater producer in Los Angeles who excelled at putting on the works of minority playwrights; director of the Boston Children's Museum, where young impressionable minds are expanded; and president of the William Penn Foundation in

KENNETH BRECHER
William Penn Foundation

TITLE: Former President, William Penn Foundation

AGE: 48

FAMILY SITUATION: Married; 1 child

EDUCATION: B.A. in English, Cornell University; Rhodes Scholar, and Diploma in Social Anthropology, Oxford University; advanced study, The Institute of Social Anthropology, Oxford University

HISTORY: Ford Foundation Foreign Area Fellowship for Anthropological Research among the Wausha tribe of Central Brazil (1969–71); Associate Artistic Director and Acting Artistic Director, The Mark Taper Forum (1977–86); Director, The Boston Children's Museum (1986–93); President, William Penn Foundation (1993–94)

HONORS AND SPECIAL ACCOMPLISHMENTS: Overseer, Institute of Contemporary Art, Boston; Advisor to Fund for Cultural Innovation, MacArthur Foundation; Museum Program Panel, National Endowment for the Humanities; Board, Aspen International Design Conference, Anthropology Resource Center; Cultural Advisory Board, Olympics Arts Festival; Editorial Advisory Board, *Arts & Architecture*

BUSINESS: Cultural affairs and philanthropy

CURRENT ACTIVITIES: Consultant to foundations and cultural institutions

Philadelphia, whose mission includes improving life in the inner city. His varied experiences have given him special insight into the power of diversity.

Brecher recounts an experience he had at a community meeting of nonprofits. In attendance were representatives from the Chinese and Latino community as well as from one of the area's settlement houses and a local foundation.

"The leader from the Chinese community," Brecher recalls, "was very excited because her group had just obtained control of a parking lot, and she was planning to use the revenues the lot generated to help fund her organization.

"The woman from the settlement house said she could never do that, because her group felt it shouldn't take money from the community." The lot, she said, should either be free to the community or have the lowest parking prices in the area, because her group saw its job as serving the community.

The Latino person said she could foresee all kinds of problems if her group got a parking lot. "Members of the community might think our organization would now be in the money, or wonder how we had gained control of it. They'd want to know who we had to make a deal with, and what that deal would ultimately cost us. And they might ask why we weren't building affordable housing on the land instead."

"And," Brecher added, "the middle-class white person said he wasn't sure the Chinese group should be running a parking lot at all, because it might affect its status as a tax-exempt nonprofit.

"There were four different cultural responses to the same set of circumstances," Brecher explains, summing up what appeared to be a simple story about a community group gaining control of a parking lot. "The Chinese group is getting kudos from the community, because they're showing they know how to be entrepreneurial," Brecher points out. "The settlement house is performing as the nineteenth-century liberal, in asking how you can think of charging the community. The Latinos are trying to find their place in society, without raising their profile too much, and the white, middle-class MBA is saying, 'Watch out for the IRS.' "

"The lessons businesses, nonprofits, and government can learn from this are simple," Brecher continues. "Not only is the marketplace more heterogeneous than ever before, but the solutions we fall back on, the decisions we make, are culturally specific and they're limited. They are just one way of looking at a problem. There are others that might be more effective."

Everyone is prejudiced to a greater or lesser extent. Prejudice is a natural emotion that starts early in life in our relatively isolated families and neighborhoods. We often attend segregated schools, play in racially or ethnically unmixed schoolyards, and socialize with friends who look like us; all the while our stereotypes germinate and grow. As a result, each of us possesses a unique collection of prejudices and stereotypes. Although it's not politically acceptable to be openly prejudiced these days, some of these stereotypes are so ingrained that we are not even aware of them.

These prejudices either are magnified or shrink, according to our experiences with people who are different from ourselves. Often our reaction to these people is that we don't understand them—the way they look, act, talk, or dress—and conclude that they may pose a threat to our beliefs. To protect ourselves, we maintain a distance from strangers.

At its most fundamental, our rejection of unfamiliar people is based on ignorance and insecurity. We conclude there are two worlds: our safe, known sphere and the outer world populated by threatening strangers. Strangers provoke a full regalia of emotions—fear, envy, admiration, revulsion, and insecurity—not because they are inherently ferocious or worthy of envy but because of what they reflect about ourselves. This limits our ability to understand the world, limits our ability to tap into the diversity of the workforce, and limits the best business decisions we can make.

In today's competitive business environment, we cannot afford self-imposed limits. We cannot afford to undervalue people whose core identities are different from those of western European, white, heterosexual males. We cannot afford to ignore the rage and hurt lying dormant inside people. We cannot afford to eliminate anyone's potential contribution. If for no other reason, economic conditions will not permit us to say that those who are different are inferior. Confronting prejudice head on becomes vitally important to an organization's success.

The best leaders become aware of their own prejudices. They recognize that they are products of the institutional environment in which they work, and also realize that this is no excuse. They are very aware of the stereotypes that the mainstream culture holds about special groups, and they are committed to trying to change.

Understanding their own reactions is the first step in the process. The next is to confront directly their own feelings of xenophobia, the fear of strangers. Successful leaders do not tiptoe through their organizations, reluctant to confront the institutional and perceptual barriers that separate people. They meet them head on. This is exactly what Brecher did.

"There is a housing project in Philadelphia right next to where we were funding the construction of a new theater," he recalls. "People kept telling me it was filled with guns and violence and it was just so dangerous. I heard this three times in one day, so I canceled my afternoon appointments and walked over there. My heart was beating, and you know what I found when I got there? I found children. I found mothers. I found people getting their dinners ready. I didn't find people lined up with guns. I found human beings trying under very difficult, very reduced circumstances, to lead decent lives, and many of them were succeeding in doing so. People had been telling me what danger I would be in if I went there, and I came back and said I hadn't been to a terrifying place. I had been to Oz. I looked behind the screen, and what I found was children."

Brecher's decision to directly confront the situation is typical of successful leaders. When faced with someone different, the best leaders are quick to ask, "How does this person make me feel? How do I interact with him differently from the way I act with others?" By asking these questions, successful leaders are distilling their own cultural and family roots—along with the deep-seated assumptions, mores, heroes, villains, and messages that were part of their upbringing—to see how all these factors are affecting their interaction with this person who is different from them.

They carefully watch how they ascribe personality characteristics to this new person, and ask themselves why they have these feelings, and whether the feelings are warranted. They try to distinguish between real cultural differences, that need to be respected, and stereotypes that need to be rejected.

Leaders understand they must work hard to become comfortable with people who are different from them. They must learn about the others' values and cultural heritage; they know that they must interact with others to become aware of the differences in language, communication styles, and interpersonal relationships. Because they are able to confront their own prejudices, they are able to deal with those of others. This is critically important inside organizations in which the combination of a personal superiority/inferiority belief system, coupled with the ability of institutional power to impose that system on others, turns personal prejudices into something larger, more powerful, and far more destructive. That is why leaders must understand their own prejudices, confront them, and model the behavior they want their organization to embrace.

In Brecher's case, dealing with diversity was not just about culture, color, or sexual orientation—it was about gender as well.

"When I was at the Children's Museum, I inherited a staff that was ninety percent women, and I learned how to work with women as a result. It was very hard on them. They suffered under me, because I had so much to learn. Eventually, a group there decided to help me. I began to learn that I shouldn't walk into a room and tell people what we were going to do. I learned I should come in and ask, 'What are you thinking about? What are your recommendations? How would you solve this?' This was delegation of a very different kind. And their solutions were often very different from the ones I would have employed as a white middle-class male."

And what they wanted was different as well. Not all diverse people aspire to be like the dominant, mainstream culture, and part of the job of the leader is to make those people comfortable within the organization as well, so that they, too, can contribute fully.

To do that, Brecher explains, "you break down the barriers between the older generation and the younger. You break down the barriers between homosexual and heterosexual. You find every way that you possibly can to bring people to the table and give them the support they require." In other words, you make them feel at home. Deep within the best leaders is an understanding that people must feel comfortable at work, in order to give their best and be optimally productive.

"All business—whether you work for a profit-making company, a nonprofit, or government—is about problem solving," Brecher says. "And you can't find the most creative solutions to problem solving unless people are free to be who they really are, and not the person others expect them to be. You have to make them feel at home, to encourage the kind of performance you want. When people don't feel comfortable, they may become anxious or angry. They shut down and don't do their best work."

One of the keys to making them comfortable is to ask what it will take for them to work most productively. And in doing so, Brecher often goes against the grain. "Our society," he explains, "has told us that in the workplace it is absolutely inappropriate for us to be who we would be with our friends. In the workplace we often have to present the idea that we do not have real lives."

That is wrong. The new leaders listen and tap into people's real selves. They allow their employees to reveal and express who they really are, in an environment that is free from prejudice and discrimination.

The amount of change Brecher is talking about is substantial. Yet he is convinced that any leader, no matter what her background or experience, has the potential to accomplish it. Successful people steeped in traditions and old habits can change, he says, but it usually requires a catalyst—the death of a mother or father, the loss of a job, a divorce, or delayed parenthood—to do it.

At those moments, "people are looking for affirmation, and very often when they look at another culture, they find it," Brecher says. "An anthropologist is a perfect example. He goes off and spends two years among the Indians in Brazil, and what does he really learn? He learns about his own family, religion, and culture. You think you're learning about somebody else, but in fact everything is in comparison."

None of this learning is easy, as Brecher is the first to admit. But it is necessary. Leaders must have the courage to have tough conversations with themselves about the difficult issues behind diversity. And they must deal directly with people issues and problems every day and, as Brecher points out, "most of us are not trained to deal with these things, and there are never any easy solutions."

"It's difficult, because there are not many role models," he adds. "You can hire consultants for the next twenty years, but many of them have never dealt with the real issues of race in the workplace. You can hire people who say they know how to solve this particular problem, but when it comes right down to it, they have a formula that does not apply to you."

Still, the leaders must press on. They—and we—have no choice. We need everyone's talents, if our organizations—and our society—are to thrive. This is something most people know intuitively.

"When I was in Boston, we did research on the developmental nature of racism in young children," Brecher says. "We asked parents of different cultures and classes what they wanted for their kids, and everyone said the same thing. They wanted their children to be successful, although they defined success differently, and they all said they wanted their children to own houses and live anywhere they wanted to live. They might not have wanted to be exposed to new people themselves, but they realized it was important for their kids to be able to deal with people different from themselves. It was like the parent who doesn't know how to swim who says, 'My child is going to learn to swim,' or the parent who is terrified of computers but who buys one for his five-year-old, because be believes this is a skill his child needs to succeed.

"What our society needs is a broader range of skills than we have right now," Brecher adds. "The parent who says, 'If my child can work with people of completely different backgrounds, races, cultures, and languages, then my child will have a better chance of success' understands that. This is a skill we all must learn."

As the percentage of white males in the workforce decreases every year, diversity is a given in today's organization. The natural tendency of leaders, who tend to be white males, is to see that decline as a problem. Brecher sees it as a wonderful opportunity.

"The real issue is to use the workforce we are given in different ways, and to prepare our people differently, in today's competitive environment. To accomplish this will require leaders to have a better understanding of the diverse kinds of people they now find working for them."

But the opportunities diversity presents don't end inside the organization's walls, Brecher quickly adds. "Any corporation in this country whose objective is profit would benefit greatly from understanding that there is almost always a wider market than they think for their products and services. And that market is more international and diverse than they might imagine."

To reach that market, just as to reach today's new workforce, requires understanding the thought processes of people who are different from you.

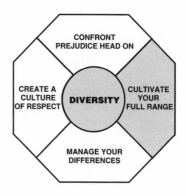

CONFRONT
PREJUDICE HEAD ON

CREATE A
CULTURE   **DIVERSITY**   CULTIVATE
OF RESPECT   YOUR
                             FULL RANGE

MANAGE YOUR
DIFFERENCES

CULTIVATING YOUR FULL RANGE

Leaders must wear many hats—negotiating one moment, issuing orders the next, striving for consensus at the end of the day. Business demands that you develop an array of skills and perspectives. To develop them, leaders must learn how to cultivate the full range of their personalities.

We each have within us a male competitive capability and a female collaborative one. This does not mean that only men exhibit masculine leadership, nor does it mean that all women are collaborative. Both traits are within all of us, and the best leaders reach deep inside themselves to cultivate each of them to lead effectively.

The ideal leader is a full, robust person who blends the best of his or her male and female sides to create a new kind of "androgynous leadership," one that is more powerful—and more nimble—than either masculine or feminine leadership alone.

With androgynous leadership, the decisiveness and accountability of male leadership has been preserved, but blended in are such qualities as collaboration and open communication, traits that are traditionally viewed as feminine.

Learning how to put diverse leadership styles to work gives an organization a competitive edge.

Joan Claybrook's brother could have told you, back when she was growing up nearly fifty years ago, that his sister would end up running a large organization. What he didn't know was that the organization would turn out to be Public Citizen, a Washington, D.C.–based public-interest group with 100,000 members, devoted to improving

JOAN CLAYBROOK
Public Citizen

TITLE: President

AGE: 57

FAMILY SITUATION: Divorced

EDUCATION: B.A. in History, Goucher College; J.D., Georgetown Law Center

HISTORY: Research Analyst, Social Security Administration (1956–66); Special Assistant to Administrator, National Traffic Safety Bureau, U.S. Department of Transportation (1966–70); various public-interest groups, including Founder and Director, Public Citizens' Congress Watch (1970–77); Administrator, National Highway Traffic Safety Administration, U.S. Department of Transportation (1977–81); President, Public Citizen (1982–present)

HONORS AND SPECIAL ACCOMPLISHMENTS: Georgetown Law Center Board of Visitors; Board, Consumers Union, Citizens for Tax Justice, Trial Lawyers for Public Justice, Advocates for Highway and Auto Safety; Advisory Board, California Wellness Foundation; Co-Chair, Citizens for Reliable and Safe Highways

HEADQUARTERS: Washington, D.C.

BUSINESS: Consumer advocacy

NUMBER OF EMPLOYEES: 75

BUDGET: $9 million

government, law, health, and energy policy. But there was never any doubt in his mind that Joan would be in charge of something important.

"Even when I was small, he used to call me 'commander,' " Claybrook, one of the original "Nader's Raiders," recalls with a laugh.

And yet when you ask Claybrook, who has become an extremely effective social activist, what is the first thing she thinks of when you say the word "leadership," she responds: "Gandhi. Because he led without commanding, without demanding that people follow. He led by his personality. By inspiring others. By the ideas he had. By his vision of the future. By his suggestions of ways of changing policy. He led with the power of his purpose.

"I think in many ways Ralph Nader is like that," she adds. "The power of his ideas is so fascinating and commanding that people adopt them as their own. What my mother said about Ralph is absolutely true. She said, 'He says what I'm thinking. I just haven't articulated it yet.' "

It is interesting to think about what Claybrook, who has spent thirty years representing the needs of the general public before the Washington power structure, believes is necessary to accomplish change. She says three things are required.

The first is a powerful idea, one that is logical and inherently compelling. Unless there is a compelling vision, such as having air bags in every new car—a goal Public Citizen worked for and achieved—no one will support it.

Second, the idea must be benevolent and represent the needs of an extremely wide group. Targeting a specific tax cut to help a particular industry might generate more jobs, and allow public companies within that industry to pay a greater dividend to their shareholders, but it is not good public policy and it would never gain widespread support, because the benefit is too narrowly focused.

And third, the change agent must be active and shrewd. Gandhi, Nader, and English reformist John Wilkes (about whom Claybrook wrote her college thesis at Goucher) knew exactly where to apply pressure in order to get government to change. They understood the political process, and were committed to doing what needed to be done within that framework.

The interesting thing about Claybrook's three prerequisites for change is that one of them—benevolence—is what we would consider to be a female characteristic. One of them—acting on shrewdness—is usually considered to be male. And the third—the power of the idea—is common to both male and female leaders. In other words, to accomplish their goals, leaders must be able to blend their male and female sides.

Most organizations are shaped by male values. That is not surprising. Traditionally, men have held leadership posts in most organizations. Male leaders tend to get their philosophies from either the playing field or the battlefield and tend to see leadership in terms of transactions. They exchange rewards for services rendered, and punishment for services not rendered well. The dominant charac-

MALE LEADERS

Male leadership is being increasingly questioned, to the point where "male bashing" has become commonplace. But the fact that it is understandable does not make it right. While it is true that there are things wrong with male leadership it is also true that there are many things right with it.

Strengths	*Weaknesses*
• Sets strong boundaries.	• Isolates employees and departments
• Assigns clear responsibilities and accountabilities	• Deters collaboration and teamwork
• Responds rapidly	• Responds inflexibly
• Weeds out weak performers	• Discourages risk through competition
• Keeps sensitive information confidential	• Starves creativity and innovation through lack of information

teristic of a male culture is a firm, entrenched hierarchy. Power comes from position within the hierarchy. The male leader tends to see himself in a situation where he must constantly battle to preserve independence and avoid failure. Hierarchies tend to breed competition, as people (usually other men) continually ask themselves, "How do I measure up?" The focus in this kind of organization is on the goal and not the process. How a task is accomplished is not as important as whether it is accomplished.

In this kind of environment, information is power to be hoarded and disclosed only on a need-to-know basis. Communication usually flows in one direction—from the top down—and the leader tends to communicate to preserve independence, avoid emotion, and maintain the status quo.

On the other hand, female leadership seeks solutions in which

FEMALE LEADERS

Female leadership, which has recently been the subject of numerous books praising it as the leadership of choice in the new workplace, does, indeed, have many things to recommend. But despite its strengths, it has almost become politically incorrect to examine its weaknesses. That is just as wrong as dismissing male leadership out of hand.

Strengths	*Weaknesses*
• Enhances teamwork	• Blurs boundaries
• Fosters accountability through peer pressure	• Weakens accountability through lack of supervision
• Encourages innovation through collaboration	• Encourages complacency through lack of competition
• Improves quality through attention to process	• Responds slowly because process needs to be worked through
• Increases opportunities for continuous improvement because of open access to information	• Risks divulging confidential information

everyone wins, or at least no one loses. The focus is on encouraging participation, sharing power and information, and enhancing other people's self-worth.

Female leaders create a web culture, an organization in which the leader is not at the top of a pyramid, but in the center. This fosters collaboration rather than competition. The leader's authority comes from the connection to the people around her, rather than the distance she can keep from the people she is leading. In a web culture the focus is on the process, rather than the goal, and on creating joint commitments and open communication in all directions. The leader tries to create a sense of community, preserve intimacy, and avoid isolation.

Subconsciously, we expect people to fit into our gender preconceptions. Those very preconceptions can inhibit leaders from using all the techniques in their leadership tool box, as the strengths and weaknesses sides of the tables show. A man may rely on autocratic decision making, instead of a more participatory approach, because he fears looking like a "wimp." Similarly, a woman may seek consensus to avoid being thought of as a "bitch."

The trouble is that the business costs of gender-based inhibitions can be huge. Not using the most appropriate leadership techniques can delay a project, damage it, or even destroy it. The ideal leader is androgynous. By androgynous we don't mean some gray, washed-out sexless abstraction. We mean a full and robust human being who expresses the best of both genders and understands that leadership blends the best of both men's and women's cultures to create a healthy, high-performance organization. We mean someone like Joan Claybrook.

Not that Claybrook is always lauded for her efforts. Far from it; in a *Washington Post* profile, she was described as "an evil, small-minded woman" by Representative John Dingell (Democrat from Michigan), the powerful former chairman of the House Energy and Commerce Committee, who has regularly opposed Claybrook on auto issues. On the other hand, longtime consumer advocate Esther Peterson says, "Joan is extremely positive and straightforward, very effective, very tough, very direct. She'll go to the end for whatever she believes in."

The fact that Claybrook is described in these contrasting ways is not surprising. Public Citizen is an organization of tremendous energy and strong-willed entrepreneurial people, who grapple with incredibly difficult, politically charged, controversial issues, such as creating a better way of providing health care and completely overhauling the way we finance elections. It is the group responsible for winning a nearly complete ban on the use of silicone-gel breast implants and for striking down provisions of an energy bill that would have allowed the disposal of radioactive waste in landfills, sewers, and incinerators.

Claybrook's challenge is to figure out how to manage all the ideas, egos, and conflicts that she confronts every day—both inside and outside her organization—and focus all that energy on improving the world we live in. She must empower her people, and still build a cohesive team with a coordinated agenda. The very complexity of her task, she says, forces her to draw on the multiple parts of personality. She needs both her male and female sides in order to negotiate with others, build consensus, make tough decisions, confront people she disagrees with, and liberate members of her team so that they can do their best work.

"I like to operate by consensus, and I feel very strongly about that," Claybrook says. "I like things to happen as much as possible from the bottom up, rather than the top down. But sometimes that is just not possible, and I have to step in. Sometimes I'll have a private negotiation with the individual who is dragging a project down.

"I'll give you an example," she continues. "We had been working on the single-payer issue for health insurance, and there was legislation that had been introduced that wasn't perfect, but our Congress Watch lobbyist thought it was the best we would be able to achieve. She wanted to support it, and build it up in Congress. Our Health Research group leader didn't think we should go with an imperfect vehicle for something that was so important. We went round and round. Eventually, I brought in an outside intermediary, and I did everything else I could think of to get our health-group leader to come around and eventually he did."

It was an example of Claybrook's male and female sides coming together to get a task done.

"My job requires a great deal of diversity," she says. "There are times when I have to be a researcher and a student, and there are others when I have to be a soft shoulder for people to lean on. And there are still other times when I have to battle and fight— sometimes internally—to create something new." The challenge, she says, is to balance all the different parts of her personality to accomplish the task at hand.

A case in point is how she helped pass a National Highway Traffic Safety Administration law that mandated air bags for cars, along with a whole host of other safety features. Claybrook's initial efforts to get the bill passed were defeated by Dingell in 1986, so in her typically dogged style she came back eighteen months later, this time with backing from the insurance industry. Still, the bill failed to pass in the House. Undeterred, she began lining up additional support in the Department of Transportation and began searching for the right moment to try again.

"Finally, in 1991 there was a big transportation bill—a $150 billion spending program—being introduced and we decided to make our bill part of that one. This time we started by educating the senators, because we had problems in the House. Well, we got it through the Senate, but we needed a member of the House Energy and Commerce Committee who would stand up to Dingell, so we could get the bill passed in the House. We finally found someone who agreed to be our leader, and we started lobbying to get hearings before a subcommittee. The problem was the subcommittee chair was very close to Dingell. He wouldn't agree to hold hearings. So we did some work out in Washington State where he's from, talking to his constituents and pointing out why the bill was needed, and how it would save eleven thousand lives a year, and asked him as nicely as we could to hold the hearings. Finally, he agreed. We embarrassed him into it."

Eventually, this combination of persistence, strategic ingenuity, and personal touch got the bill into conference with the House, where it eventually passed. It was a combination of consensus and confrontation all wrapped into one that got the job done.

Cultivate Androgyny Within Yourself and Your Organization

We all have within us a male competitive capacity and a female collaborative capability, and one trait tends to dominate the other. To lead most effectively, you must develop your other side. Are you most comfortable acting within consensus? Good, but the pressure of emergency situations will, at some point, inevitably require you to lead by command. Or are you one who feels that opening up the decision-making process to others threatens your authority? Maximizing quality and employee motivation, especially over the long haul, will require involving others in the process of making decisions.

Leaders must recognize that the two styles need not weaken each other, but actually can improve and invigorate each other. Balanced appropriately, male and female leadership can yield a whole that is greater than the sum of its parts. One situation will call for a set of tools from the masculine section of the tool belt, whereas the next may require female tactics.

In addition to making sure that you become comfortable with both your male and female sides, you must ensure that your organization is open to both male and female leadership styles. Ultimately, no single leader can excel equally in all tasks. Leaders, therefore, must create organizations in which different people can apply different management strengths and styles to different circumstances. They must also make sure that their organizations respect and reward different leadership styles, whether or not they exhibit those qualities. This is something that Claybrook is working on.

"I realize that, as a person in the workplace for the last thirty years, I have been influenced by, and have adjusted to, the male system of doing business," Claybrook says. "While this is not wrong per se, it is worthy of reflection. We are going to need greater flexibility and adaptability in business, as well as government and nonprofit organizations, as we undergo many fundamental changes forced upon us by societal needs, marketplace adjustments, and limited resources, in the hurly-burly 1990s. Even without the male/female context, students of organizational management and business success are talking about relationships with customers and with workers."

After three decades in Washington, Claybrook has learned a lot, primarily about what it takes to accomplish change. Specifically she says you must:

- Accept that you are going to be criticized.
- Depersonalize your battles, even if the attacks on you are personal.
- Learn to absorb anger. Don't blame others or hold grudges. Build scar tissue.
- Look forward but learn from experience.
- Celebrate your successes, and be honest about your failures.
- Secure incremental changes and keep your eye on the long-range goal.

To achieve all this demands cultivating both the female and male sides of leadership. Blending the strengths of men and of women creates a work dynamic that is both more powerful and quicker to respond than either of the separate styles. In our increasingly turbulent, complex, and unpredictable marketplace, the business costs of gender-based inhibitions can be large. Androgyny offers a competitive advantage.

The goal of today's leader, working in an era when management teams are increasingly made up of both men and women, should be to maximize the power of both, to refine it and distill it into its most potent essence. What is hard is finding the right balance, especially at a time when business is complex, and what is right in some circumstances is not always right in others.

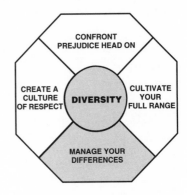

MANAGING YOUR DIFFERENCES

The best leaders have a deep appreciation for people's differences. They get excited when employees bring their unique lives and perspectives to work. The business challenge is to figure out how to manage and leverage those differences.

To do that, leaders must have a broad perspective on diversity. Their definition needs to go well beyond age, gender, and ethnicity to include differences in lifestyle, religious beliefs, working habits, and personality.

The best leaders are tolerant and less threatened by this individuality. They know that people are simply less willing to abandon their identities to the organization these days. As a result, allowing people to retain their ethnic and cultural heritage becomes a high priority for them. The best leaders learn to take the perspective of their employees, walk in their shoes, and give voice to all this diversity.

Different people require different kinds of leadership. Tailoring your style to their diversity is a prerequisite for success in today's world. Yet the best leaders know their success ultimately depends on blending all this diversity into a common vision. And sometimes that means standing up for what they know is right, even when it means going against their diverse team.

Neither palm trees nor the revitalized Miami Beach are the first things that spring to mind these days when you say Miami. Odds are many people think of the aftermath of Hurricane Andrew. And the images are dramatic: crumbled houses, palm trees with their roots exposed, sprawled across four-lane highways; overturned cars every-

CAESAR ODIO
City of Miami

TITLE: City Manager

AGE: 58

FAMILY SITUATION: Married; 5 children

EDUCATION: Degree in Business Administration, University of Santo Tomas de Villanueva in Havana, Cuba; B.S. in Public Administration, Florida Memorial College

HISTORY: Several management positions, including Vice President of trucking operations, for Maule Industries, Maule subsidiaries, and Lone Star of Florida, Maule's successor corporation (1970–79); Assistant City Manager of Miami (1980–85); became City Manager in 1985

HONORS AND SPECIAL ACCOMPLISHMENTS: Chosen as 1993 recipient of Most Valuable Public Official award by *City and State Magazine*; Theodore R. Gibson Unity Award; Hispanic Coalition and Mexican-American Council Award of Excellence for Community Service; Member, Governor's Commission on the Homeless; Board Member, United Way of America

HOBBIES: Active member of Miami Rowing Club

BUSINESS: City government

NUMBER OF EMPLOYEES: 3,500

BUDGET: $500 million

where; and in the parking lots of marinas, boats stacked on top of one another like pancakes.

What people don't know is how effective the city was in managing that catastrophe. And the city's success was in large measure due to the man behind the city—Caesar Odio, Miami city manager.

Miami is one of the most ethnically diverse cities in America—63 percent of its residents are Hispanic, 25 percent are black, and 12 percent white—so it is only natural that a Cuban immigrant would be its city manager. Odio, who serves as city manager for the city's $500 million budget, received his undergraduate degree from the University of Santo Tomás de Villanueva in Havana. His background certainly helps provide him with a deep sensitivity to diversity issues, not only within the Hispanic community but within the African-American sections of the city as well. Even though he is quick to say, "I am just a public administrator doing his job," when asked about the role his cultural background plays at the office, the fact is it helps.

Each person has his own unique perspective, set of principles, strengths and weaknesses, and interpersonal style. The best leaders come to understand deeply what makes them unique, as well as what makes them similar to those they are leading. Odio is sensitive to his own uniqueness.

"The people who ran the military boarding school I attended instilled in me the exact opposite of what they intended," Odio says, when you ask him what has made him so effective. "Some guy my age would come into my room and say, 'Shine my shoes.' And I would have to do it. And they gave us those haircuts. I asked them why they were shaving my head, and they said they were doing it to depersonalize me.

"But it had the opposite effect. It made me realize that people are different, and everyone has different needs. You have to find the best way of addressing their individual needs, if you are going to be effective as a leader."

Some thirty years later, when he was named city manager of Miami, Odio would have the chance to put these insights to work in a very public forum. He has had one of the longest tenures of any city manager in the country. In that position, Odio, formerly a trucking executive in southern Florida, has combined conservative fiscal management and positive human relations in the face of declining revenues. His success has been stunning. The city does more work today with fewer people than it did when he took over in 1985, and its formerly tumultuous relations with its unions have been transformed for the better.

Most leaders must grapple with diversity issues in their organizations, and Odio is no different. The 3,500 employees who comprise Miami's city government are just a microcosm of the city, which has its share of rich neighborhoods and ones that are poor. Odio would apply his idea about diversity not only to the municipal government but to the Miami community as well.

Instead of treating the city as a monolith, as his predecessors had done, Odio decided to work with the individual neighborhoods that make up Miami, and address their specific needs. Within an overarching vision for the city, Odio decided to manage each of Miami's different communities differently.

Why? Why not treat everyone exactly the same, and rely on the melting pot to meld the city together?

The answer is the concept of the melting pot works more as a metaphor than as a reality in today's workplace.

We all bring different values and different emotional makeup to work. This is not surprising, given that we are quite different in age, race, gender, ethnicity, physical abilities, sexual orientation, educational background, income, marital status, and the like. And the things that motivate us are different as well. While some people are driven to achieve and master the world, others are defensive and risk-averse. For some, the need is to gain respect, while others value building friendships above all else. Taking the same approach with everyone won't be as effective as tailoring your leadership style to suit an individual's needs.

But why can't we expect everyone just to blend in? If the melting pot approach to management was good enough for our grandparents, why isn't it good enough for us? The answer is simple. Times have changed. The melting-pot theory requires people to voluntarily abandon most of their distinctiveness at the door. Today, Asians, African Americans, and Hispanics are far less willing to be "melted down" than the Europeans who came before them.

No one likes to be typecast. People of all diverse backgrounds want the freedom and support to be themselves. Younger and older workers want more respect for their life experiences. Women want to be recognized as equal partners. Men want the same freedom to explore the range of their personalities as women do, and they too want time with their families. People of color want to be valued not only as equal contributors but as unique and different. Gay men and lesbians want to be recognized for who they are, and to have equal protection. And white men also won't tolerate being disadvantaged.

Odio understands this new reality. He knows employees want to maintain their unique ethnic and cultural heritages, sometimes even thinking their diversity is more important than other people's. He, as all other leaders must, understands that people outside the mainstream culture face special challenges. They often encounter isolation, prejudice from peers or subordinates, and resentment from coworkers, who feel threatened or skeptical about their performance. Also, they often feel they are "forced" to act at work in a way that is at odds with the way they truly are.

The key for the leader is to recognize these unique circumstances, be understanding of individuals' special pain, and realize that when it comes to leadership, one size does not fit all. Indeed, that is why Odio created Neighborhood Enhancement Teams.

"There was a perception in the community that we were not doing enough crime control, and there was a perception in the police department that the administration was tying their hands," Odio recalls. "I had a two-day staff meeting with the police department, and it was a tough, tough session, because we criticized each other and we all expressed our frustrations. At the end of it I said, 'If what we are doing isn't working, why don't we change it? Why don't we go to community police work, where people can see the same officers every day?' From there, I decided to add someone from my office who would work in the neighborhoods so that we could help address *all* the concerns of the community, not just crime. That is how NET was born."

Instead of running Miami from an isolated department within City Hall, Odio created eleven separate branches of his department, located in eleven very different neighborhoods within the city. Each Neighborhood Enhancement Office is staffed with an administrator and a Neighborhood Resource Officer (NRO), from the local police department. Through NET, Odio would share not only his responsibility but also his vision at the neighborhood level, and break down the walls of mistrust that existed between the community and the city administration. "Each NET is a mini city hall," Odio explains. "Each administrator is in fact a city manager. He or she [five of the eleven administrators are women] is the person who represents me in the community, and helps represent the community—and its needs—to City Hall."

And those needs vary widely. In affluent Coconut Grove, which once put a secession referendum on the ballot because its residents felt they were not being adequately represented, abandoned cars and crowing roosters are not primary concerns, as they are elsewhere in the city. Rather, residents want zoning laws enforced to decrease density, and want to make sure that the streets are kept clean. In Overtown, scene of the city's most recent race riot, the focus is on crime, the lack of jobs, and better relations with the police department.

Because Odio has a deep understanding of himself, he is able to be more open to the diverse views and opinions of these communities. But he, like the best leaders, also has personal blind spots. He needed all the help he could get when it came to dealing with the city's unions. Odio recalls that "we used to have head-on confrontations. For example, the fire union would come in and say they want five more firefighters next year, and if they don't get them, they will have five hundred firefighters at the next city commission meeting saying, 'If you want our support in the next election, you'll give us what we want.'

"And I would say, 'I am not going to give you five more firefighters, we can't afford it,' and then there would be a big blow-up before the commission. This happened every year."

In time, Odio began to understand that the unions represented another piece of Miami's diverse makeup. And just as he did with the neighborhoods, he began looking for approaches he could take to address their needs, and have the city benefit as well.

"Finally, I went to the fire union and all the other unions and said, 'Why don't we work as partners? The city is going to go broke if things continue this way.' Out of those conversations came the decision to create a group we now call the Summit, made up of union representatives and members of my office.

"Initially, there was tremendous mistrust, and even hatred. At the first meeting, I got up to walk out. I told them I wanted to do what was best for the city, in partnership with them, and I just wasn't going to listen to all the things that were spewing out of the union representatives' mouths. I was not looking for them to support me, I was looking to have a partnership with them so we could have a better city, so that we could survive during a time that is very stressful to cities. We just don't have enough money.

"Before I got out the door they called me back, and from that moment on things changed. We've opened up all our books to the unions, and they are now working with us."

Today, the Caesar Odio that we see has a deeper understanding of the unions. He understands now that they did not like his confrontational approach. And he understands why they didn't trust the city: the municipal books were closed. Odio has realized what is important to the union leadership—the protection of their members' jobs. (In exchange for the unions' help, Odio promised to cut the city's top-heavy management structure, as the first step in any cost-cutting program.) Odio's ability to take the unions' perspective, and to feel their pain, was a unique asset that added rich new perspectives within the Miami community. It helped forge partnerships, at all levels.

"I was sitting at home one day, and I see a TV report that says there aren't enough police officers on the street, because our motor pool isn't fixing police cars fast enough," Odio recalls. "I'll never forget the picture they showed: six police officers standing about, because they didn't have cars to go out in. Boy, that bothered me."

So much so that Odio went down to the motor pool and changed things on the spot. "I knew our supervisors were not people oriented, they were taskmasters. So, I went to the mechanics and said, 'If I give you the place to run, will you show the world you can do it better?' They voted 100 percent in favor, and I removed all the middle management and told the mechanics to elect their own supervisors, which they did. The result is we have no police cars waiting to be fixed."

These innovative kinds of leadership were the reason *City and State* magazine recently named Odio "most valuable public official." In the spirit of partnership, Odio asked the heads of the city's four major unions to accompany him to Washington when he received the reward.

FLEXIBLE LEADERSHIP

Different events require different leadership responses. "You have to adapt yourself to the circumstances," Odio says. At times, as when he is working with the unions, Odio is collaborative. In dealing with the local communities he is empowering.

"And in an emergency," he says, "there can be only one boss."

Hurricane Andrew was just such an emergency. How Odio took the different members of his community and channeled their efforts to overcome the effects of Hurricane Andrew is a great example of diversity coming together for a common purpose. On Saturday morning Odio got the unofficial word that the hurricane would be a bad one. "I had heard about the storm developing, and I went over to the Hurricane Center and they showed me projections that the storm would hit Miami hard," Odio recalls. "I left there, and from my car I called the fire chief and told him to get the Emergency Center ready. I then called the head of the waste department and told him to get the city cleaned today. He told me that I was going to get fired for authorizing $500,000 in overtime, but I said I didn't care. I didn't want anything flying around that could damage buildings.

"From there I called the police, and we went to our Alpha Bravo configuration, which meant every shift would have to go on overtime. No one was to go home.

"By Sunday morning, we were ready. We scattered our public-works equipment throughout the city, because we knew once the storm hit the streets would be blocked. We activated the National Guard and positioned them downtown. Their orders were 'No looting,' and there wasn't any. We arrested people as soon as they broke the glass."

But even more impressive was the response of the NET teams. "The storm hit Sunday night, and by Monday morning all the NET offices were telling us what streets were flooded and where potential crises were. For example, in Coconut Grove, boats had been blown on top of one another and were leaking gas.

"The NET teams went out to their neighborhoods Tuesday, and they reported in with horrible news," Odio continues. "People didn't have any food. See, many people could go to the market before the storm hit, and stock up. But the poor person, who doesn't earn much, couldn't. They didn't have the money. So by the second day they were hungry. But by the third, they weren't. We had gotten them food, ice, and water.

"We had firefighters out with six tankers that normally hold milk, and they were dispensing water to the parts of the city that needed it most," Odio recalls. "We handled the distribution of food the same way." Through it all, Odio was in his Jeep, driving from neighborhood to neighborhood, overseeing the process.

Odio had been assistant city manager during the Mariel boat lift in 1980, when 125,000 Cubans arrived in Miami in a little over two months. "What I have learned in managing a crisis is that the manager has to be there," he says. "You cannot just sit back and say 'I wrote a procedural manual to cover this.' You are asking your people to pay a price—risking their lives during a hurricane in this case—and you have to be there with them."

And you have to do what you know is right. "In the midst of the hurricane, I told the commissioners [who run the city], 'Hands off,' " Odio recalls. "They could fire me afterward. We felt we were doing the right thing. And it worked. We had accountants directing traffic, personnel people manning the food trucks. We brought everyone in, and they did a great job."

That is exactly what Odio told them, in a letter he sent to every city employee.

> In the wake of the destruction left by Hurricane Andrew, we were asked to forgo our human instincts of self-preservation, and protecting our loved ones, in order to care for our community as a whole. This is the responsibility we share as public servants.
>
> Never have I been prouder of you as City of Miami employees than in the days following the storm. Those who worked to patrol the streets, help repair people's homes and volunteered where they could . . . made a difference and Miami is appreciative of your efforts.

As Hurricane Andrew showed, valuing differences must be coupled with a clear purpose shared by others to help coordinate and direct the actions of employees. Without a unifying force, diversity can become unruly and divisive. But when we allow people to fully express themselves around a common purpose, amazing things can happen. All that individuality gets used for the good of the organization.

"I have a vision of the Miami I want to be a part of," Odio says with pride. And we see that vision become a reality over and over again as the diversity of Miami comes together.

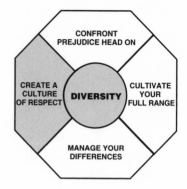

CREATING A CULTURE
OF RESPECT

How do you get diverse people to move in the same direction? By creating a culture of respect.

The word "respect" is derived from the Latin **respicere,** *which means to see, and creating a culture of respect starts with a special kind of vision from within the leader. He begins by looking at his own passions and self-esteem, in order to discover what makes him feel inspired and respected. When the leader feels good about himself, he becomes a more fulfilled person.*

These insights become the leader's building blocks for creating a culture of respect. They help him understand his organization at a deeper level and they offer a special look into the motivations of others.

The leader extends these insights into the surrounding community and creates business practices based on the principle of respect.

Leaders who act this way understand that we are all created equal, and that people who feel equal, and respected, are likely to perform to the best of their ability.

You could have the same building right across the street, with the same ovens and equipment, the same recipes and same ingredients, and I'll guarantee that your chocolate cake would taste different. The caring and love our employees put into the product is a reflection of the caring and love they feel from Just Desserts.

—ELLIOT HOFFMAN, PRESIDENT, JUST DESSERTS BAKERY

ELLIOT HOFFMAN
Just Desserts

TITLE: Cofounder and President

AGE: 47

FAMILY SITUATION: Married; 2 children

EDUCATION: B.S., New York University

HISTORY: Briefly worked in the banking industry and then ran a jewelry factory before founding his company 20 years ago

HONORS AND SPECIAL ACCOMPLISHMENTS: Numerous awards for best desserts and best bakery in San Francisco; one of 10 best bosses in California, *California Magazine*, 1988

HEADQUARTERS: San Francisco, CA

BUSINESS: Wholesale and retail bakery

NUMBER OF EMPLOYEES: 320

GROSS REVENUE: Over $14 million

FACTS: Uses 30,000 pounds of butter in a month. Advertising budget is less than 1% of sales.

Not surprisingly, the man who made that statement is a special kind of person with a special kind of philosophy about life and business. You see that in the way he interacts with people, constantly looking them in the eye, giving them hugs, and calling them by their first names. And you see it in his three business goals, which are lofty, yet straightforward. Hoffman wants Just Desserts to be recognized as one of the world's finest bakeries; he wants people to consider it a model, "albeit imperfect," workplace; and he wants the company to reach and maintain a healthy level of profits.

How Hoffman goes about achieving these goals is unusual. He does it by taking diversity one step beyond where even the best companies go. To be really effective—both in having a harmonious workforce, and in producing the best chocolate cakes—you have to surround your culture of diversity with respect. Hoffman does. Not only do immigrants of all nationalities work at his $14 million company, so do gay couples and former felons. Everyone's background and beliefs are accepted, and valued, and people are encouraged to be themselves. Employees are evaluated on two things and two things only: how well they do their jobs, and how they get along with their fellow employees.

But Hoffman's commitment doesn't stop there. He goes beyond the walls of his company, and he respects the community around his stores. He has spent the last twenty years working to make San Francisco a better place, serving on committees that are trying to improve everything from the way the city's rent-control policy is administered to how the state prison system is run. As a result, Hoffman and Just Desserts are well known. It seems a Democrat can't run for higher office anywhere in the country without making a stop at Just Desserts.

"I'm a real believer in the potential of the human species," Hoffman says. "Men, women, black, white, gay, straight, it doesn't matter. And the people who work here feel the same way. It's very inspirational to come here."

Elliot Hoffman is the reason it is. He is a person who is absolutely thrilled with his life: "I feel like a very successful human being," he says. "Gail, my wife and business partner, and I feel we are among the most fortunate people on this earth. We have each other. We have two healthy and terrific young children. Great friends. Our own home in San Francisco. We have a successful, growing, and highly regarded bakery business in one of the world's great cities renowned for great food. We employ a lot of good people from very diverse cultures and lifestyles. I am one of the most fortunate people on this earth. I have absolutely nothing to bitch about."

What do these feelings have to do with running a 31,000-square-foot bakery that operates twenty-four hours a day, seven days a week, to produce 260 items from scratch for Just Desserts' seven retail stores and countless wholesale customers?

Quite a lot, says Hoffman. "If you're not doing what you enjoy, you're not going to be fulfilled. And if you are not fulfilled, then you are going to project that onto your business and be a drag on your company."

Remember, leaders can shed light or impose darkness on their organizations. Because he is secure with who he is, Hoffman feels free to ask potentially troubling questions such as, "What's really important in life? Why are we here? What should I be doing with my life?"

Hoffman's answer is not surprising coming from someone who is a product of a Jewish working-class home (Hoffman's father was a milkman in the Bronx) who stressed family, friends, and community above money. Hoffman worked his way through New York University in Greenwich Village and came of age during the 1960s. Since he grew up "on the other side of the tracks," he is sympathetic to the plight of others, and is committed to doing something about it. "I'm here to make the world a little better place for us, for all people, my children and yours." His passions concern people, principles, and community responsibility. Ironically, this passion initially made it difficult for him to accomplish his goals.

In typical entrepreneurial fashion, Just Desserts started by accident. For his wife's twenty-fourth birthday, Hoffman made her a cheesecake that was such a hit that one of his friends asked Hoffman to supply his café with them. But when Hoffman first started business out of the kitchen of his San Francisco apartment, "profit was a four-letter word. And that was one of the things that really slowed down the growth of the business. It probably took me five or six years of running my business before I really understood that it was how you make a profit and what you do with it that really count."

Hoffman decided to make that profit harnessing the differences within his organization. He was convinced that if he could gather the diverse energy, and direct it toward achieving his business goals, success would be inevitable. Given that he lives in a city known for its diversity, it is not surprising that diversity is an important part of Hoffman's business strategy.

"I'd say that seven or eight years ago we began to realize that we were going to have to deal with the issue of diversity," he recalls. "We saw our own workforce in San Francisco becoming more diverse. It wasn't just white males and white women, there were more Hispanics joining us, there were more gays and lesbians, and we realized we would have to build a culture of diversity."

That takes time. It's an ongoing process, and the leader must be patient, because people don't easily change their attitudes and stereotypes. To spur the change process, Hoffman began by applying to Just Desserts the same principles of respect that he had developed for himself and his family. He listened carefully to the concerns and aspirations of each person.

Hoffman believes that "leaders need to genuinely respect people for who they are. As the faces, colors, cultures, and lifestyles of America grow and change, the issue of diversity will confront every leader."

Hoffman confronts the issue head on and does it in the simplest manner possible. He puts diverse people side by side in the workplace every day and lets them be themselves. "From the beginning, we were very clear that we didn't care where you were from; what color, race, or age you were; whether you were gay, lesbian, straight, man, or woman; all opportunities were open to you as long as you did your job effectively, and you got along with your fellow staff members.

"As we've grown, so has our diversity," Hoffman adds. "When people come to visit, many comment on the people they see working as they walk through the bakery. On our main baking crew, there's Phouc from Vietnam, who has been with us for twelve years; Tika, from Indonesia ten years; Mike, the white guy from New Jersey, fifteen years; Miguel and Javier from Mexico; the list of cultures and styles goes on and on. It's certainly not Utopia, and we have our disagreements like everyone else, but it is never over race, culture, or lifestyle. We have learned to live and work with each other, and I'm very proud of the level of human respect at Just Desserts."

"We must thoroughly trash the artificial barriers to opportunities in our business. The best *people* and not the best men, women, whites, or blacks deserve the opportunities. Our diversity really can be our strength. As leaders, we ought to embrace it and promote it at all levels."

Hoffman ensures that happens in a number of ways. The starting point is the institutional environment, which is built on the values of fairness, mutual respect, understanding, and cooperation. At the busiest times of the year, everyone pitches in to get the job done. Hoffman will help glaze cakes, and his wife will join the people who package them. The feeling is constant: "We are all in this together."

And the "we" doesn't depend on who you are. "We had this huge order a couple of years ago," Hoffman recalls. "It took about twenty people to package it, over a weekend. I had ex-prisoners, gays, lesbians, blacks, white men, women, welfare mothers, my thirteen-year-old and his friends. We were a human packing machine. And I stood back and said to myself, 'This is incredible. Look at the human diversity we have here, with everyone coming together to get the job done.' "

Shared goals guide the efforts of every employee. The company's 320 employees know and agree with Hoffman's diversity objectives and agreed upon operating norms—"we will treat each other with respect"—and common vision—"diversity is the source of our strength."

Hoffman has a deep understanding of the corporate culture at Just Desserts. He can read the mood of the bakery better than anyone else, and is the first to know when someone is upset or angry. Hoffman is also quick to confront any institutional bias, such as sexist language in company publications or promotions that benefit one group over another. He knows the effect this has on people's performance.

Hoffman started by bringing diversity to the top of the company and then moved it down through every aspect of the business. There are policies that prohibit discrimination, programs in diversity awareness, and celebrations for people of all races and nationalities.

RESPECTING THE COMMUNITY

Hoffman extends his deep respect for people to the community at large.

"You can do well by doing good, and I say bullshit to the person who says that if you're still an idealist at thirty you have no brains," Hoffman adds. "Well, I'm forty-eight now and the day I stop being an idealist, please put me out of my misery. As working people, we and our employees spend half of our waking lives at work. Why can't it be fulfilling and have meaning?"

Hoffman extends this kind of approach to how he thinks about money and to the role he thinks businesses should apply in the community.

"If business is to be the dominant social institution in the future, we have to mix social goals with business goals," Hoffman says. "When we evaluate a company's 'bottom line,' we should include whether they've hired more people, and improved their products, their workplace and their community, in addition to turning a profit. I'm certainly not advocating that we disregard individualism—we as a society are just totally out of balance between individual and community interests and needs. If we don't change our ways and come home to important life values, human values, I'm afraid that the fabric of society will be shredded.

"I really believe that business has to play a larger role in changing society," Hoffman adds. "Business knows how to get things done, how to think outside the box, and we need to bring that creativity to society."

Hoffman does his best to ensure that happens. When someone buys one of his Rain Forest Crunches (a vanilla layer cake with toffee made from Brazil nuts), Just Desserts donates $1 to the Rain Forest Action network. Closer to home, Hoffman has teamed up with the San Francisco County Jail to turn what was once a garbage-strewn vacant lot adjoining his bakery into an elaborate organic garden tended by parolees among others. The half-acre plot is home to the Garden Project, which is designed to help former inmates make the transition back to society. The project aims to "empower its students to heal their environment, their communities, and ultimately themselves." Just Desserts, along with area restaurants, buys the produce, and the eighty or so gardeners share in the proceeds. Hoffman has hired six of the "farmers" to work full time at Just Desserts. Hoffman balances humane, compassionate leadership with business savvy. It's how he tries to accomplish his goal of becoming a model workplace.

Like all the other leaders in this book, Hoffman's philosophies about leadership start inside himself. Hoffman has a deep respect for himself and his family. It's so deep in fact that in 1994 he did the unthinkable for most entrepreneurs. He left his business for a year, and took a sabbatical.

"We all say our families are absolutely primary in our lives, and then we spend most of our lives at work," he says. "I decided that if I was really successful, by my personal definition of success, then I could arrange my life and my business so that I could take a tiny portion of my life—one year—to devote to my wife and two kids and myself."

That, of course, takes us full circle. Hoffman has a deep respect for himself and his family, which extends to the community, which comes back to him in the form of satisfied customers, who are willing to pay a little bit more for his products because of what Hoffman and Just Desserts represent. That allows Hoffman to respect himself, by taking time off, and the process begins again.

Hoffman passionately believes that you "can provide your customers with great products and services, offer your employees a good workplace, and you—and your company—can make a positive contribution to the community, and make money."

The secret is to tap into the talents of your diverse employees and have them work up to their fullest potential.

"I don't even have to talk about diversity anymore," Hoffman says. "It is just wonderful. It really feels great. It used to feel a little scary, like 'Gee, how do you get this group going? How do you get so many different cultures and lifestyles moving in the same direction?' We're doing it and it's mainly through respect.

"The leaders of tomorrow's businesses need qualities like passion and compassion. We need to inspire, not merely mandate. We need to gather and focus energy, not merely command and control. We need to genuinely respect our people for who they are."

Elliot Hoffman is doing just that. As a socially responsible entrepreneur, he's an idealist with strong roots firmly planted in reality. He has a unique ability to connect others, and he balances his humane compassionate leadership with business savvy. Hoffman is honest about himself and what he wants out of life. He admits his strengths are painting visions, touching people, and caring about his community. By his own admission, his weaknesses are in operations and the specifics of the business.

The payoff falls directly to the bottom line. The company is named "best bakery" in San Francisco by every area publication year in and year out. And the business continues to thrive.

For some, the story of Elliot Hoffman may sound a bit unreal and Pollyannaish. How could anyone be so warm, so content with life, and so compassionate to others? But if you think it through, the question is probably best asked in reverse. How come so many of us are unfriendly, unhappy, and unforgiving? Maybe Hoffman can teach us something about successful living.

CREATIVITY

We are all creative. No, not everyone is going to write a sonnet, paint a picture, or win the Nobel Prize. But we are all capable of original thinking. The most creative leaders are truly imaginative, probing and curious, and willing to take calculated risks. That means that they are willing to travel into the unknown, confronting self-doubt when they have to. And when they make mistakes, or suffer defeat, they are the first to share their lessons, and to bounce back.

The creative leader pictures possibilities and sees opportunities that others don't see. He entertains offbeat ideas, and reconfigures problems to find new solutions. He pushes himself to break with tradition and always asks: What new products can we develop? And how can we add more value to our customers?

This positive, forward-looking approach extends to his people. The leader has faith in the capacity of others, and believes that his organization can solve its own problems and create new business by unleashing the creativity of the workplace. To him, this makes good business sense because he sees people as knowledge assets inside the organization. Their minds are as filled with potential as his, and worth many times their book value, if they are used to their fullest.

To ensure that that happens, the creative leader creates the right conditions for people to express their creativity. This is best done by interacting with them. The leader asks penetrating questions, encourages people to remake themselves and their ideas, and supports "out of the box" thinking. He encourages dialogue and dissent—indeed he fosters creative conflict and multiple viewpoints—and encourages risk taking and experimentation.

For this to work, the creative leader must also be willing to encourage another kind of risk—an internal risk inside himself. He must allow ideas to come to the surface, let people push up against him, and allow them to share the limelight. This leads to an environment that nurtures and rewards creativity. The leader must attack all the systems that undermine creativity: abusive bosses, fear, intimidation, and bureaucracy. He knows that people need a flexible and safe culture in order to do their best work, a place where they are not smothered by politics, outdated policies, and competitive one-upmanship.

These leaders begin by developing their own inventive minds and focusing on their own innovative talents. Once they nurture their own creativity, it is easier to unleash the creativity in others. As Todd Mansfield of the Walt Disney Company has learned, the secret is to discover what people do well, and then ask them to do more of it. But people won't tap their creative gifts unless they feel they are working in a trusting, challenging environment. If people feel threatened, insecure, or uninspired, they cannot—or will not—do their best work. This is something that Robert Koski, the head of Sun Hydraulics understands.

Sidney Harman at Harman International Industries teaches us how to combine the power of machines with the power of people. This combination can create a sustainable competitive advantage, but only if technology enriches jobs and liberates people's minds.

Dr. Mitchell Rabkin of Beth Israel Hospital knows how to keep that advantage going by concentrating on the human side of his high-tech work environment. By making the most of the relationships with patients and coworkers, he rewards the soft innovations inside the hospital.

These four competencies together can help mobilize the creativity of any workforce.

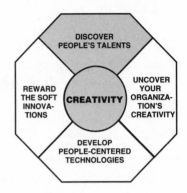

DISCOVERING
PEOPLE'S TALENTS

People are born with natural gifts. Unfortunately, many of us take these gifts for granted. We fail to make full use of our talents and instead spend much of our time trying to improve our weaknesses.

But research shows that maximum productivity comes from getting people to focus on their strengths and having them manage around their weaknesses.

Successful leaders focus first on their own natural strengths and discover their creative potential, making it easier for them to unleash the creativity of others.

Such leaders hire people who are flexible and inquisitive. They help employees discover their talents, and they link those talents to the task at hand. Then the best leaders create the right environment for people to experiment, take risks, and fulfill their creative potential.

The secret is to discover what people do well—and ask them to do more.

It was not the most promising match. There was the Walt Disney Company, known the world over for its creativity, hiring Todd Mansfield to be head of commercial development for the Disney Development Company, which is responsible for developing the company's resort lodging and real estate. There was nothing wrong with Mansfield. Far from it. A graduate of prestigious Claremont McKenna College and Harvard Business School, Mansfield began his working life as a management consultant and moved into real-estate development. He had always been successful.

TODD MANSFIELD
Disney Development Company

TITLE: Executive Vice President, Disney Development Company

AGE: 37

FAMILY SITUATION: Married; 3 children

EDUCATION: B.A., Claremont McKenna College; M.B.A. Harvard Business School

HISTORY: Director of Community Development, Disney Development (1986); project management, Hines Interests (1982–86); Management Consultant, Booz, Allen and Hamilton, Inc. (1979–81)

HOBBIES: Reading, rollerblading, skiing, and camping with his family

HONORS AND SPECIAL ACCOMPLISHMENTS: Chairman, Enterprise Community Development District; Member, Florida Greenways Commission; Vice Chairman Kissimmee Osceola Chamber of Commerce

OFFICES: Orlando, Florida

BUSINESS: Designs, develops, and operates real estate and new business opportunities compatible with Disney's entertainment mission

NUMBER OF EMPLOYEES: 325

GROSS REVENUE OF THE WALT DISNEY COMPANY: $10.1 billion (1994)

FACTS: Disney has developed over 14,000 hotel rooms, over 2 million square feet of office space, 3 championship golf courses, and over 75 shops and commercial facilities.

The problem was Mansfield was a linear thinker in a company where the thought process is anything but. And that is true in every part of Disney, even real estate.

Disney executives don't view their resorts as just places for people to stay. Rather, they see them as part of the entire "Disney experience." That's why the shrubbery is trimmed to resemble Disney characters such as Dumbo, the soap in the hotels looks like Mickey Mouse, and each of the resorts has its own theme, whether it's the Dixie Landing, Wilderness Lodge, or the Yacht and Beach Club.

In this kind of environment the challenge for Mansfield was

to find a way for his creativity to come to the fore. There were many who came before him, from Walt Disney himself to Michael Eisner, producing such American attractions as Disney Land, Epcot Center, and Touchstone Pictures. While Mansfield is operating on a smaller scale, as executive vice president of Disney's Development Division, one of his jobs is creating a new town from scratch.

He and his team are building an entirely new community—to be called Celebration—not far from Disney World in Orlando. While the description of the future home of twenty thousand people makes it sound like a Norman Rockwell painting come to life ("There once was a place where neighbors greeted neighbors in the quiet of summer twilight, when children chased fireflies, the grocery store delivered and there was one teacher who knew you had something special. . . . The people at Disney are creating a place that celebrates this legacy"). The reality will be far different. Celebration will be thoroughly up to date. Everything—from the school system and library to the health center and office buildings in town—will be state of the art, or beyond. All information will be on computer, and the residents will be linked to the schools and the hospital by fiber-optic cables.

The creativity involved is staggering. Simply thinking of creating a new community would seem to be beyond most of us. But, as Mansfield points out, it shouldn't be. We all have this kind of creativity inside us. The best leaders know how to draw it out and channel it for the good of their organizations.

MAXIMIZING THE ORGANIZATION'S CREATIVITY

On one level, creativity does, indeed, just happen. Somebody asks "what if," or someone else looks at one thing and imagines another, and a new product or idea is born. But the process does not have to be haphazard. The leader can harness the creativity of his staff. This involves a three-part process.

First, the leader understands the unique talent each employee has. In every case, it is there. It just has to be discovered.

Second, the leader structures the employees' job to nurture that creativity. Unproductive rules are eliminated; bureaucracy is kept to a minimum; and within the context of what's best for the organization, employees are given as much flexibility as they need.

Third, he creates the right environment, one that supports risk taking and experimentation.

Of the three, the last may be the most important. People need to feel comfortable, secure, and self-confident, before they are willing to try anything new.

The challenge for any leader is figuring out how to create the right environment that stimulates all this creativity. Mansfield does this in several ways:

He begins by looking for people who are inherently flexible, who have the ability to "think outside the box," no matter what their jobs will be. Mansfield believes past performance is the best predictor of future performance. He looks for patterns of behavior, thoughts, and actions that produce a high degree of satisfaction and pride and generate both psychic and financial rewards. He listens for what people yearn to do. He watches what gives them satisfaction, and where there is steady contribution over time.

Once he discovers the talents of his team members, he works hard to match those skills with the job that needs to be done. "You cannot make people into what they are not," Mansfield says. "Friction and performance problems occur when you place the wrong person in the wrong job, and they end up trying to do things they are not good at."

Mansfield tells a story that illustrates his point: "We had hired a talented finance executive who had incredible charisma and personality," he recalls. "We needed someone new to organize and energize the department because it had a history of being dysfunctional, and the people who worked there were unhappy. He was a deal person, and great at it, but he didn't have a good operational focus, which is needed in the day-to-day running of the department. Not only did he not have a feel for it, he was a bull in a china shop. Eventually he and I came to the conclusion that he wasn't in the right role. He wasn't tapping into his strengths. He wasn't the kind of person to handle day-to-day operational issues. A lot of people were annoyed with him, although they liked him personally.

"So we redefined his job, and put him in a new role that was very conceptual—he would develop new business opportunities for us,"

Mansfield adds. "He got very energized by it. He was great at build-ing external relationships, developing contacts, and networking."

Strengths develop best in response to another person, especially when that person is a trusted, supportive leader. Mansfield played that role and was able to help his associate make the transition into a new job.

Having placed the right people in the right jobs, Mansfield then sets clear, challenging, and creative goals. That is in keeping with the environment that Disney Chairman Michael Eisner has worked hard to create. On one of Mansfield's early days on the job, Eisner stopped by to see how Disney's Celebration project was going. Mansfield got a taste of what one of those clear, challenging goals was all about.

"You are not in the real-estate business," Eisner said. "You are in the entertainment business, and the buildings you put up should support that larger mission. Figure out how to make history with this town. That's your standard, make history."

When you think of your job in those terms, you go about creating projects in a decidedly unusual way. Today, this is reflected in the way Mansfield manages. He sets precise goals—both in the project's creative objectives, and when it should be completed—and then he gives people a lot of latitude, to ensure he does not get in the way of their creativity. "If you create a high standard for somebody on your team, I am convinced it propels them forward, if they are a moti-vated, charged kind of person," Mansfield says. "They want to demonstrate they can meet the goal."

This works well because creativity is a high priority at Disney. "We subvert the financial objectives, at least at first, to the creative," Mansfield says. "Eisner firmly believes, and I've come to appreciate and agree with him, that you first need to come up with the idea, break the mold, set the standard, and only then do you confirm that you can do it profitably. If you take this approach, in the end you have a better product, which can make more money than if you set out without that objective."

But setting goals isn't enough, so Mansfield stimulates alternative thinking. He understands that people differ in how they express their creativity. Some people build on existing work, while others ex-periment with new ideas and make new assumptions. Research sug-gests that people with very different styles can be equally creative,

Perhaps more than any other company in the world, Disney is known for creating an environment that supports calculated risk taking, experimentation, and the free expression of ideas. As Chairman Michael Eisner says, "No idea is a bad idea."

To encourage that thinking within its own business, Disney Development's Peter Rummell has developed Ten Guiding Principles:

1. **Committed to growth.** We are 100 percent committed to intelligent growth for our business and our people.
2. **Hire the best.** We will hire and retain professionals who are smart, hardworking, and prepared to deliver on their commitments.
3. **Personal responsibility.** Each of us must take responsibility for our careers and personal growth.
4. **Control our egos.** We all have egos, but it is important that we keep them under control both internally and externally.
5. **Be ethical.** We will be ethical and moral in our dealings with our clients, our vendors, and fellow employees.
6. **Emphasize accountability.** We will emphasize accountability and strive to eliminate bureaucracy at all times and at all levels.
7. **Value performance.** We will value performance. We must be diligent in measuring individual contributions.
8. **Communicate.** We must communicate. This is not just from the top down, but in every direction.
9. **Buy, not make.** We should permanently integrate into our organization only those functions that are essential to our business.
10. **Community enrichment.** We will improve the communities where we live and work.

but they'll express it differently. At Celebration, "we went after the best, most diverse ideas we could find, always looking to improve them ten percent, and then connect one good idea with another. In the education area, for example, we put together a consortium of advisors that would have been on anybody's top twenty list of education experts."

Mansfield also works hard to create a liberating environment that allows people to be creative in their own ways. But no matter what role they play, he encourages them to ask "what if." "Even with somebody who's not in a purely creative role, like a construction manager, I still like to see them thinking about new ways of doing their job."

As part of a new area of Disney World in Florida, now under development, Mansfield's division was building some cottages on a lake that he wanted to create for honeymooning couples, and VIPs who needed a high degree of privacy. "Our people had put together some floor plans and hired an architect, but it just wasn't there. These were cottages that were on one the prettiest lakes in all of Florida, and it didn't take advantage of the lake. It wasn't oriented toward the water. It was oriented inward, which missed the point.

"So I pushed it. I asked, 'Did you think about having the cottages oriented to the water, what would happen if we did?' " Mansfield challenged his team to generate as many alternatives as possible. After much discussion, the team came up with some creative alternatives, a final decision was made, and there was no going back.

CREATIVITY CAN BE MANAGED

The best leaders know that the most effective way to get employees to be creative is to "accentuate the positive." The leader has them capitalize on their strengths and manage around their weaknesses.

Nobody likes to admit weakness. In our fantasies, we all like to think we excel at everything all the time. The myth we grew up with says people can accomplish anything, if they just put their minds to it. That's fine—in our dreams. But believing this is true can be damaging, especially in business. People who believe they excel at everything quickly learn the hard way that they don't. And their performances, and that of their organization, suffers.

The typical cure for dealing with our weaknesses is almost as damaging as the disease. We devote a great deal of time and effort trying to improve what we do poorly. The power of positive thinking says if you concentrate long and hard enough on a problem, you can solve it, and with a typical "can do" attitude we set off to try to improve our personal weaknesses.

In managing organizations, the idea of attacking problem areas is frequently expressed in terms of what is known as a Pareto distribution. Managers "learn" that they are supposed to devote 80 percent of their time to the 20 percent of the company that is underperforming. But if you take this approach with individuals, and try to overcome their weaknesses, or with organizations, focusing primarily on problem areas, you and your organization will lose in two ways. First, you will diminish your strengths. Strengths will atrophy if you don't develop them, and by definition if you are trying to correct your flaws, you are not developing the things you are good at. Second, no matter how hard you try, weaknesses can never be turned into strengths. With a great deal of effort you might turn a negative into a mild positive. But think about what you could have accomplished if you had devoted that effort to building up your strengths.

This is exactly how Mansfield goes about running the real-estate division.

"The traditional way organizations evaluate people is just not effective," he says. "And we were just as bad as everyone else. When we'd sit down to evaluate associates, we'd spend twenty percent of our time talking about the things they did well, and the other eighty percent talking about what needed to be improved. That is just not effective. People have a range of capabilities. Perhaps you can sensitize them to things they are not good at, but to expect someone who isn't naturally gifted at doing something to do that something well is just a real waste of energy. You ought to spend your energy determining what they're gifted at doing, and get their responsibilities aligned with that capability." This is a lesson Mansfield first learned himself, and then applied to others.

At Disney, Mansfield has been pushed through the ranks quickly. He is still under forty. And along the way, the company environment, coupled with support from Mansfield's immediate boss, Peter Rummell, has helped Mansfield learn what he is good at—the integration of the human and business elements, which involves building relationships, motivating others, and creating a team environment, where people can do their best work—and equally important he has learned what he is not good at. He is too trusting and has occasionally allowed himself to be taken advantage of.

To be fair, that is a weakness and a strength. Because he believes the best about people, Mansfield gives them the freedom to create their best work. But people are given the benefit of the doubt—repeatedly. Mansfield is not confrontational, and he finds it hard to have tough conversations with people he has relationships with. That makes it extremely hard for him to fire people.

"Obviously, we have to let go of the people who are not measuring up," Mansfield says. "If we carry deadwood, in the end we will not have a viable enterprise for the 350 good employees that we have. Still, I find it very painful."

But since he has moved up through the organization so quickly, Mansfield has been forced to learn how to deal with weak performers. He makes sure they know what is expected of them, offers to help them achieve their goals, and then confronts them when they still don't measure up. That helps him a great deal. Still he concedes "releasing" employees is a problem for him. Mansfield could spend a great deal of time trying to overcome this weakness. But in the end he realized it is better to manage around it. Mansfield has the head of his human-resources department, a woman he describes as "a miracle worker," compensate for his weakness. This is what leads to maximum performance, managing around your weaknesses.

But how do you know what you are not good at? Donald Clifton, chairman of The Gallup Corporation, suggests you can tell by examining your feelings when you are in a difficult situation. You probably have a weakness, if you:

- Feel defensive about your performance.
- Experience slow learning.
- Develop obsessive behavior.
- Don't profit from repeated experience.
- Feel a lack of self-confidence.
- Lack futuristic thinking.
- Suffer burnout while in the task.

When confronted with these symptoms the solution is straight-forward. First, concede there is a problem. Admitting weakness is an act of courage and growth. After admitting it, manage around it. How? Mansfield does it by "enlightened delegation." Other solutions would include: simply stop doing what you are not good at, subcontracting, partnering with someone who has the necessary skills, or developing support systems to overcome the problem. Our strengths can overpower our weakness, if they are managed. If you can manage around that weakness, anything is possible, including, in the case of Mansfield's division, the creation of a new town.

Walt Disney said, "If you can dream it, you can do it. Always remember that this whole thing was started by a mouse."

UNCOVERING YOUR ORGANIZATION'S CREATIVITY

The key to innovation is good leadership. Unfortunately, too many leaders hamper, or even crush, the creative contributions that their employees bring to work.

To build a creative organization, the leader first must believe that there's a rich pool of talent hidden inside his organization.

Once he believes the talent is there, the leader's job is to bring it to light. He does that by establishing an environment that allows people to celebrate, and make full use of, their creative gifts. People simply will not expose their creativity unless they feel their work environment is safe and trusting.

To leverage these intellectual assets, the leader encourages spontaneity, nonconformity, and independent thinking. He nurtures self-expression and innovation. And he examines the work culture—its systems, the way people are promoted, and the organization's overall bureaucracy—to ensure that the company is nurturing, not negating, the creative process.

Ultimately, the leader never manages creativity. Rather, he learns to uncover it, unleash it, and channel it in the best direction for the business.

There are watercolor pictures of birds hung throughout the hallways of Sun Hydraulics, a leading manufacturer of fluid-power pumps, in Sarasota, Florida. The pictures in the building, which borders a bird sanctuary, make a telling point about managing organizations, says Sun's founder and chief executive Robert Koski.

"All birds look alike until you start studying them," he says. "I tell my people to study the birds they see outside our building.

ROBERT E. KOSKI
Sun Hydraulics

TITLE: Founder and Chairman

AGE: 66

EDUCATION: A.B. in Historical Architecture, Dartmouth College

HISTORY: Founded Sun Hydraulics in 1970

HONORS AND SPECIAL ACCOMPLISHMENTS: Past Chairman, Fluid Power Systems and Technology Division, American Society of Mechanical Engineers; Past Chairman, Selby Botanical Garden; Past Chairman, National Fluid Power Association; Joseph Brahma Medal, Institute of Mechanical Engineers, United Kingdom

HEADQUARTERS: Sarasota, Florida

BUSINESS: Design and manufacture fluid-power control valves

NUMBER OF EMPLOYEES: Over 400

GROSS REVENUE: Approximately $50 million (1995)

FACTS: The company followed its preincorporation plan so closely that 10 years later they were within a percentage point (correcting for inflation) of their most optimistic projections.

" 'What are we supposed to see?' " they ask.

" 'Just study the birds and explain to me what you see,' " I tell them. And pretty soon they start pointing out different markings on the birds, or how they catch fish in different ways, or whatever.

"Until you study something, you don't see it," Koski adds. "It isn't until you begin to see the differences between people, the differences in their knowledge, values, and needs, that it starts to be interesting."

The clear implication of Koski's comments is that if we took the trouble to look more deeply and closely at one another, we would begin to see the gifts that we each are able to bring to the organization. "But you have to do more than just look," Koski says. "You also have to make your work environment risk free. People don't always expose their gifts. People become very tight when they perceive they have something at risk. You have to work hard to ensure that this doesn't happen, if you want to develop creativity within your organization."

Creativity? Inside a business that designs and manufactures a line of fluid-power pumps? Why would creativity possibly be important in a business like that?

Koski, who can be direct to the point of bluntness, says that is an easy question to answer. The key competitive advantage in the years ahead will be the ability to innovate in an information-rich environment. The key to innovation is leadership. Good leadership, he adds, goes beyond hiring capable people and giving them the funds they need to make them successful. It also includes the ability to refurbish the innovative capabilities of the organization, and that means inspiring and unleashing the creativity of your work force. It means creating new products and new work processes. It also means ensuring that the environment enables and supports the expression and implementation of employees' ideas.

How did Koski come to these conclusions? Through years of experience at other firms that did not do business this way. Having seen and worked in companies that seemed to hamper, deflect, or even crush the human spirit they were supposed to harness, Koski swore things would be different when he started his own firm.

If Only I Were in Charge

"If only I were in charge." People in the middle of organizations probably say that phrase more than any other. If only I could do things the right way. If only there wasn't all this bureaucracy. If only we could take some risks. If only my boss would get out of my way. If only . . .

Most people don't get a chance to put their beliefs into practice, but Koski did when he founded Sun some twenty-five years ago. His company was built on the premise that "the ultimate quality of a corporation is largely determined by the character of its employees and the environment created around them." From the beginning, Koski set out to get the most out of those employees. He decided to do that by establishing a trusting environment. The best way to nurture that environment, he decided back then and still believes today, is to keep everyone's ego—including his own—in check.

Within organizations there is always a tension between the need to nurture people's creative egos and keeping those egos in check. The best way to handle that tension, Koski has found, is to channel people's gifts toward the organization's goals.

"I think ego is one of the things that, one way or another, really kills most organizations," Koski says. "Our challenge is to transfer everyone's individual ego into a group ego and align those egos with the company's goals. We keep trying to find heroes to worship inside organizations, and I think that is a big mistake, because for every winner, there are a bunch of losers.

"I don't want to be a saint, sitting on a pedestal, because that is a dangerous position. You're going to get knocked off, or you'll knock yourself off. The better course of action, if you are a leader, is to do whatever is necessary to get other people's egos attached to the goals of the organization. You've got to get ego out of the individual and into the organization as much as possible, in order to maximize creativity."

Koski gives an example of how this works within Sun Hydraulics. "We have at least two people involved in anything that happens at the company," he says. "The second and/or third or fourth person helps to refine the original author's idea. As a result, the idea gets better. Authorship gets diluted and becomes invisible, but the essence of the idea, or the new product, gets refined and improved. In the end, what you have done by following this kind of process is looked at a lot more options. This enlarges the creativity process.

"The creativity is where the fun is. If you want to attract high-quality engineers, this is the way to do it. Our willingness to do these things, as part of managing new ideas and new innovations, is the reason people come here and never leave."

That is not an exaggeration. In Sun's twenty-five-year history, not one of the company's senior engineers has ever left for another job.

"THE BEST MANAGEMENT IS THE LEAST MANAGEMENT AND IDEALLY NO MANAGEMENT."

A corporate setting such as the one at Sun—where there is a trusting environment and minimum organizational structure—helps people learn, adapt, change, and express themselves. It gives them the ability to ask tough questions about the business.

If the kind of organization that Koski has created sounds at odds with most business structures, it is. Koski believes that the traditional organizational structure drives out good people. The worst thing a company can do, he says, is create an organizational chart. Why? Because once the structure is written down, people either tend to stay inside their organizational box, not doing a single additional thing, or they defend their turf, the area inside the box, or both. This habit is very difficult for an organization to change.

That's why the organizational structure at Sun Hydraulics is deliberately fuzzy. People can tell you what they do for a living, and whose approval they need to get something accomplished, but they can't sketch out an organizational chart because there isn't one. There are no titles.

Well, that is not exactly true. There is an exception, the woman who has taken it upon herself to care for the hundreds of green plants that adorn the Sarasota factory and office. She has a business card, complete with title. It reads: SUN HYDRAULICS CORPORATION, MARIE OLSEN, PLANT MANAGER. But other than that, there is no crisp delineation of duties.

There was no clearer example of this than when Koski set out to hire a company president, someone who would handle day-to-day operations. Once Clyde Nixon began work, he took—with Koski's encouragement and support—a full year wandering around to learn as much as he could about the organization, its suppliers and customers, trying, in Koski's words, "to see what he thought he could do." Nixon visited with the 250 people who worked for the company worldwide. (There is a manufacturing plant in Coventry, England, and a distribution facility in Switzerland.) The entire purpose of this yearlong "apprenticeship" was for Nixon to figure out where he could help the company become more creative. Today, Clyde Nixon sits as a peer alongside his colleagues in a long, open office, quietly helping to guide the operation.

But creating a trusting work environment goes beyond eliminating needless organizational boundaries. Koski says you must examine all the systems in the company to see if they promote or undermine creativity. And he understands that building a nurturing environment means that he must allow employees to fail occasionally, in order to grow.

For example, "We have a woman here who knows a lot about manufacturing and what goes on inside this factory, and for a year she went around trying to tell people what to do," Koski recalls. "She finally came to me in tears, and said it had been the worst year of her life and she was going to have to leave, because she couldn't get anything done. She asked me if I could help her be effective or find another job.

"I told her I wouldn't help her directly, that she shouldn't leave, but I would give her some ideas about what she should do at Sun. I asked her who she was finding to be her biggest obstacle in getting work done, and she named a couple of people. I said, 'I know these people, and their thinking processes are very straight. Have you asked them for their help? You haven't? Well, then why don't you just go to them and honestly express your frustration, because if you think you have excellent ideas that are worth implementing, you ought to be able to implement them. Maybe the problem is the way you are trying to achieve your objectives.' It worked!"

There are three points Koski wants people to take away from this story:

- First, a leader must eliminate the "intimidation" and "hassle" factors that get in the way of people's sharing their creative gifts with others. Sometimes those factors are in the work environment. Other times they are inside the egos of employees.
- Second, establishing a trusting environment, and having employees recognize it is there, takes time.
- Finally, people must be given the freedom to fail. Out of failure an employee can learn a great deal and become a much more effective person, one who is able to help Sun Hydraulics innovate.

Organizations that encourage creativity capitalize on employee attributes, and cultivate a culture that supports experimentation and stimulates creative behavior. At Sun, Koski relies on what he calls "divergent thinking." He encourages himself and others to temporarily suspend their knowledge, experience, and expertise, in order to explore whether an idea might work. He wants people to ask tough questions of each other and to admit when they don't have an answer.

This is in contrast to "convergent" thinking, which tends to reject ideas quickly, by saying such things as: "It does not fit," "It will never work here," and "We tried that before." We fall victim to the cancers of comparisons, competition, and criticism. This shuts down people's creativity, making them resentful and hesitant to take risks. When this happens they fall back on old familiar ways. That is not acceptable, given what is happening in today's marketplace.

To solve tomorrow's problems will require new knowledge and new approaches. Divergent thinking is designed to ensure those tools are in place.

And at Sun, divergent thinking has been put into practice. For example, part of the process of machining metal parts to precise tolerances calls for heat-treating the metal. Everyone knew how to do that. The process hadn't changed in sixty years. However, if you could create a new process, which succeeded in heat treating the metal at a lower temperature, you could make more precise parts. That would open up entirely new product lines for Sun. Without consulting with Koski, people in the factory created a new automatic furnace capable of hardening metal but using less heat. This enabled them to design new valves.

"This entire project represented twenty percent of the book value of the company, but I was never asked my opinion and never asked to approve or disapprove the project," Koski says with pride. "The people involved didn't think it was necessary to contact me because I was considered incompetent to make decisions about the new process. I just didn't have the technical background. I could have stepped in, if I had chosen to, but I didn't. I never challenged their ideas. I let the creativity come out naturally. The people got more and more confident, and today we have a huge success on our hands. They made it work!"

You can see through Koski's focus on creativity that he is fostering a leadership style that makes full use of the ideas, talents, experiences, and perspectives of all employees at all levels. In order to do that, the leader must have the inner security not to be threatened by releasing the potential of other people.

ADULTS AS CREATIVE PARTNERS

Notice that as Koski goes about uncovering his organization's creativity, he puts an obligation on all his employees to work to their fullest potential. "I'll help build the environment that will allow creativity to happen, that will allow you to do your best work," Koski is telling them, "but you have to live up to your end of the bargain.

"Most organizations foster parent-child relationships with employees by their organizational-chart structures," Koski says. "The boss says: 'I'll tell you what to do, and what you are responsible for doing, and I'll tell you when it is done well enough. Your only responsibility is to try hard to do it.' We don't believe in that. We want adult-to-adult relationships."

That's why during the hiring process Koski spends an inordinate amount of time trying to determine whether a potential employee wants to be a real adult—whether he or she has a realistic assessment of skills and weaknesses. Koski believes that managers spend a huge portion of their time resolving problems caused by employees who don't have a good idea of their competencies.

This assessment of self-awareness, however, is not intended just to eliminate potential problems. Each employee is expected to choose the range of activities in which she will contribute best to the organization. Frequently, that leads to a natural expansion of the individual's responsibilities. For example, one person whose activities were initially largely administrative began slowly to use her considerable interpersonal skills in her routine interactions with fellow employees. Eventually, everyone at the company began coming to her with personnel issues. Today, that woman is an important human-relations resource.

By letting people play to their strengths, and aligning those strengths to the company's goals, Koski builds a high level of specialized knowledge within the organization.

What Can Robert Koski Teach Us About Creativity?

In the course of building Sun Hydraulics, Koski has learned what must happen if an organization is to be creative.

- Smart people learn from their own mistakes. Wise people learn from the mistakes of others.
- Reality doesn't count. Perceptions are what matters.
- If anybody really thinks deeply about things, it's easier to be intellectually humble. The water never gets shallower, it always gets deeper.
- When asking people for business advice, the strongest opinions generally come from individuals with little direct experience—and they are usually wrong.
- Articulate people rise in power and assume control. Knowledgeable people, if not also articulate, become discouraged and either leave the organization or settle into middle-management positions as passive obstructionists. The process takes about eighteen months.
- If you want to get out of the hole, first start digging.
- In times of rapid change, experience is your worst enemy.
- When people are too serious, they probably won't take risks.
- Getting there isn't half the fun, it's all the fun.

Koski's approach to creativity pays off. Not only is Sun recognized as the industry leader, but it has turned in the kind of financial performance any company would envy. Year in and year out, sales increase 20 to 35 percent, in an industry that is growing only a third as fast, and Sun's profits are usually twice the industry average.

Perhaps the best proof that this approach works came from an executive at a rival firm. He said: "Everyone who competes with them sees Sun as the industry leader. The company's standards are exceeded by no one I know."

DEVELOPING
PEOPLE-CENTERED
TECHNOLOGIES

The power of machines and the power of people are an awesome combination. By investing in highly skilled, motivated people, and letting those people work with state-of-the-art machines, successful leaders get the largest possible return on their technological dollar.

The best new leaders spot and take advantage of these strategic opportunities. They engage in breakthrough thinking, and reconfigure problems to find fresh solutions. By managing people and technology, they are able to advance their business.

However, the best leaders know that the more advanced their technologies become, the more humane their treatment of people must be. Technology well applied should enrich jobs and liberate people. It should also make them the masters both of their fate and of machines—and not the other way around.

To make that happen, successful leaders know that their employees must be involved in every aspect of the technology, from choosing it to using it. And these leaders know something else: capable people must be protected from being reengineered out of a job, if that is humanly possible.

It isn't surprising that Harman International is one of the world's leading high-technology companies. After all, founder and chief executive Sidney Harman was one of the handful of pioneers who created the high-fidelity industry back in 1952. Today the Harman companies manufacture high-quality high-fidelity audio and video

SIDNEY HARMAN
Harman International Industries, Inc.

TITLE: Chairman and Chief Executive Officer

AGE: 77

FAMILY SITUATION: Married; 6 children

EDUCATION: B.S. in Engineering, City College; Ph.D. in Social Psychology, Union Institute

HISTORY: Founded Harman-Kardon (1952) and arranged for its sale in 1977; Deputy Secretary, U.S. Department of Commerce (1977–78); repurchased Harman International Industries privately (1978); Harman became public again (1986)

HONORS AND SPECIAL ACCOMPLISHMENTS: Founder and active member of Program on Technology, Public Policy, and Human Development, John F. Kennedy School of Government, Harvard University; Senior Advisor, Aspen Institute for Humanistic Studies; Trustee, The Carter Center; extensive writing on productivity, quality of working life, and economic policy in *Newsweek*, *The Washington Post* and *The Christian Science Monitor*; coauthor of *Starting with People*; board member, Center for National Policy, National Symphony Orchestra; member, National Alliance of Business; Council on Foreign Relations

HEADQUARTERS: Washington, D.C.

BUSINESS: Manufacturer of high-fidelity audio and video reproduction equipment

NUMBER OF EMPLOYEES: 6,850

GROSS REVENUE: $1 billion +

products for consumer and professional use in living rooms, automobiles, concert halls, recording and broadcast studios, and in theaters around the world. For years it has been on the cutting edge of manufacturing excellence. Harman companies created the first stereo receivers, the first widely available transistorized components, the first wide-band electronics, the first high-fidelity all-in-one systems . . . The list goes on and on.

It also isn't surprising that Harman International dominates the audio business today. Its brand names—JBL, Harman-Kardon, Infin-

ity, Lexicon, Soundcraft, Studer, Becker, and AKG—are synonymous with high-fidelity audio, and are even better known than the
company's technological advances.

What is surprising is what Sidney Harman likes to talk about, and
where he puts the emphasis within his company. In a firm where you
would expect to hear constant discussions about sound waves, baffles,
bites, and chips, instead you hear over and over again Harman talking about the "power of the human mind, and its fundamental
genius to create extraordinary products and results."

"Technology and computers," he adds, "are never going to over-
run the capacity of the human mind, thank God."

While Harman has great faith in the power of people, his
challenge is to raise the consciousness of his employees, and liberate them from both potential organizational and self-imposed re-
strictions on their ability to create. Technology, Harman believes,
can be that liberating force. "Our technology must serve a legitimate need and also serve the human mind," says Harman, who
founded the Program on Technology, Public Policy, and Human
Development at the John F. Kennedy School of Government at
Harvard.

"It's a mistake to have technology assume a dominant role, to
make people become servants to our technology," Harman says.
"The goal should be to make technology the servant of the people,
freeing them to do what they do best—create."

And that ability to create has never been more necessary, in these
days of increased competition and businesses' constant reengineering of the way work gets done.

BEYOND REENGINEERING

The restructuring and reengineering of corporate America has had
the desired effect. Organizations now have fewer people, and those
who remain are working more efficiently. But for many companies,
reengineering is just the first step. The next step, says Harman, is to
use technology to harness the power of the workforce.

The use of technology in American business goes through three
distinct phases. In phase one, technology is used to accomplish work
faster. Manual tasks are broken down into their smallest parts, and

those individual components are then automated. That's what the assembly line and the personal computer are all about. In phase two, technology is used to redesign the way work is done, in order to make the process of producing the end product or service more efficient. This is the reengineering phase that many companies are going through or have just completed.

But before they can move on to phase three—where the technology will liberate the workforce, giving the organization a sustainable competitive edge in the process—companies must deal with the aftermath of phase two. Reengineering helped companies break down old functional fiefdoms and redeployed solo workers into multidisciplinary teams. And because reengineering got companies to focus on their core capabilities, they found it easier to get the right products and services to their customers.

The result? Increased productivity, driven by a massive influx of new technology and corporate restructuring. Companies were able to lay off large numbers of employees, because the reengineering and technology made it easier to do the work without them.

That's the good news for the company.

The bad news is reengineering left thousands of workers scared, angry, mistrustful, cynical, and worrying about when their jobs were going to be "reengineered out." To compete and thrive in the years ahead, organizations, as Harman quite correctly understands, will need to draw on all the talents of every employee. Employees will need to apply their creative abilities to organizational problems, and will need to generate new ideas, and invent new ways of producing goods and services. Constantly, they will have to ask themselves what new markets they can tap; where they can add value.

But employees won't do those things if they are angry, cynical, or constantly worried about losing their jobs. Sometimes those jobs can be reallocated, but sometimes no new jobs are created and they are lost permanently. It is up to companies to manage these changes with fair, honest, and responsible practices, and it is up to individual workers to commit themselves to lifelong learning.

"We must develop processes and manufacturing technologies that make us more cost efficient," Harman says. "As we do, it understandably threatens jobs. The more efficient you become, the fewer peo-

ple you need to do the work. But we believe that if workers feel secure—truly secure in their jobs—you can experience productivity
beyond your wildest imagining."

Is the answer to guarantee jobs? No. Companies need to shed labor in order to remain competitive. But this could be done more
constructively by allowing people to create new businesses within
their companies, which would provide some semblance of employment security, Harman says. He feels companies have a responsibility to provide safe and ergonomically sound work, offer continuous
training to help people learn about the technology that is coming
on line, and give them plenty of freedom to enjoy it. Above all else,
Harman tries to create an environment that protects employees
from being "reengineered" out of jobs.

How? "You can only deal with it in an environment that permits
you to be seen as honest," Harman says. "You deal with it by stimulating creativity and unleashing people's best efforts. You deal with it
by developing programs that don't guarantee jobs but seriously increase the security of employment. Our Off-Line Enterprise program is intended to do that.

"Off-Line says to employees that there are many opportunities for
us to build operations not necessarily related to your core work. We
will establish a reservoir of such jobs, and if people become redundant in what they are doing now, we will try to shift them to those
Off-Line jobs." This is good for Harman's people, because their jobs
are protected, and they will be able to stay in the company, keep all
their benefits, and work in a job that is respectable.

"I am absolutely convinced this idea affects people's commitment
to the organization," Harman adds. "If I'm not concerned that I'm
working my way out of a job by cooperating with this new way of doing work, then of course I'll cooperate. I'll cooperate with people I
trust. Trust is fundamental, and Off-Line is an expression of trust."

The original idea was to train people in services that Harman buys
on the outside—gardening, painting, security, that sort of thing.
But, instead, they concentrated on things that are more a part of
their business.

"We have a lot of scrap in the plant. In the process of making
speaker cabinets, we punch out millions of twelve-inch circles, ten-
inch circles, and eight-inch circles of wood. Over the years, we paid

hauling companies to come and cart that stuff away because it is scrap.

"Now we take those circles of wood, and make Movado-looking clocks out of them," Harman explains. "We buy inexpensive clock movements and attach the mechanism to the wood, and sell them through our own marketing companies to high-fidelity dealers who use them as giveaways to hospitals and charities. We are creating a useful product out of scrap, and are creating useful jobs for our people who have become redundant on the line.

"We've also started an outlet store, which is staffed by production workers," Harman adds. "They've been going to class learning the theory of acoustics, of electronics, and how to sell, install, and service our products, and they are so excited about it.

"The time to do things like creating off-line enterprises is when your business is healthy, as opposed to when it is in crisis." It is in the good times that companies are best positioned to create new ventures. But to make it work, employees have a major responsibility. They must be flexible and open to innovation, willing to use and apply the new technologies and be willing to redesign their work in order to improve quality and efficiency.

PEOPLE AND TECHNOLOGY WORKING TOGETHER

The key to Harman's approach is investing in people and technology. These are the two major assets in companies today. Both are critical, but technology depends on people to make it work. To maximize your technological assets, you must invest in your human assets.

"If we maximize our technological assets, we free our people to do their best work, and thus maximize our human assets," Harman says. "To dismiss so profoundly the people who make the product, because of your fascination with technology, is nothing less than insane."

You won't find a bigger advocate for technology than Harman. Yet he understands that the more advanced technologies become, the more sensitive management must be in their treatment of people. That is why Harman involves people in every aspect of technology, from choosing it to using it. He educates his employees as broadly and deeply as possible, so that they can understand the new tools. He empowers them to make decisions and make the best use of the technology they can. Harman inspires his people to be as entrepreneurial as possible when it comes to applying the new technology.

This only works if Harman spreads his insights around the company. Harman makes sure that all managers—including himself—understand the employees' fears and feelings about technology. The easiest way to do that is to literally stand in their shoes.

"All of our senior executives are required to, and do, spend eighteen days a year working on the production lines," Harman says, explaining a program that is called Senior Executive Service. "This does two things. If you work here, in whatever capacity, you have to believe manufacturing is important. If you don't, then our system is in trouble.

"But even if you believe technology is important, we don't want you to deal with it in the abstract. You have to deal with it in person, by working on the line. This is no photo opportunity. You get there at a quarter to six in the morning, and you work until two-thirty in the afternoon, and then, still dressed in your jeans and work boots, you go upstairs to your office and your regular job in the afternoon. This way executives learn firsthand about the manufacturing process, and the value employees bring to that process."

Often executives' perspectives change as a result of the process. They realize that the employees on the line are more than pairs of hands. They are people who have creative ideas and can contribute to the good of the organization.

"After a very brief period of doubt, people on the line realize that managers are willing to get their hands dirty," Harman says, explaining the program's other benefit. "We're often incompetent and embarrassed when we start to work, and we need them to teach us what to do. It changes in a significant way the nature of the relationship. It is no longer the executives' company, it becomes 'our company.' "

One of the benefits that Harman gets back, in exchange for treating his people so well, is their uncompromising commitment to the success of the company. For example, when the California earthquake in early 1994 destroyed Harman International's major production facility just outside Los Angeles, the response to the disaster was unanimous.

"Our people were heroic," Harman recalls. "They performed. They coalesced. They were glorious. They put the thing back together in a matter of days, even though it meant driving for hours on backroads to reach the plant, because the highways were closed. We had the critical stuff working in three days, and not one of the other plants in the area was working three months later. Management was there, of course, but it was the people on the line who truly made the recovery possible. There was a partnership between management and workers."

Is the Harman approach to blending people and technology perfect? No. And Harman adds, once you think things are as good as they can get, they will deteriorate.

While Harman is no "fan of modesty," he says you must constantly guard against hubris. "When things are going well, there's a tendency to think either that you've got the master touch, or that it is always going to be like this. Good times, unfortunately, don't last forever, and you must fight against these feelings."

What makes Harman so successful is his philosophy about creative work. He is a restless, independent man who is curious and eager to learn. He sees opportunities others don't. He makes room for the unexplored and the underdeveloped. He is widely innovative, always thinking about how to unleash the creative potential in his firm. At the core, he believes that people are capable of amazing things, if they put their minds, and the available technologies, to work.

Says Harman: "Technology should be the servant of the people. You have to believe in the majesty of the people. When you free people of the legitimate fear that technology is their executioner, then magical stuff can happen."

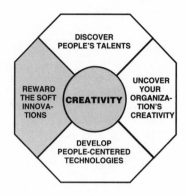

REWARDING THE
SOFT INNOVATIONS

We are all suppliers and customers of interpersonal relationships. Each day we have many opportunities to add value to someone's life in the way we treat them. Successful leaders know how critical it is to manage these relationships well.

Every interaction is a moment of truth—an opportunity for someone to delight a customer, show respect for a coworker, exhibit quality, and express creativity. These moments are built one person, one conversation, one commitment at a time. The leader's challenge is to get everyone to make the most of these moments of truth—to do the right thing, the right way, the first time, every time. These are the soft innovations inside a business, and they really make a difference.

Successful leaders know that relationships will deteriorate over time, if they are left unattended. Customers will become alienated and the organizations will eventually rust. This is why leaders give special attention to the humanity of their organizations.

You're in Boston on a business trip and you have just completed dinner. Suddenly, you feel a tingling in your arms. It's probably nothing, but then again, isn't that kind of tingling one of the signs of a heart attack?

You hail a cab to take you to the hospital. But which hospital? This is Boston, after all, with some of the best medical facilities in the world. You can go to Massachusetts General, Brigham and Women's, New England Medical Center, or any number of other facilities within a ten-mile radius. They are all as good as it gets techni-

MITCHELL T. RABKIN, M.D.
Beth Israel Hospital

TITLE: President

AGE: 64

FAMILY SITUATION: Married; 2 children

EDUCATION: A.B., Harvard College (1951); M.D., Harvard Medical School (1955)

HISTORY: Associate Professor of Medicine, Harvard Medical School (1962–82); Massachusetts General Hospital, Acting Chief, Endocrine Clinic (1964–66), Assistant in Medicine (1963–71); Visiting Lecturer on Health Service, Harvard University School of Public Health (1976–present); Professor of Medicine, Harvard Medical School (1983–present); President, Beth Israel Corporation (1984–present); physician, Beth Israel Hospital (1966–present), and President (1966–present)

HONORS AND SPECIAL ACCOMPLISHMENTS: Doctor of Science, Brandeis University (1983) and Massachusetts College of Pharmacy and Allied Health Service (1983); Governing Council, Institute of Medicine (1992–present); Honorary Physician, Massachusetts General Hospital; member, Medical Advisory Board to Hadassah Medical Organization (1981–present); Board of Directors, The Partnership Group, Inc. (1985–present); member, Advisory Board, The Leadership Institute, University of Southern California (1992–present)

HEADQUARTERS: Boston, Massachusetts

NUMBER OF EMPLOYEES: 5,672

GROSS REVENUE: $445.8 million (1994)

cally and professionally. Suddenly you remember a conversation with a colleague whose mother went into Boston's Beth Israel for some kind of major operation and all she did was rave about how nice the doctors, nurses, and even the support staff were. You remember his saying she had been a patient at three different hospitals in Boston, and the experience at Beth Israel was like night and day compared to the other two. And so you tell the driver to take you to Beth Israel.

Clearly, the decision of which hospital to go to could be a matter of life and death. But on a smaller scale, this kind of scenario is played out this way every day. We live in an age when the speed of change is so fast, and the number of players in the marketplace so large, that it is virtually impossible to find a competitive edge.

Technology isn't the answer. Very few technologies are proprietary, and people can copy you in a matter of months, or less. There is no edge in financing. The cost of money is basically the same for everyone. And there is not much of an edge in trying to control costs. Everyone does that today, and people receive market-rate wages, and the cost of goods sold is constant, no matter where you look.

The only edge, when you come right down to it, is people, and this is something that Dr. Mitchell T. Rabkin, chief executive of Beth Israel Hospital, understands. "Everybody has the same machines and the same skilled people to use them," says Rabkin, who has been in charge of the hospital since 1966, giving him perhaps the longest tenure of any hospital administrator in the country. "You can't gain a competitive advantage in urban Boston by saying we do coronary-artery bypass better. Technical competence we have, but our competitive edge is warm, personalized patient care. Strategic advantage in our business—indeed in any business—will go to those who can manage the human side of the business."

At Beth Israel, a major teaching hospital of Harvard Medical School located on the edge of suburban Brookline, just south of Fenway Park, there doesn't appear, on the surface, to be much time for warm, personalized care. The 408-bed, 80-bassinet hospital is a busy place; some 40,000 people visit the emergency room each year, another 24,000 are admitted, 6,000 children are born there, and about 200,000 patients visit the hospital's outpatient specialty units.

On top of this, you have the changing nature of the health-care system. With the push toward cost management, the very nature of the way health care is delivered is changing, and it is becoming a consumer's market. Doctors' practices are going public. For-profit hospitals are expanding, and government reimbursement programs, and beleaguered insurance companies, are putting even more pressure on hospitals to keep down costs. At Beth Israel, for example, 54 percent of all surgery is now done on an outpatient basis. The days when a patient checked in Tuesday afternoon, for minor surgery on Wednesday morning, and then went home the following Monday are gone forever. Rabkin says simply: "To be successful tomorrow, a hospital will have to be skilled in creating efficient and technically effective operational schemes that also lead to a warm and personal experience for patients."

CREATING A HIGH-TECH, HIGH-TOUCH ENVIRONMENT

The first thing Rabkin does is acknowledge the pressure hospital employees are under. But having done that, Rabkin is quick to stress that pressure is no excuse for not creating a "high-tech, high-touch environment."

Having established that goal, what does a leader do? A picture in Rabkin's office lends a clue. Hanging on the wall is a photo of several boats racing into the wind. Underneath, the caption reads: "We cannot direct the winds, but we can adjust the sails."

"There are times when things are tough, but think about a bunch of sailboats in a race, and a squall comes along. Everybody's got the same lousy weather," Rabkin says. "We all have the wind, and the rain, and everything else. The question is how sound is the boat? How sound are the sails? And how sound is the crew? If we are sound, and we are determined, we can adjust the sails and move forward."

The first way that Rabkin does that is making sure that everyone knows exactly how those sails should be set. All the employees at Beth Israel—from the people at entry level to Rabkin himself—know exactly what their roles are.

"The capacity of the hospital staff to make appropriate decisions, to do the right thing, the right way, the first time, every time, depends on defining clearly the roles and working relationships of each individual," Rabkin says. "You have to articulate the mission clearly and you have to reiterate it in a whole variety of ways, verbally, in writing, and in action."

It's an important point. It's not enough that someone in the lab knows what her job is. She also has to understand where her job fits in as part of overall patient care. Otherwise gaps can develop.

Rabkin provides an example. "Say your job is to deliver the trays from the kitchen to the eleventh floor, and mine is to get them to the patients' bedside," he begins. "But nobody has specified the space between us. So you take the trays from the kitchen and leave them just outside the elevator, saying, 'If that Rabkin weren't such a lazy guy, we'd have those patients fed by now.' And I'm waiting over by the rooms saying, 'If you weren't such a lazy SOB, this process would work a lot better.' I think a large part of the problem in American business deals with definitions of roles and relationships. We try to make the definitions as clear as possible, so that the process works well and people can work to the best of their ability.

"But importantly, the capacity also relates to how our employees feel about themselves, their relationships within the hospital, and their commitment to the hospital's mission," Rabkin adds. "Those feelings emerge out of how individuals are treated by the hospital, whether they know and share in our purpose and direction; and also whether they perceive the institution as nurturing of them, their personal integrity, and intelligence; and supportive of their personal growth and advancement. I think it's very hard, particularly for entry-level people, if they feel denigrated, then to be able to reach out to patients, or to reach out to other employees, and think, This is my hospital."

In other words, it is hard for employees to treat patients well unless they feel they are being treated well by their employer. So Rabkin works hard to create a level playing field, a place where everyone in the hospital is a customer to someone else, whether they are dealing with patients or with other employees. Respect is the key to making this work.

Rabkin ensures a "high-touch" environment by sensitizing employees to what patients go through in a hospital, and how the staff can make a difference. To do this he talks at every orientation session. As part of his presentation, he gets new employees to discuss the experiences they had when they were patients, be it in Beth Israel or elsewhere.

"Someone will say it was very pleasant, the nurse was kind and helpful, I had some concerns and she told me what to expect, and held my hand at night when I was very nervous. Or someone else will say it was terrible; they disregarded me completely, and treated me like I was an idiot, or a lump of stone.

"In both cases," Rabkin says, "I'd point out that they were making judgments about their hospital stays not on the technical qualities of

the work, but on the human-to-human interactions. We are all pro-
fessors of interpersonal relationships, whether you are the chief of
surgery or the person who answers the phone. We can all tell who is
good and kind and warm and helpful, and who is a son-of-a-bitch.
And people make judgments about an organization that way.

"Every time you do something as an employee, interact with anybody—patients, other employees—you're saying something about
the Beth Israel Hospital and I want you to be saying something that
reinforces and enriches the institution, and by virtue of that, enriches your own experience."

Rabkin's next strategy will surprise many. He makes sure that patients know what their rights are, so that the Beth Israel staff know
how they must act. Patients are told they are entitled to individuality
and dignity, to participate in decisions that affect them. They have a
right to privacy and a full explanation of why they are being attended to in a certain way.

The patients have a reciprocal responsibility. They are expected
to be on time, to provide complete information about their past ill-
nesses, to be open and honest, to show consideration of others, and
to pay their bills on time. But the primary purpose of the patients'
bill of rights is to make patients aware and to put the staff on notice
of that awareness.

The last part of Rabkin's strategy involves making sure that employees treat each other with the same kind of respect that they ex-
tend to patients. "Employees," after all, says Rabkin, "are people,
too. I do not see how we can go the extra mile, day after day after
day, being asked to treat patients with warmth and dignity and concern, unless we ourselves feel that we're being treated with warmth
and dignity and concern by one another.

"People have basic needs to know, to share knowledge, and to interact positively and gratifyingly with each other," he adds. "This is
simply an outgrowth of being human. Such needs do not change
with advances in medical science and technology, nor with the stric-
tures of cost controls. You must keep that in mind when dealing with
people. If you just look at someone as an extension of her job, you
are bound to miss a lot."

That is something Rabkin learned firsthand. "I remember vividly
one man who used to sweep the floors. He and I had never said

much more than good morning. One day I sat down at lunch with him in the cafeteria and we were chatting, and I asked him how long he had been working here, and he said seventeen years. I said that is quite a long time.

" 'Well, I have been working at Children's for nineteen years,' he said.

"It turned out that he had been working eight hours a day at Children's and then coming over here for another full shift.

"I thought that was pretty interesting. We went on talking, and I asked him how many kids he had, and he said nine. I said to myself, Okay, a typical family with no possibility for social advancement.

" 'Where are they and what do they do?'

" 'Well, my oldest is a professor of microbiology at Stanford, and the next one teaches law at Yale and . . .' It turns out that this man had put every single kid through graduate school, but what you saw walking down the corridor was this guy pushing a broom. What I came to realize in talking to him was here was a man of extraordinary strength and determination, and very few people knew it. And you wonder how many other people working here are like that?"

There are many ways in which you can see the richness of individuals, and sometimes that richness is at some discrepancy with the costumes they wear and the roles they are assigned. To ensure that Beth Israel's employees see beyond the costume, Rabkin deliberately puts them in different roles throughout the year. "I think this is very important, because I've seen here, particularly years ago, extraordinary instances of people ignoring the humanity of someone who's in a low-level position," Rabkin recalls.

"Indeed, I have experienced this. Every year we have an employee-appreciation week, and during one day of that week, the administrative staff serves the food in the cafeteria. And this physician comes along, whom I have known forever, and he looks right through me as I plop some spaghetti on his plate.

"I said, 'How about it, Charlie,' and you could see he was thinking, 'Who the hell is this guy to call me Charlie,' and then he focuses and says 'Oh, hi, Mitch, what are you doing there?' He just didn't see me, because of the job I was doing."

In an effort to teach young doctors not to do that, Rabkin had first-year medical students put on the uniforms of various people in the hospital—nurses, housekeepers, and so on—and spend two or three days with the people who do each job.

"Obviously, they can't do most of the work, but they can help and observe," Rabkin says. "They learn a lot through the experience. They learn what work is done. They learn the attitude these people bring to their jobs. And, of course, they were treated exactly like the people in these jobs by everyone else in the hospital, since they were wearing the clothes of whatever role they were learning, and no one knew they were first-year medical students. I think it was useful for these students to learn about the hospital before they arrived in their own role, with a white coat and a stethoscope."

WALKING THE TALK

At the heart of Rabkin's leadership style is his concern for the patient and the quality of the care he or she receives at Boston's Beth Israel. Rabkin wants to create an environment in which everyone identifies with this mission. So he models the kind of behavior he knows is required to liberate the creativity of everyone in the organization. He picks up trash on the floor, says hello to everyone, answers all the letters he receives, and writes the organization's two weekly newsletters—one oriented to medical staff and one oriented to all employees—so that everyone knows what is going on. And he does everything he can to make sure employees are treated fairly.

In most hospitals, there is a major distinction between doctors and nurses. Rabkin minimizes that distinction at Beth Israel by putting nurses on salary rather than hourly pay and emphasizes their clinical professionalism through a long-standing, hospitalwide program of primary nursing, in which one nurse is in charge of supervising each patient's care. This is done through a twenty-four-hour nursing-care plan she creates and carries out with her nursing colleagues, working directly with physicians.

"The philosophy of this place is not simply to understand the psychology of the patients and make it a good place for them," Rabkin says. "Rather, the philosophy is to understand the psychology of being a human being and make this the kind of place where if you're going to be a patient, it'll be good to be a patient, and if you're going to be an employee, it'll be good to be an employee."

It is exactly this kind of approach that is going to make leaders successful in coming years. In the twenty-first century, which will be the age of information, we will need leaders who understand the nature of human beings and human enterprises. Rabkin is that kind of leader. He has a deep understanding of the human condition at its strongest and weakest hour. He knows the power relationships have to nurture life and health or poison and destroy another person. He is in the business of selling healing relationships, and he does a very good job.

How does Rabkin ensure he is sending the kind of message he wants? He says the secret is to be consistent. Specifically, he says it's:

- The way you behave with people.
- Your public utterances.
- The way you deal with difficult news.

And just like his organization, Rabkin has evolved. He has learned to listen more and talk less, something that does not come easily to people trained as physicians. "There are two sides to every story, and you better learn the second side before you open your mouth." He is not anxious about disagreements, but he has learned you don't go into them without a win-win solution in mind.

The payoffs from Rabkin's approach are clear. Not only is Beth Israel constantly recognized as one of the best hospitals in the country, it is almost always included on lists of the best places to work. For proof, all you have to do is look at turnover rates. Nationwide, when turnover of nurses was at 19 percent, at Beth Israel it was about a third of that.

Beth Israel's combination of participation, respect, and a focus on one-on-one relationships allows people the freedom to live the hospital's mission every day. It also allows them to make their own decisions about how to create a healthy, healing environment.

As Beth Israel approaches the twenty-first century, Rabkin's challenge will be to apply what he has learned managing a hospital to the complex world of integrated health delivery networks. The business of health care will change, but the principles of high-tech, high-touch healing environments will never waver.

*I*NTEGRITY

With a net worth estimated at $250 million, Malcolm Forbes was frequently asked how he decided where to invest his own fortune. His answer never varied.

"I bet on the jockey, never the horse," said the man whose magazine proudly bears the slogan "capitalist tool." "I don't need to know what industry the company is in, or what its financials are. All I need to know is what kind of person the CEO is."

Forbes understood a fundamental truth. The character of an organization is established by the character of the people who work there. And that character is determined by the integrity of the leader. Integrity is a timeless virtue that is central to living a healthy ethical life. Ethics may twist and turn, being subjected over time to economics, law, psychology, and management whims. And ethics means different things to different people as they debate what is right—and what is wrong. But the concept of integrity never changes.

The kind of leader that Forbes was looking for, and most people want to follow, is driven by fundamental, undeniable principles. These principles are deeply ingrained in the leader's makeup, shaped over a lifetime of development and introspection. They serve as a moral compass, an internal guidance system that has fairness and justice as its magnetic north. It is important to note that integrity has nothing to do with a leader's personal views, or political agenda. It is more fundamental than that. At its heart it is about the leader's being a centered and grounded person.

Because they are grounded by principles, leaders with integrity have the courage to be themselves. They are not afraid of tough issues and stand firm in the face of struggle and adversity. Their integrity grows out of their own sense of self-worth. This does not mean they are naïve. They know that people are a mixture of altruism and self-interest, and cannot always be counted on to do the right thing. Still, they know that consistency is better than hypocrisy, and acting ethically is better than deceiving. To them, how we produce things is just as important as what we produce. The means are fundamental to the ends.

Now all this sounds nice, but the real test comes when the leader must put the principles of ethics and equity into practice. Do her actions match her words? Does she set an example? Does she act consistently on the small issues as well as the larger ones? Does she insist that ethics are everyone's responsibility?

Ultimately, by employing these precepts, the leader builds a culture of institutional fairness, a place where people have the courage to voice their opinions, where pay is fair and equitable, and where reputation matters. The end result is an ethical community, where a fair and balanced return for all of the organization's stakeholders—customers, employees, shareholders, labor unions, suppliers—is the goal.

Indeed, Dwane Baumgardner, chairman of Donnelly Corporation, has made balancing the needs of those stakeholders his company's number-one priority. He knows that if any one of his stakeholders feels he is not getting a fair shake, he can withdraw support and undermine the organization.

In carrying out his strategy, Baumgardner has learned something that Robert Beyster, head of Science Applications International, has known for more than a quarter of a century: Good ethics is good business. Companies with the best reputations attract not only the best employees but the best customers.

Taking the ethical high road isn't easy. While most people want to do the right thing, business is a constant struggle to put integrity into action, to close the gap between rhetoric and reality. That's why the leader must be a role model. That is something that Gregory Favre does at *The Sacramento Bee* every day.

But all this begins, as Assistant Secretary of Housing and Urban Development Roberta Achtenberg exemplifies, with personal courage. And often this means standing up for what you believe is right, and making short-term sacrifices for longer-term gains in relationships and reputation.

Without integrity, the organization will turn against itself. Lack of integrity destroys communication, cooperation, and creativity—and ultimately it destroys the company, period. Unethical behavior exacts a hefty fee. Not just on the spirit of the organization, but on its bottom line as well. That's why Malcolm Forbes always wanted to know what kind of person was running the organization he was thinking of investing in.

PROMOTING
INSTITUTIONAL FAIRNESS

Every organization must achieve a fair and balanced return for all its stakeholders: its customers, employees, shareholders, and suppliers. Without that balance, the organization will never be strong and secure.

Today's stakeholders are a demanding group, and balancing their needs is a tricky business. If any of them feel taken advantage of, they can withdraw their support, and undermine the organization.

Issues of fairness are particularly challenging within the walls of the organization. Fairness issues range from how decisions are made to how people are treated and compensated. If the leader does not resolve these issues equitably, the organization will turn against itself.

Successful leaders put the principles of fairness and equity into practice. They believe people have a right to a just workplace, where they are heard, can disagree, and can participate in the overall governance.

In return, people must participate as mature partners in the enterprise, following rules, resolving conflicts on their own, and supporting the organization's multiple stakeholders.

Creating an environment that will allow this to happen starts with a fair-minded leader.

Dwane Baumgardner, the chairman of Donnelly Corporation, has set a difficult goal to achieve, and he has picked a tough industry to achieve it in. Donnelly, which serves 250 customers in 25 different countries, supplies windows, mirrors, and interior trim parts to the auto industry, and you'd be hard-pressed to pick a more competitive business anywhere in the world. The car industry is shrinking—and the companies that remain choose to go with a finite number of suppliers.

DWANE BAUMGARDNER
Donnelly Corporation

TITLE: Chairman and Chief Executive Officer

AGE: 54

EDUCATION: B.S. in Physics, Missouri School of Mines and Metallurgy; Ph.D. in Engineering Optics, University of Rochester

HISTORY: Joined Donnelly in 1967 as Manager of Research and Development. Promoted to Vice President of Technology (1977); appointed President and Chief Operating Officer (1980); appointed Chief Executive Officer (1982); appointed Chairman of the Board (1986)

HONORS AND SPECIAL ACCOMPLISHMENTS: Chairman, International Management Council's Top Management Advisory Committee; Director, SL Industries, Sligh Furniture, Holland Economic Development Corporation, Economic Alliance for Michigan, and Economic Club of Grand Rapids; Chairman, Deans Advisory Board, Seidman School of Business, Grand Valley State University; Executive Advisory Committee, Aquinas College

HEADQUARTERS: Holland, Michigan

BUSINESS: Production of automotive mirrors, windows, interior trim, and coated glass for electronics industry

NUMBER OF EMPLOYEES: 2,800

GROSS REVENUE: $350 million

FACTS: Listed in the book *The 100 Best Companies to Work for in America* as one of the top 10. Average absentee rate is 1.6%, compared to national average of approximately 3%.

But that, Baumgardner is quick to tell you, is exactly why he has set his sights so high. The industry is forcing his $350 million company to constantly bundle more products together, and forcing it to come up with new products.

To compete in an environment as competitive as this requires balancing the needs of four competing groups of stakeholders:

- Customers, who are at the center of everything the organization does.

- Employees, whose talents produce products for the customers.
- Shareholders, who invest the financial resources essential to support the growth of the company.
- Suppliers, who provide the materials, subassemblies, and services needed to make the products for its customers.

You can't focus on one group to the point of excluding any of the others, Baumgardner says. "If any stakeholder is not receiving a fair return, then he may decide to withdraw support from the partnership, and that would weaken our organization. Our customers can obviously source their business from someone else, if they don't feel like they're getting a fair return for what they are paying us. Shareholders can always liquidate their investments and put their money in another company. All of us, as employees of the company, can invest our time and energy elsewhere, if we think we are not being treated fairly. And suppliers have the same option.

"There is a critical interconnectedness among our stakeholders," he adds. "In the past, management has not always had the integrity to hold all the stakeholders accountable to ensure a fair return for all. While achieving a profit is of critical importance, characterizing the fundamental purpose of the business in this narrow sense will ultimately tend to work against achieving truly outstanding results over the long term. That's why we must communicate the pressures and the challenges we face to all our stakeholders, so they will understand the big picture. We want them to embrace this idea willingly and enthusiastically in a world of competing opportunities."

In other words, Donnelly must be fair to all its stakeholders, or the company is doomed to fail. And it is fairness and equity that are at the core of the company's business strategy. These principles influence everything the company does. You might wonder what the concept of institutional fairness has to do with maximizing return to shareholders, or making car mirrors for that matter, but at Donnelly they are key.

And it begins with Baumgardner. He is a unique blend of competencies. A scientist—Baumgardner earned his Ph.D. in optics—and an expert in psychology, he is a religious man, who studied for his

MBA. Baumgardner is a deep thinker. He understands the principles of human behavior and how they relate to running a business. He believes there is a commonality linking us all together as people, and we are all looking to be respected and treated fairly. Baumgardner believes people have a fundamental right to be heard and that they have the right to disagree, to dissent, and to question workplace decisions. He also wants employees to be able to resolve conflicts and feel protected from abusive people. He believes people have the right to be treated fairly in the workplace.

Baumgardner understands the fundamental principles of equity because he is not arrogant. There is a humility to him. This allows him to listen to employees and solve conflicts fairly. "I'll be walking around the production floor, and someone will tell me about a work situation that they are having trouble with. Maybe they are having a conflict with their supervisor. I'll spend some time with them and give them my best shot at what I think they can do to resolve the issue. I'll do that instead of going to the supervisor and saying, 'Your team is having a problem with you.'

"We'll sit there and talk, and I might say, 'Maybe this is where your supervisor's coming from, maybe this is the problem he has. Here's an approach you might take in helping get the problem solved.' "

You can see humility at work here. There is no exaggeration of self-worth, no desire to blame or rescue, no abuse of power, no need to impress others. Rather, Baumgardner is comfortable within himself, sees people as assets who need to be nurtured and developed, and is willing to build deep, honest relationships with them.

"This belief in equity and fairness is part of my fabric, it's part of me as a being," Baumgardner says. "It's built into this unconditional respect I have for people. You can't have that unconditional respect if you don't have a sense of fairness and believe you are going to try to treat everyone fairly."

There is nothing moralistic about Baumgardner. He is not interested in winning at the expense of others. He is not obsessed with greed, insecurity, or jealousy. Rather, he is comfortable sharing power and trusts people to work out for themselves what is right, just, and fair. Baumgardner's beliefs mesh perfectly with the family business he joined more than a quarter century ago. Donnelly Cor-

poration has built its business strategy on four fundamental concepts, known as the "Scanlon principles," a socioeconomic plan developed by MIT Professor Joseph Scanlon in the 1950s.
 The four principles are:

- Identity. Everyone must understand the business, its vision
  and mission, its customers, competition, products, opportunities, stakeholders' needs, and the market it competes in.
  Once everyone knows what the organization is all about, it
  can develop a clear set of values to guide everyone's actions.
- Participation. The company must empower both individuals
  and teams to achieve their full potential. That means giving
  people the authority and responsibility to implement the
  ideas and solutions they have.
- Equity. Equity requires a fair and balanced return to *all* of
  the organization's stakeholders. But it goes beyond that,
  Baumgardner says. "Any organization that consists of two or
  more people is certain to have issues of fairness that will arise
  from time to time. If these issues are not resolved, they will
  tend to dissipate the team's energy. This saps the energy required to do the work of the organization."
- Competence. An organization cannot hope ever to become a
  model of the productive enterprise unless there is a commitment to achieve high levels of personal, professional, and organizational competence. People, and the organizations they
  work for, are always learning and are always in a state of
  becoming.

"All these principles," says Baumgardner, "when applied together
provide the foundation needed to become world-class."
 As a leader, Baumgardner has tried to institutionalize these beliefs into Donnelly's business strategy. "You must take these values,
these philosophies, these Scanlon principles off the shelf and introduce them into day-to-day relationships and weave them into the
fabric of the organization."
 Why?
 "It's the only way to build a long-term foundation for survival," he
says. "If you want a corporation to survive a hundred-plus years, and

to be strong, and be capable of renewing itself, you have to have the human element more deeply woven into the way you do business. Otherwise, it's like sand in your hand, and you'll never make it through the rough times."

INSTITUTIONAL FAIRNESS AT WORK

Donnelly Corporation is made up of two separate sides—operations and governance. Operations is comprised of everything you'd normally associate with a manufacturing company: procurement, production, research and development, and marketing. Also within the operations side is what is known as the "work structure." Every employee is a member of a team that meets regularly to discuss how work can be done most efficiently.

On the governance side, there is the "equity structure." It is responsible for all aspects of institutional fairness, everything from hearings on work grievances to promotions. Authority is delegated to the representatives, and "unanimous agreement" is the goal. The equity structure plays a central role within the company. It does not eliminate conflicts. Indeed, it does not try to. And its goal is not to create one big happy family. Rather the equity committee comes as close as humanly possible to guaranteeing a fair resolution to disputes.

Says Baumgardner: "The purpose of the equity structure is not to make decisions that satisfy each individual member of the organization, but to make decisions that are in the best interests of the total organization. Only when the best interests of the whole are met can individual needs of employees be met."

Both management and employees take these committees seriously. For example, when Donnelly was struggling through the recession in the late 1980s, senior management revealed the extent of the problem, and then asked the equity committee for suggestions. The committee recommended that the pain be shared across the board, saying there should be salary reductions for all employees who earned more than $40,000 a year. The amount of the reductions ranged from 3 percent for people making $40,000 up to 17 percent for the most senior managers. The proposal was accepted by management. And because employees believe that the company treats them like equal partners, they were willing to cut their own salaries.

Donnelly consistently demonstrates the importance of its employee stakeholders. The equity and governance committees assure employees their voices will be heard, and the company's pay structure guarantees that they will share in Donnelly's success. In addition to constantly surveying the industry, to make sure its people are among the highest paid, the Scanlon plan calls for monthly companywide bonuses, based on corporate profits. The bonuses at Donnelly tend to average 3 to 7 percent of salary. If a loss is experienced, then a negative bonus is "awarded" for the month. Negative bonuses must be made up before a positive bonus is earned and paid.

Building adult relationships, Baumgardner says, is the key to the company's future. He believes his greatest challenge is to increase the "strategic maturity" of the workforce. To make Donnelly's operating philosophy work, the company needs people who can resolve disagreements and conflicts on their own; who follow the rules of the organization; who understand the principles of fairness and equity; and who recognize that responsibilities go along with rights.

Since many people have never worked within a self-governing environment, Donnelly has developed guidelines for them. Among them:

- Be aware when discussions reach a point of diminishing returns.
- Don't let the pressure in a meeting build to the breaking point.
- Care should be taken not to allow win/lose situations to develop.
- Reaching consensus does not mean that every member must be in complete agreement.
- Every member must support whatever decision is finally reached.
- Everyone must take responsibility to voice concerns and share ideas.

If you can get people to understand more deeply the principles of human development, let them grow and mature on the job, and learn the responsibilities of corporate citizenship, greater competence and commitment will result. This approach will unleash the power within people, and then the leader can amplify this power and become a steward of his organization. In Baumgardner's view, the development of employees is the engine driving growth at Donnelly.

There is, unfortunately, one major problem with this approach. It takes time and patience. For example, when the company was thinking of instituting a no-smoking policy back in the 1980s, the most efficient thing would have been for Baumgardner to send out a memo saying that, effective immediately, Donnelly had become a smoke-free company.

But that is not how Donnelly does things. Instead, Baumgardner approached the head of the equity committee and explained that he was getting numerous complaints from people who were afraid of the consequences of secondhand smoke, and he asked for the committee's help in resolving the issue.

The equity committee discussed the problem, which took time. They eventually decided to ask people to voluntarily quit smoking. They established a six-month deadline. More time.

When the deadline had come and gone with minimal compliance, the equity committee recommended setting up smoking rooms, to keep secondhand smoke to a minimum. It later recommended making the smoking rooms as austere as possible, both to keep people from lingering and as an added inducement to get them to quit. In all, it took years to create a smoking policy that everyone in the company was comfortable with. It is the price the company pays for full participation. But given the payoff, it appears a small price.

"In 1980, when I became president, we were a $30 million company," says Baumgardner. "Since that time, Donnelly has been through a recession—the biggest one since the depression—and we've grown to over $300 million in sales, that's twenty percent compound growth. Just recently we acquired the largest mirror company in Europe and reorganized our entire operation. Through it all our values have remained the same."

Still, this performance is no reason to gloat, says Baumgardner, staying in character. "We are still evolving. Donnelly is still in a state of becoming. The company has changed many times over the last eighty-five years. We still have a long way before we can claim to be a model of a productive enterprise."

Our goal is to become a model of the productive enterprise—a company that is known not only for the success we have achieved, as measured in traditional terms, but for how the company has gone about achieving it. We would like to be known for the values that we have, and the way we have applied those values to truly stand out and be a great company.

—DWANE BAUMGARDNER, DONNELLY CORPORATION

FOSTERING ETHICS AND ENTREPRENEURSHIP

Good ethics is good business. Companies with ethical reputations attract the best employees, people who are honest and honorable. They also attract and retain loyal customers, consumers who like doing business with honest and honorable people.

Companies earn their reputation for integrity by making ethics a high priority for each and every employee.

To be successful, good leaders must also surround themselves with entrepreneurs—creative people who work hard and share the risks and rewards of the business.

The challenge is to foster good ethics and good entrepreneurship at the same time.

We are confronted daily with business decisions that put ethical concerns in conflict with short-term economic pressures. These situations are difficult, because people are a confusing mixture of self-interest and altruism. They look out for the good of the group—and of themselves. As a result, the "right" business decision is not always obvious.

Thoughtful leaders are mindful of these conflicting motives, and the complexity of ethics and economics. They deal with this by tapping into both sides of their employees' motivations, and by creating a work culture that values ethical behavior, hard work, and employee ownership.

When Robert Beyster, a former researcher at the government institute Los Alamos, founded Science Applications International Corporation (SAIC) with just $10,000 more than a quarter of a century ago, he was more concerned about having an environment where he could do a good job for the customer than anything else. "I just set

J. ROBERT BEYSTER
Science Applications International Corporation (SAIC)

TITLE: Chairman and Chief Executive Officer

AGE: 70

FAMILY SITUATION: Married; 3 children

EDUCATION: B.S.E. in Engineering and Physics and Ph.D. in Nuclear Physics, University of Michigan

HISTORY: Westinghouse Atomic Power Division, Los Alamos Scientific Laboratory and General Atomic (1950s); established and managed Traveling Wave Linear Accelerator Facility of General Atomic (1957); founded SAIC with $10,000 in 1969 as professional service-oriented government contract research organization

HONORS AND SPECIAL ACCOMPLISHMENTS: Fellow, American Nuclear Society; fellow, American Physical Society; member, Scientific Advisory Group to Director, Strategic Target Planning Staff of Joint Chiefs of Staff; consultant to Defense Science Board; member, National Academy of Engineering. Coauthor of *Slow Neutron Scattering and Thermalization*

HEADQUARTERS: San Diego, California

BUSINESS: High-technology research and engineering

NUMBER OF EMPLOYEES: 18,000

GROSS REVENUE: $1.9 billion

FACT: 91% of SAIC's stock is employee owned.

out to create a good place to work for me, and anybody else who wanted to join me."

That simple objective turned out to be a powerful magnet. Today SAIC is the largest employee-owned technical company in the United States. Its 16,000 employees generate more than $1.6 billion in sales a year by providing diversified research, engineering, software, and systems-integration services to corporations and governments worldwide. SAIC computers and instruments do everything from ride on space shuttles and oceanographic research vessels to keep oil flowing through pipelines under the Arabian desert.

What is the secret to this nonpublicly-held company that produces better than a 20 percent return to investors year in and year out? Ethics, employee ownership, and entrepreneurship.

"Employees are very smart, and you may as well take advantage of that brain power," Beyster says from the Washington office of his San Diego–based company. "We founded the company on the principle that those who contribute their efforts to building the company should share in its ownership commensurate with their contributions." Today, employees own 91 percent of SAIC. This is clearly by design, as a framed saying from Beyster's wife on the wall makes clear: "None of us is as smart as all of us."

Now, some employees hope—and some bosses fear—that employee ownership means lifetime employment, complete with automatic annual raises and no heavy lifting. In other words, a lot of people think that employee ownership is all about benefits, and not about earning those benefits, that it's about opportunities, but no responsibilities. Others in business believe that ethics is something that is soft and mushy. They feel it is impossible to measure, and monitor, and not related to bottom-line profitability.

Both parties are wrong. When you combine ethics and ownership, amazing things happen. How do you get those kinds of results? Beyster says it is a three-part process.

• You focus on the responsibilities of employees. You must create a culture that values hard work and high performance.
• You need to structure your organization so that it rewards those values and not "entitlement" values, such as seniority for its own sake.
• You must create an entrepreneurial environment that unleashes all the potential within your organization, within the confines of ethics and integrity.

Accomplishing these three tasks is not easy, given that employees have altruistic *and* self-interested motivations. Indeed, Beyster believes it requires an organization to follow six specific steps.

Step 1. Make Ethics Everyone's Number-One Responsibility

Beyster knew from the beginning that SAIC's long-term profitability would be maximized if the company acted ethically and with integrity. You simply cannot prosper over the long term by cheating the public and taking advantage of your stakeholders. In the end, unethical behavior will get punished. To make sure SAIC acts ethically, Beyster communicates—clearly and consistently—that ethical behavior is the foremost responsibility of every employee.

"First of all, because it is right," he explains. "But second, unethical behavior costs the enterprise in many ways. People who do things such as hoard information, circulate rumors, or play one person against another hinder teamwork. That adds a bundle to the organization's internal expenses.

"Unethical behavior," he adds, "can also add to external expenses by losing accounts, engendering lawsuits, or inciting fines or other government action."

SAIC constantly briefs employees on ethics, and has set up a hotline so that they can report any ethical irregularities. "We're in the science and technology business, an industry that has had its share of ethical lapses—environmental problems, defense-contract overbilling, and so on," Beyster says. "So we have taken very strong steps to ensure that all our employees understand our commitment to toeing every ethical and legal line."

But Beyster goes even further, making sure his company leads by example.

"During the bidding process for a government contract, we've occasionally, inadvertently, come across some piece of information we shouldn't have," he says. "It may have come to us from some source who didn't know what he was doing, or didn't understand the importance of the information that he gave us. Legally, that put us in a situation analogous to insider trading. In those cases, we've had our lawyers report the incident to the government, and sometimes that has cost us a contract, because the government believed that the information could have given us an unfair advantage.

"In such cases, the short-term costs may seem high, but they are worth every penny," Beyster adds. "We simply have to discourage people from crossing the ethical line in any way, since it could be quite damaging to our company. When we have to make hard decisions, we try to do it on the basis of what's right and what's wrong, and try to do it on the basis of what's best for the customer."

Managers often lack solutions when ethical demands and economic realities conflict. We often justify and rationalize unethical, if not illegal, behavior, in the name of business. Even subtle unethical behavior, such as deceptions and game playing, undermine the trust in an organization. Beyster understands this. That's why he takes the high road, when his company stumbles upon "insider" information. He knows taking the right course of action will result in people feeling better about themselves, their colleagues, and their company.

Beyster assumes most people are willing to do the right thing. But he is not naïve. He knows people can be vulnerable when put in difficult, ethically murky situations. He knows there are unethical people out there, and that there are also ethical people working in unethical environments. That's why he tries to increase people's awareness of the ethical dimensions of business. It is also why he models integrity and leads an integrated, ethical life. He understands the power of reputation.

Beyster is a man of moral toughness. He has the courage to pursue his principles of fairness, honesty, and ethics, even while withstanding the real-world pressures that come from building an entrepreneurial company.

Step 2. Encourage Everybody to Work Hard

With the ethics of the company agreed upon, everybody needs to work hard for the good of the organization. Hard work is important to morale.

"People should contribute to their full potential, especially if they expect a piece of the rock in terms of employee ownership," says Beyster.

"These days when money is tight, a lot of people are trying to handle two or more jobs within a company, simply because the budget is tight and the organization cannot afford a second or third person," he adds. "And when these people see others abusing the system by coasting, or working some angle to get by doing the minimum, that incites resentment and ill will. Once again, teamwork and camaraderie suffer, and internal expenses go up."

Initially, Beyster wanted to surround himself with people who held the same values as he, people who were totally motivated by the work and work environment and loved what they were doing. But his beliefs changed over time. He realized that by focusing exclusively on finding those people he was ignoring another potentially qualified group of employees, people who were constantly looking for "what's in it for me."

Says Beyster: "They were simply more motivated by carrots, and when we gave them something they did just fine."

Over time Beyster grew to be comfortable with both groups. What he can't stand is people who have an "entitlement philosophy," and are totally "out for themselves."

Step 3. Promote an Active Interest
in the Organization

The best way to ensure that people work harder, smarter, and ethically, says Beyster, is to make sure they are interested in their work and in their organization.

"We are always looking for ways to give employees a say in their jobs, and in ways for their ideas to be aired," he says. "We have over a hundred committees in our company, and they are not just for show. They meet and make changes. The employees on those committees feel more a part of the company. I also tell employees that if they can't get their idea heard through normal channels to bring it to me, or any other senior manager, directly."

But that is just one way Beyster tries to promote interest within his organization. The other is to let employees have a direct stake in SAIC's profitability.

"We really encourage people to be entrepreneurial within the company," he says. "Most technology companies our size have about five hundred contracts. We have about five thousand. And while the average contract is $300,000, we have a lot of small contracts, some as small as $25,000. If somebody wants us to do something, even if it's fairly small, we will do it, if it might lead to something else."

Beyster says he does business this way to push ownership as far down the line as possible. "Because we have five thousand contracts, it means we have a large number of profit-or-loss centers. That's five thousand opportunities for an employee—or usually a team of employees—to act as entrepreneurs," he says. "Letting people manage the risks and successes of these contracts really helps to get them interested in the health of the company as a whole."

Step 4. Use Equity to Reward Performance

Letting employees have profit-and-loss responsibility is good if you want them to take a vested interest in the company. Giving them equity is better because it provides two tangible benefits. First, it is a type of compensation that lets workers reap a part of what they helped sow. In a word, it's fair. Second, it's a kind of motivation, a carrot designed to have people work harder and smarter. This is vitally important at a company such as SAIC, where 77 percent of employees have advanced degrees in such things as geology, oceanography, and nuclear engineering, and tend to care as much for their disciplines as they do about their company.

Ownership gives these people a tangible incentive to care more about the company. They know if they do they will share in the increased harvest. "From the very beginning, we have used ownership of the company to reward people for the high-performance work we are trying to encourage," Beyster says. "What we most needed at the beginning were contracts. So we said anyone who brings in a $100,000 contract can buy a certain amount of stock. And you could buy a significant piece of the company for not very much money back then. In the years since, the rules governing stock purchases have gotten much more complex, but the basic principle has remained the same.

"We do reward seniority, through 401-K and other retirement plans, and if an employee has been with us for ten or fifteen years, that can add up to hundreds of thousands of dollars for retirement," he adds. "But we continue to make a real effort to reward performance. When people accomplish something major, we often use stock instead of cash as a bonus. I don't mind people making a lot of money, if the company is successful."

Beyster realizes giving away ownership is a difficult concept for many leaders, especially those who founded their companies. That's why he has started the Foundation for Enterprise Development to explain the benefits of employee ownership. It is a difficult sell. One of the fears that leaders of rapidly growing companies have is that if they don't own at least 51 percent of their company's stock, they will lose control.

"Most of these guys have 90 percent of the stock, or more," Beyster says. "I've told some of them, 'Why don't you try owning 80 percent and see what happens. And then 70 percent, and go down to 60 percent, and take it slowly and see if you can give it to people you feel comfortable with,' "

Beyster thinks differently from many leaders. He knows everyone is responsible for the ultimate success and failure of the business. He believes that if you share the wealth other people will help you become successful. Yet he is the first to tell you that if you measure your success solely on how much money you make then your salary becomes your only measure of personal success.

Step 5. Set an Example

Beyster knows his plan of using equity to reward performance will only work if people believe it is fair. If the senior managers—including the founder—of SAIC reserve most of the stock for themselves, then there is not much incentive for anyone else.

"Currently, I own about 2 percent of the outstanding shares," Beyster says. "So you could say that I've lost 98 percent of the company since I founded it. But in fact I've gained tremendously. You cannot take percentages to the supermarket, only dollars, and 100 percent of something very small is not much, but 2 percent of something very big is a lot. By 'giving away the store,' I've made the company grow far faster than it would have and I've increased my own earnings. That wasn't my strategy back when I started the company. I just wanted to make sure people were treated fairly and rewarded for their work. But that is the way it has worked out.

"My reasoning back in the beginning was that I should demonstrate a nongreedy attitude," he adds. "I didn't mind other people making money, if the company as a whole was successful, and I figured the best way to show people I was serious about this was to give loyal, high performers equity in return for their work. If you set up the right culture—where employee ownership is seen as a reward, not an entitlement—I really believe that it does help the company grow faster, making everyone from top to bottom better off in the long run."

Beyster understands that people need to be recognized and rewarded fairly for their contributions, that these contributions must be valued and perceived as equitable, and that people have the right to share in the financial success of their company. In return, employees must understand the organization's financial obligations and multiple stakeholders, and give their full effort at work.

Step 6. Don't Get Cynical

In business, there are natural tensions between ethics and entrepreneurship.

"Someone once said about democracy that it is the worst form of government, except for all the others. Well, employee ownership is like democracy," Beyster says. "Yes, it can be abused. If you don't work hard at setting up the right culture, you can give employees stock and they won't appreciate it. Even when you've done everything you can to avoid that, it can still happen. It is easy to get cynical."

But it's important that the leader doesn't, adds Beyster, who has seen his company's earnings triple and sales rise more than fourfold in the past decade, as a result of his sticking to what he believes. "The alternatives—the pure profit motive, the drive to impress Wall Street every quarter, the excessive CEO salaries—destroy the inner fabric of a company." Employee ownership isn't perfect, not by a long shot, but as SAIC's numbers show it's better than any other way of dividing the pie.

HAVING COURAGE

A leader must stand for something.

As public leader and private citizen she is the same person wherever she goes. She knows what is important in life and develops a set of principles that guides the way she lives. We call this approach to living character. Showing courage is the ultimate expression of character. Being courageous means standing up for what you believe, and questioning the status quo, even when you are confronted with angry dissenters.

Leaders can either stimulate or stifle this courage within their organizations. In many organizations, people are attacked for speaking their minds. After being treated this way for a while they become resentful or passive, and unwilling to take risks.

But organizations need as many acts of courage as they can muster. Courageous people help an organization to ask tough questions, sharpen its ideas, and renew itself. This is why successful leaders teach others how to be courageous.

This isn't easy. Indeed, it takes courage for the leader to surround herself with courageous people.

The phrase "federal bureaucrats" conjures up images of dowdy men and women in gray suits sitting behind desks piled high with papers.

But the scene in Vidor, Texas, was out of a Clint Eastwood movie, not the bureaucrat's handbook. Federal officials, holding walkie-talkies and cellular phones, positioned federal marshals and state troopers around the public housing authority in East Texas, which had a long and troubled history of excluding African Americans. They were going to integrate the facility for the first time.

ROBERTA ACHTENBERG
U.S. Department of Housing and Urban Development

TITLE: Assistant Secretary for Fair Housing and Equal Opportunity

AGE: 44

FAMILY SITUATION: Life partner; 1 child

EDUCATION: B.A., University of California at Berkeley; law degree, University of Utah Law School

HISTORY: Civil-rights attorney for 15 years; teaching fellow at Stanford Law School; Dean, New College of California School of Law; San Francisco Board of Supervisors (1990–93)

HONORS AND SPECIAL ACCOMPLISHMENTS: 1989 Management Volunteer of the Year, United Way of the Bay Area; 1993 California State Senate's Woman of the Year for Third Senate District; Executive Director, National Center for Lesbian Rights

HEADQUARTERS: Washington, D.C.

BUSINESS: Enforcing United States Fair Housing Law

NUMBER OF EMPLOYEES: 772 (155 in headquarters; 617 in field offices)

BUDGET: $76 million

Attorney Roberta Achtenberg, Assistant Secretary of Housing and Urban Development (HUD) was the "bureaucrat" in charge of the operation. She was there "because it is my job."

"Every American has a right to fair housing. The right to live where you choose, to raise a family, to own a home, in dignity and without fear of discrimination," she explains. "It cannot be denied to anyone because of race, color, national origin, religion, sex, familial status, or handicap."

Her mission is simple to state, simple to understand. Accomplishing it is not simple. There is nothing more personal to an American than where he lives. Most people choose to live in communities where the residents share their beliefs, and look and act as they do. People will fight—sometimes legally, sometimes not—to make sure they can live the way they want.

To take people on, when they act contrary to law, takes courage.

Such courage involves risk, a willingness to speak out despite potential costs, and requires a certain amount of daring, as well as confidence in yourself and your opinions.

Roberta Achtenberg, who is in charge of HUD's office of fair housing and equal opportunity, is such a courageous leader. She is a product of immigrant parents who helped put her through college and law school, and taught her that she owed it to herself, her family, and her community to eliminate injustice. Although she never had a formal plan for how her life would turn out, no one who knew her is surprised that Achtenberg, who in school was voted most likely to succeed, has turned out to be so accomplished.

Achtenberg knows who she is and what she stands for—equal opportunity for all. Throughout her life, she has cultivated a well-developed conscience, an internal guidance system that helps her make decisions. So it was only natural that she became a civil-rights attorney, and was serving as an elected member of the San Francisco Board of Supervisors, when she was appointed to HUD.

It is one thing to have principles, but another to put those principles into action. Too many leaders spend their lives taking actions that are inconsistent with what they say they believe. Achtenberg is not one of them. It didn't take long, once she was in Washington, for Achtenberg to start living up to her words. She began with her own department. After all, how can you stand for fair housing, when your own house is not in order?

The team she inherited needed a lot of support. When Achtenberg took over her job, she found a staff that had been exploited and was self-doubting—as a result of being undermined by their previous manager every time they expressed an opinion contrary to his. They were timid and poorly trained. "It's as if they and their work had been devalued significantly over a period of time."

This was the place where Achtenberg would begin her work. "Charity, after all," she says, "begins at home."

"I don't think it is good enough to say that our goal is equal opportunity, and not try to figure out how to make our staff into a team, and see that the team gets the kind of support it needs," Achtenberg explains. She would show her employees what she had learned about courage—about the need to speak out, to be active and responsible, and to stand up for what you believe.

It is hard to take unpopular positions, question conventional wisdom, and push up against the existing power structure. It is even harder to convince others to go along with you when you do. But if HUD's fair-housing office was going to be successful, it needed a full team of courageous people. Achtenberg knew that meant she would have to instill trust and safety back into the department.

"I had to constantly reassure members of this family that there was a reason to trust, and that there would be a free and fair exchange of ideas," she said.

Achtenberg also knew that organizations can either stimulate or stifle courage. It is easy to dismiss, exclude, or pass people over for promotion when their ideas threaten their boss. Indeed, that is exactly what had happened under the last head of the department. But in today's workplace, organizations need as many individual acts of courage as they can muster. These acts allow the organization to regenerate itself, to ask tough questions, and to move forward. When done well, these courageous initiatives sharpen ideas, elevate commitment, and make the organization a better place to work by stimulating healthy organizational change.

You could see the effect of Achtenberg's changes in the actions her people took in Vidor, Texas, a town with a history of racism, that had served as host to the Klu Klux Klan.

"In late 1993, the secretary and I decided the department had to take over the housing authority," Achtenberg explains. "During the previous eighteen months, a number of African Americans had tried to live in Vidor, but had been driven out because of racism. In fact, HUD was a defendant in a lawsuit that said the department had engaged in all kinds of practices that had actually furthered discrimination and promoted segregation. Indeed, a federal district court had found us guilty of doing the exact opposite of what we were supposed to do.

"Our predecessors had stonewalled," Achtenberg explains. "We decided that the best thing to do was seize the housing authority and make it safe for African-American residents who were living in neighboring communities to move to Vidor. We wanted to turn it into an example of a place where people could learn to live together, rather than an example of how one race could dominate another."

She knew deep inside that seizing the housing authority was the right thing to do; still there were a couple of moments of hesitation. It's lonely standing up for what you believe is right. It's only human to feel that way. But having acknowledged those feelings, you can't be too cautious, conforming, or compromising. You must remain a strong, centered person.

"By taking the action we contemplated, we recognized that we would be putting other people's lives at risk. My job was to do all the groundwork to make sure that people would be able to move in, that there would be adequate security, high-quality housing, and that the schools would be receptive to the children.

"I needed to go and personally speak with each one of the families that were going to move in to satisfy myself that they were doing this freely. We are talking about very poor people, and when I saw where they lived, there was no doubt in my mind that they were putting themselves into better surroundings. Still, I had to make a judgment about whether or not these people were knowingly doing what they were doing. I had to make sure that they knew what the risks were, even though we were going to do everything we could to protect them. In the end, when I called the Secretary of HUD and the Attorney General, I felt great with my decision. These people knew they were taking a chance, but they also knew this is what they wanted to do."

Achtenberg connects with the heart and the pain of others. She saw the struggle in very personal terms. One of the families that was thinking of moving into Vidor was a single mother with four small children. Achtenberg, who is also a parent, spent a great deal of time agonizing over what the decision to move into an openly hostile environment would mean to that particular family.

"I have never been that poor, but still I could identify to some extent with the struggle these people were going through. I think that is very important in this line of work. If you ever get to the point where you can't identify with the people you are supposed to be trying to help, it is time to do something else.

"This woman with the four small children wanted to move into Vidor because the schools in the district were better. We had made a special arrangement with the superintendent to have one of her kids tested immediately, to see if he needed to be put into a special class. So she was trying to improve her children's lot, but she was in agony wondering whether by doing it she would be putting their lives in jeopardy."

Today that family is one of twenty African-American families who live in Vidor, and there has not been a significant incident since they moved in. "There is not a day that goes by that I don't think of that place, and the fact that I'm based in Washington. It was the right thing to do, but it was also right for us to be extraordinarily cautious and not foolhardy about putting other people's lives in danger."

There were many acts of courage here: Achtenberg and her staff certainly acted courageously. They responded to a crisis, took a risk, and challenged the majority in Vidor. But so did the African-American families who were willing to move into the community. They confronted raw prejudice and had the courage to pursue a better life.

STANDING UP FOR WHAT IS RIGHT

But courage is not just about standing up for things you believe. It is also about doing what is right for people whom you don't care for, when there is an important issue at stake. Achtenberg is willing to do that as well.

For example, in Berkeley, California, three vocal opponents of a group home for recovering addicts were under investigation by HUD after a fair-housing group filed a complaint against them. A similar situation occurred later that year in Seattle. A citizens' group fighting against the location of a community housing facility for recovering alcoholics and drug addicts was subjected to demands for its membership lists and financial information by a HUD investigator. In addition, they were asked to sign a "conciliation agreement" pledging not to speak against the project, or to contact elected officials to oppose it. Enormous penalties were threatened for failure to sign the agreement.

When Achtenberg discovered what was going on, she took immediate steps to stop it. She knew deep in her heart that the rights of these vocal opponents were being violated, and that the Constitution protected them as well. She issued a directive to her staff and held a press conference, where she announced HUD would no longer allow investigations involving such things as leafleting, holding neighborhood meetings, or writing letters to the editor or elected officials, activities that were all covered by the First Amendment.

"When confronted with a complaint that someone relentlessly ha-
rassed and intimidated a neighbor, HUD will stand up for the
proposition that there is no place for such behavior in America,"
Achtenberg said.

"When confronted with a claim that neighbors engaged in peace-
ful political protest, however, HUD will stand up just as strongly for
the proposition that in America people have a right to participate
actively in the public affairs of their community. From now on,
[HUD] investigators in the field will have to make a very clear showing that the facts being alleged in a complaint, if true, rise to the
level of intimidation, interference, or coercion within the meaning
of the federal Fair Housing Act," Achtenberg added.

Admitting her department was wrong took courage. She also
knew that you must be credible when you express your courage. You
must temper your personal views, acknowledge the legitimacy of op-
posing positions, and be prudent and fair-minded, while still acting
courageously and with conviction.

THE COURAGE TO BE YOURSELF

Perhaps Achtenberg's greatest act of courage was in becoming the
first openly lesbian federal official to be confirmed by Congress as
an assistant secretary of a federal agency. Despite an open debate in
Congress, and public ridicule from the infamous Senator Jesse
Helms, Achtenberg's nomination passed. Thinking back over the
experience, Achtenberg says: "People will treat you the same as anyone else, if you are open and respectful of who you are."

Letting the world know she is a lesbian is consistent with who
Roberta Achtenberg is. "Ever since I realized I was a lesbian, it just
never made any sense for me to act otherwise," she says. "I never
said, Golly, the right thing to do is be out. It was much more like I
couldn't imagine being any other way."

Achtenberg knows who she is and who she is not. It is important
for her to be a "whole person, being the same person at home and at
work." She believes you cannot live different rules and values in your
private and public life. Her coming-out experience is an example of
her wholeness. Part of being courageous means being demanding of
yourself and others. That explains why she holds people in privi-

leged positions to a higher standard. She is not tolerant of people in high places who are gay and who do not come out.

"In a way, it is an act of betrayal," she says. "They are in a different position than people who essentially are prevented from coming out because, if they did, they would be putting themselves—or their children—in jeopardy."

Being demanding of yourself can lead to personal risks. Achtenberg imposes high expectations on herself, and has found others can be even more demanding. It is a burden to be a role model. Many people put her on a pedestal, she says, and don't acknowledge her flaws.

"I understand that it is important for there to be people to look up to," she acknowledges. "But having people look up to you can be difficult. I wouldn't trade my life for anybody's, but I do have to say that I think among the hardest parts of my life is the fact that some people think I am different from them, and that can get burdensome."

Achtenberg doesn't think she is better than anyone else. In fact, she believes everyone is capable of extraordinary acts of courage. She says this with a sense of authenticity and humility. To Achtenberg, security is not based on possessions, positions, credentials, or comparisons with others. Rather it flows from her ability to follow her principles, no matter what the obstacles. It takes courage to do what Achtenberg has set out to accomplish. Her goal is nothing less than changing the way America works, believes, and behaves.

"The country, in my view, lives with a dissonance that I think at some point will become unbearable," Achtenberg explains. "We say we are for fairness, justice, and equality; that we're the greatest democracy on earth and that this is a place where a person can become anything.

"But at the same time, there is a very dark underside to the American psyche, which thinks very different and contradictory things. That part is racist, prejudiced, and has helped build systems that exclude whole groups of people. We preach one thing, and often do another, and that dissonance is defeating.

"I want to try to bring those things a little bit closer together, and I don't think the way you do that is by creating less opportunity for people, but by creating more opportunities for those who have been systematically excluded from enjoying those opportunities."

And that, of course, takes courage.

PUTTING INTEGRITY
INTO ACTION

There's an ethical twist to every business decision. Good leaders remind us to pay attention to that fact.

Most people want to be ethical. But business is a constant struggle involving conflicts and compromises, and doing the right thing is not always easy. So when it comes to ethics, the leader must show his people the way.

Every successful leader has a moral compass—a gut sense of what is right and wrong. The challenge is to put these principles to work, both on and off the job.

The best leaders walk their talk. There's a connection between their values and their behavior on the job. The successful leader is quick to jump into the ethical morass. He confronts tough issues head on, speaks passionately about what is right, and is the first one to question those who justify unethical behavior in the guise of "good business."

None of us possesses pristine ethics that have never been relaxed. But when it comes to integrity, there is only one road, the high road.

The seeds of Gregory E. Favre's moral integrity were planted early, back when he was growing up in the Deep South. His parents brought him up to believe in fairness and the importance of certain timeless virtues: Truth is better than dishonesty; fairness is better than inequity; integrity is better than immorality.

"My father started out as a local politician," explains Favre, who is now executive editor of *The Sacramento Bee*, as well as Vice President of News for McClatchy Newspapers. "He bought the local newspaper

GREGORY E. FAVRE
The Sacramento Bee

TITLE: Executive Editor

AGE: 59

FAMILY SITUATION: Married; 2 children

EDUCATION: 2 years at Tulane and Louisiana State University

HISTORY: Grew up working on family newspaper in Mississippi; Assistant Sports Editor, *Atlanta Journal* (1957–63); Managing Editor, *Dayton Daily News* (1963–69); Editor, *Palm Beach Post* (1969–72); News Director, WPLG-TV Miami (1973–75); Editor, *Corpus Christi Call-Times* (1975–76); Managing Editor, *Chicago Daily News* (1977–78); Managing Editor, *Chicago Sun-Times* (1978–84); joined *The Bee* in 1984

HOBBY: Making desserts

HONORS AND SPECIAL ACCOMPLISHMENTS: President, American Society of Newspaper Editors; News Executive of the Year (1992), California Press Association; Board, Inter American Press Association; past president, California Society of Newspaper Editors; Board of Advisors, Newspaper Management Center at Northwestern University; Board of Advisors, University of California Graduate School of Journalism; Board of Journalism Advisors, Foundation for American Communications

HEADQUARTERS: Sacramento, California

BUSINESS: Newspaper publishing

NUMBER OF EMPLOYEES: 1,100 full-time; 1,200 part-time (excluding carriers)

CIRCULATION: 280,000 daily; 355,000 Sunday

FACTS: The first issue of *The Sacramento Bee* (then *The Daily Bee*) was published February 3, 1857. In 1992 *The Bee* received 2 Pulitzer Prizes, the paper's first since 1935.

later in his life. He instilled values in each of his ten children. Although he was a white man who grew up in southern Mississippi, he went to a black church much of his adult life. He was very outspoken, and very strong in his beliefs, and he was willing to stand up for them. I think he was probably one of the first editors in the state of Mississippi to run a picture on page one of a black who wasn't arrested, or wasn't in sports."

These principles of justice and equality were lived every day in the Favre home, and Gregory Favre has retained his parents' passion for ethics and integrity throughout his entire life. Today, they are illustrated in his day-to-day behavior, and the business decisions he makes. His beliefs about right and wrong are extremely important to him on and off the job.

"Three things you don't fool with are my family, my newspaper, and my integrity, and I really mean that," Favre says from his office at the paper. "You can call me a lot of things, but I never, ever, have done anything in this business that I'm ashamed of. I might have done some things wrong. And I've made mistakes, God knows I've made mistakes, but I've never done anything I'm really ashamed of."

Favre cares deeply about journalistic ethics. To Favre actions speak louder than words, and he has shown that consistently through the years when his principles have been tested. He makes sure that his actions are consistent with those beliefs, even if it costs him his job.

"I had worked for Cox newspapers for about fourteen years, and was editor at *The Palm Beach Post,* when in 1972 Mr. Cox decided that all his newspapers would endorse Richard Nixon for President. Our paper had been very strongly anti-Nixon, very strongly anti-Vietnam, and had believed that Watergate was more than a simple break-in. So it was a very obvious choice for me, once we couldn't convince Mr. Cox that our paper shouldn't run the endorsement. I quit. I had a wife, and two young kids, and no job.

"He had the right to do what he did. Mr. Cox owned the newspaper. But my feeling was I couldn't be true to myself if I continued to work there, so I left. When Rupert Murdoch bought the paper in Chicago (*The Chicago Sun-Times,* where Favre was managing editor), I also left. I just couldn't work for him. I still had my wife, and my two kids were in high school and college at the time, so thank God I was able to get another job. I have a good wife, who's managed to support me in these decisions, and two kids, who when they were old enough to understand, were willing to go along with what I had to do."

These experiences have obviously had an effect on Favre, the leader. He is not someone who easily rationalizes away an unethical decision because it is in the company's best interest. As he is confronted with business dilemmas, he realizes that there is an ethical element in virtually every business decision he makes. With each one he is challenged to reinvent what it means to be an ethical leader.

SHOWING THE WAY

The leader's role in setting the ethical tone of the organization is critical. People spend an inordinate amount of time watching what their leaders do. And if those leaders don't act ethically, you can be sure that the organization won't either.

Employees want to be proud of their leaders. They want to be led by people who maintain the highest ethical standards, not someone who is likely to cheat or deceive them or others. People learn from the leader's ethics and take comfort and guidance from them. Ultimately, the organization is a reflection of the leader's ethics, the people he chooses to hire, and the way he conducts business.

Favre models his ethical behavior every day. He leads by example. There is a sense of moral leadership about him. He puts aside his personal ambitions for the sake of his reporters and the newspaper as a whole. He gets his ego satisfaction out of the paper's performance.

Modeling the right behavior is just the beginning. He also takes great pains to make sure that employees understand the importance of integrity, and that they build ethical relationships inside and outside the newsroom. Ultimately, those relationships are more powerful than a list of desired principles, or an ethical code.

Favre knows there are lots of opportunities every day for him to walk the talk and get his ethics right or wrong, and he holds himself to the highest standard. When prospective employees ask what it is like to work at *The Bee*, Favre has them talk directly to employees. Their word has more credibility than his. What those potential candidates are told is Favre keeps his word, acts consistently, admits mistakes, and treats all employees fairly.

The way he interacts with colleagues serves as a guide for employees, giving them an interpersonal benchmark, ultimately leading to a healthier company. To ensure that happens, Favre tries hard to create the right working environment so that his employees can do their best work in the most ethical way possible. This is particularly difficult in a newspaper environment, where there are pressures of daily deadlines, and two hundred people with two hundred egos all competing to be on page one.

Given this situation, Favre—who defines his job as being 50 percent psychologist, 50 percent priest—works hard to show employees how ethical standards apply to their day-to-day jobs.

"About once a month, we have a brown-bag lunch, and I'll invite twenty to twenty-five of our people, and I will pose two or three ethical questions that we have been faced with here at the paper. We will discuss them and we will try to get a sense of what the staff feels, and what I feel about these issues.

"We had one not too long ago that involved an incident in Somalia. There was a picture on the wire of a group of Somalians dragging the body of a dead American serviceman through the streets. At the time we were in the middle of a very heated, very bad, racial situation in town. We had a fire bomber who had bombed a synagogue, the NAACP headquarters, the Japanese-American League, and a Japanese-American councilman's house. In all, there had been five fire bombings, all racially motivated. The community was in a state of high tension and fear.

"We decided not to run the picture, because of the racial overtones. You had ten or twelve black Somalians laughing over the death of a white serviceman. I thought it painted an unfair picture of the emotions of many Somalians. And I thought it would exaggerate the racial tensions in our community. We discussed this and at least half of the twenty-five people there would have run that picture with no questions asked.

"My feeling is that as an editor you have to do what is right," Favre adds. "We have a policy here of protecting teenagers, and very often we are the only media in town who will not give the name of a teenager arrested for a crime. In the fire-bomber example, the person who was arrested was only seventeen. Everybody in town used his name, with one exception, *The Sacramento Bee*. That's another one we debated, and I was in the minority among the staff."

As these debates show, there is almost always creative tension in the newsroom. Favre is not afraid to confront the tension directly, although sometimes, as he will concede, his temper can exacerbate the problem.

"I worry a great deal about whether or not I have enough tolerance," he says. "I have a temper. I used to worry about it when I was much younger, and less so now. For years, there was a hole in a wall at *The Atlanta Journal*, from where I hit it when I was assistant sports editor." Favre acknowledges his dark side and does what he can to keep it from taking over.

"My tolerance level goes down, as employees rise through the ranks. I have a great deal of tolerance, when it comes to dealing with a reporter just starting out. I have less tolerance for mistakes when it comes to her city editor, even less for my managing editor, and I have less tolerance for my mistakes than I do for anybody's. Still, my feeling is that if you can control your anger you can use it to make yourself a better manager." In Favre's case, that translates to his being as tough as he can be professionally, and as soft as he can be personally.

BUSINESS AND PERSONAL ETHICS
SHOULD BE THE SAME

People tend to compartmentalize their lives, separating business values and personal values. They somehow believe it is a good idea to keep the two apart. For the best leaders, however, there is no sharp distinction between personal and business ethics. They have a single, concrete code of ethics that covers all situations. For these leaders, a strong connection exists between one's personal, deeply held values and the way those values are played out in practice on the job.

Gregory E. Favre is consistent. He does not apply different values or standards to situations depending on whom he is talking to. He has a personal code of ethics, a collection of values and beliefs that form the underpinning of how he thinks, how he reacts to others, and how he conducts his life.

Favre has developed a deep moral and psychological integrity, a kind of wholeness as a person. He balances the traits of his head (problem solving, logic, initiative) with the traits of his heart (courage, generosity, fairness, idealism, compassion). This wholeness allows him to rely on both parts of himself and confront head on any potential ethical problem by using a wide range of skills.

Favre's ability to link his personal and professional lives has enabled him to walk the fine line between newspaperman and senior

manager with profit-and-loss responsibility. Because he has confidence in his own ability, he is not afraid of the conflicts inherent
between those two roles.

For example, Favre believes that newspapers have an overwhelming obligation not only to serve their communities but to be fair. So
when his paper slams a group of car dealers, or takes on the local
real-estate industry, he feels compelled to stand before their trade
groups to explain why his paper did what it did, when they ask. That
means standing up for what he believes in and taking the heat. He
can do that because he knows deep inside he made the right decision. He knows in his heart that when confronted with tough issues,
good people will do the right thing if they rely on the principles of
integrity.

"We are trying to make this the kind of newspaper where people
in every department can talk to one another," he says. "In most
newspapers, the editorial department will wall itself off from everybody else—advertising, production, and circulation. But I don't do
that. When the general manager of the company and I have a clash
of egos, or a clash of opinions about what we are trying to do, we listen to each other, or all sides, and we make a collective decision.

"Every Tuesday and Thursday, fifteen of us—including another
five people from the newsroom—meet, and we talk about common
problems and common opportunities. We understand and respect
each other's territory. We understand that there's a separation of
church and state in the news business between editorial and advertising. There always was and there always will be. But that doesn't
mean that we have to fight with each other, and it doesn't mean that
we can't cooperate together to try to make this a better newspaper."
Indeed, out of these Tuesday and Thursday sessions has come the
decision to start special sections to serve the reader better.

Favre believes that most people want to be ethical. The secret is to
create an environment that allows them to experience their natural
tendencies. Yet he also realizes that being ethical is not always easy,
and that it often requires substituting short-term losses for long-term
rewards. The most challenging ethical choices occur day to day
when the immediate cost is evident (fewer newspapers sold) and the
long-term payoff, or advantage, seems remote.

But paying the price for ethics today is a way of making an investment in a longer-lasting and larger good down the road. The decision to do just that is having a tangible pay-off at *The Sacramento Bee*. Circulation is growing, at a time when most newspapers are just happy to be treading water, and the paper has won two Pulitzer Prizes under Favre's direction.

But Favre points to something else, when you ask him for an example that proves his approach to leadership works. "A few years ago, the school administration in town did a survey, and one of the things they asked was 'What institution in this community do you respect the most?' Some 60 percent of the people said *The Sacramento Bee*. Now, 60 percent of the people in town probably don't agree with us politically. We're probably to the left of many of our readers. Still, 60 percent of them respect us more than any other institution. To me, that was the best thing that could happen to this newspaper, because it says that we're serving our readers well.

"We are living at a time when communities as we knew them are breaking up; public places are becoming scarce; values are disappearing. Newspapers are probably the last hope of keeping people together," Favre believes. "We have to learn to produce newspapers that are expert, but not aloof; warm, but not cute; informal and fun, but not haphazard; agenda setting, but not patronizing."

COMMUNITY

At a time when there is a weakening of commitments, when diversity and technology are pushing us away from one another, when there is ever-growing cynicism and self-interest, and a breakdown in the social compact between individuals and organizations, people need communities more than ever.

It's an inherent need. We are community-forming animals. We look for opportunities to belong, achieve, and learn together. Communities help us feel safe and hopeful and give us a sense of pride. They allow us to live and work in harmony with each other. People are willing to invest a lot of themselves to feel this way.

There are all kinds of communities—factories, offices, volunteer organizations, government agencies, sports teams, churches, the list is endless. We are held together by neighborhoods, occupations, and political affiliations. Each one of these communities is a human enterprise, a complex living system. In each case, people come together to pursue a common purpose, to make a contribution, and to create value for themselves and others.

All these different communities have one thing in common. They need leaders. Leaders are community builders. They understand why people need community. They know how to tap into the power of community. And they know how to build community by inspiring the commitment of others. Their job is to get the most out of the communities they lead.

Healthy communities are networks of relationships—mature adult relationships of diverse people who come together to form common bonds. They share aspirations and concerns and solve complex problems. These relationships are built little by little and work best when people uphold their commitments and responsibilities to each other. The leader knows those relationships must be managed well, or the community will not survive for very long. His job is to create an atmosphere of trust and cooperation, with an emphasis on hard work and mutual respect.

Leaders build communities at many different levels. The workplace is the most central institution. Employees are its principal members. But the workplace cannot be an island of self-interest. It must interact and support the larger community. It is the bridge that links people to their surroundings. These surroundings include a larger community of customers, shareholders, suppliers, and families. And around that community lie our civic institutions, society and the environment, a mutually interdependent and supportive network.

We need mature leaders—for business, in government, in the church—who see the value in building healthy, socially responsible enterprises, and who interact well with their multiple publics. These are leaders who have a broad perspective on life and business, who are concerned about others, and have a deep appreciation for community life, the environment, and the long-term sustainability of society.

The business rationale for building community is clear. Employees want to work in supportive environments; customers want to do business with companies that are solid and responsible; healthy organizations produce more value for their shareholders over the long term; and society needs them if we are going to survive and prosper.

Our collective sense of community is what binds us together.

It takes a mature leader to build a healthy community. The leader's understanding of himself and the world around him provides the foundation on which the community is built. There are few finer examples of maturity than Leith Anderson, pastor of the Wooddale Church.

For any community to work, people must feel a sense of pride.

That is Shirley DeLibero's area of expertise. As head of New Jersey Transit, the country's third-largest bus and rail operation, she has instilled her people with a sense of pride and holds them responsible for hard work. The results have been truly amazing.

Even though the workplace is a small microcosm of a much larger whole, when a leader is able to forge a true sense of community, as Jack Callahan of Allstate does, the leader can transform his entire organization into a very powerful entity. Leaders like James Rouse, who built the Rouse Development Company and now heads the Enterprise Foundation, know the importance of giving back to the entire community, and leaders like Horst Rechelbacher, chief executive of Aveda, understand the importance of protecting the environment.

CULTIVATING MATURITY

It takes a mature leader to build a community. Leaders who are mature build the strongest commitments and inspire the highest performance within their organizations.

The mature leader starts with a sense of purpose—a deep set of convictions about life—that helps him see what's important in business.

He leads with a positive outlook. To him, life's cup is half full, not half empty. By focusing on people's positive contributions, he taps into the best they have to offer.

The mature leader has an intuitive sense about people. He appreciates their desire to become something more than they are, and knows they want to be part of something bigger than themselves. By fulfilling these needs, he is able to inspire commitment.

The mature leader also understands the world around him. He is keenly aware of his customers and his markets, and he knows how the environment influences the health of his organization.

Ultimately, the true test of his maturity is how he manages success and his own ego.

It's Sunday morning, about nine-fifteen in Eden Prairie, Minnesota. Traffic has been increasing steadily along Shady Oak Road ever since about eight-thirty. It's now at its peak. By nine-thirty over three thousand people will be gathered inside Wooddale Church listening to pastor Leith Anderson.

Why have all these people come to the church with the two-hundred-foot spire? Many of them are searching for something. There is a void in their lives and they are looking to the church to help fill it. But while that may be the initial lure, it is the people in the church community,

---

LEITH ANDERSON
Wooddale Church

TITLE: Senior Pastor

AGE: 50

FAMILY SITUATION: Married; 4 children

EDUCATION: B.A., Bradley University; M. Div., Denver Seminary; D. Min., Fuller Seminary

HISTORY: Youth Pastor and Senior Pastor, Calvary Baptist Church, Longwood, Colorado (1967–76); Senior Pastor at Wooddale since 1977

HONORS AND SPECIAL ACCOMPLISHMENTS: Author of *Dying for Change, A Church for the Twenty-first Century*, and *Winning the Values War*; coauthor of *Mastering Church Management, Who's in Charge*

BUSINESS: Church

NUMBER OF EMPLOYEES: 50, including 13 full-time pastors

BUDGET: $3.4 million

FACTS: 3,500 people attend services at Wooddale on a typical Sunday morning

---

and the man who leads them, that keep them coming back, not only on Sunday but throughout the rest of the week as well.

When Leith Anderson became pastor twenty years ago, he was the youngest person on Wooddale's staff. He is now the oldest. Anderson is a man who understands himself, people, and the culture of America. He is an optimistic realist. Anderson is able to see what is both good and painful to people and knows what makes up the true essence of a successful life. He is everything you would expect of a good pastor. What you might not expect is that Anderson is a national expert on church management. And he is both an entrepreneur and a good businessman.

Consider:

Anderson knows about marketing. Concerned that his huge five-thousand-member congregation wasn't responding to the needs of the entire community, he held focus groups shortly after Easter to find out why non-churchgoing Christians who lived nearby in suburban Minneapolis weren't attending.

Anderson knows about profit-and-loss responsibilities. His fifty-employee church stays within its $3.4 million budget. And the church is not only fiscally sound, it is successful—so successful, in fact, that it has been able to spin off a handful of churches in the area.

And Anderson knows what makes a healthy organization. He runs his church like the most successful companies profiled in this book. He has moved from having a hierarchical management structure, to having an organization run by teams. Instead of managing by rules, he now leads by vision and values. At a time when organizations are struggling to figure out how to engage people and build commitment in the workplace, we can learn a lot from Leith Anderson and how he built a church community committed to spiritual relationships and a strong bottom line.

What makes a true community is a critical mass of people who come together to share mutual interests, aspirations, and a common purpose. At the Wooddale Church, many people just don't show up for church on Sunday out of obligation, they want to be there. Anderson has created a healthy community of people who are highly committed to the purpose and the activities of the church.

He achieved this primarily through an understanding of himself and of his congregation. Anderson sees himself "first as a Christian who is committed to Jesus Christ, and desires other people to be. That's my primary motivator. But I have also been trained as a sociologist. I want to understand how people function, so that I can be effective with them. I want to wed together both my Christian and sociologist sides."

This background allows him to weave together a leader's vision with a pastor's heart. Anderson leads from the inside out—listening, analyzing, interpreting, enabling, and empowering others. But he also leads from the outside in. He is always conscious of where the church fits within society. It is important, he says, that leaders be "ethnologists," always analyzing the culture in which they operate.

"The key question is whether the church considers culture to be the friend, or the enemy, of the gospel of Jesus Christ," he says. "If culture is perceived to be the enemy, then the church becomes separatist and eventually sectarian, and possibly a cult, because the culture is kept at a distance. But if culture is perceived as a friend of the gospel, there is contextualization to the culture. If the culture changes, then the church needs to change and be reinvented in terms of its relationships."

In other words, the church needs to evolve to deal with a changing culture, just as companies need to evolve to deal with a changing marketplace. Adapting to the new environment, in both instances, means constantly challenging the assumptions that brought the organization to its present state.

"It may be as simple as recognizing that the time of church services was once set by the milking schedule of cows, but today it may need to be set by the kickoff time of the NFL," Anderson says. "Not a lot of people milk cows anymore, but a lot of people do watch football."

MAKING THE CONNECTION BETWEEN
LEADER AND FOLLOWER

This is a man with a sense of task, a sense of purpose about life, and great integrity. He has dedicated himself to the healthy development of people and their families, focusing on people's health and strengths. And he tries to spread that positive attitude to his church congregation. "We shouldn't identify our sicknesses and attack them as much as we should identify our health and spread it around. We're trying to do that."

That will take a lot of effort, Anderson believes. He is troubled by the pressures and expectations under which people operate.

"I was in a museum recently and there was a ten-year-old kid ahead of me who was wearing a T-shirt that said, 'Coming in second is being the first loser.' That's really sad, but that's what people believe, that you've got to be first.

"I think that is one problem our society has; another is we have had it too easy. We've become a nation of whiners, and it is ridiculous what we complain about. In most parts of the world, where people have more serious problems than we do, people don't whine, because they don't have the expectations we do. Our expectations are totally unreasonable. For example, people have an idealized view of marriage, and if the marriage does not match up to this idealization, they walk."

These are the sorts of messages Anderson communicates through the church. It is part of his effort of making sure that the lessons people learn in church leave with them and carry over into their everyday lives. "The true mark of a successful church," he says, "is when you spread health throughout the community."

Anderson believes that if his church doesn't find a way to relate to the way people really live, it will have no chance of forging any kind of relationship with the community. "There's an African proverb that says an empty stomach has no ears," he explains. "That means if you are going to lead someone with a Christian message who has a void in his life, you should first fill that void. By doing so, you will give him a way to connect with the church."

Indeed, Wooddale's slogan, "a place to belong, a place to become," grew out of focus-group research that Anderson conducted with members of the community. "That slogan represented about what 70 percent of the people who live within a five-mile radius of here were looking for," Anderson says.

In responding to market needs is Anderson changing what the church stands for? Not at all, he says, stressing that the mission is still guided by the overall teachings of the church. "We are not changing our central product, but we are packaging it in a way that's palatable. "We're a less religious society," he adds. "People used to come to church, and then find relationships. Today, people have relationships, and through their relationships they find the church. There are many people who don't understand how to access a church. We provide multiple opportunities through all the social activities we offer here for them to test the system. We have thousands of people who come to this building in nonchurch activities every week, and they can check out the facility, read our literature, and understand how we operate. Then, if they want to show up at a church activity, they're already comfortable with at least the externals of the system.

"We have a member of our church, Jim Nelson, who as far as I know didn't come here because of religion. I think he came because of the softball team. Then he went through employment difficulties, and because he wanted to build new relationships, he volunteered to work on a Habitat house. Today, he is employed by Habitat as a supervisor. And I would say in the last two years he's made a commitment to become a Christian, but we reached him initially because of the softball league.

"People are yearning for meaning and relationships," he says. "That's why you must go where people are. You must start with where their interests lie and offer activities that match. Like Velcro, we offer a lot of different places to hook on to." Anderson isn't kidding. Even a partial list of what the church has to offer is daunting: music groups, divorce-recovery workshops, singles' Bible studies, volleyball leagues, women's retreats, "Mom's time-out," aerobics class, blood-donor club, employment counseling and placement, sons'-fathers' campouts, Christmas coffees, men's breakfasts, bowling leagues, midweek children's club.

All those activities help to satisfy the belonging needs of people in the community. People can connect with the church at three levels— the celebration, the congregation, and the cell. The celebration services are large-group gatherings for worship. As many as three thousand people can gather at one time for one of the three celebration services held every Sunday. The congregations are Christian-education units of no more than one hundred people that meet for fellowship, learning, and sharing every week. The cells are small groups that provide opportunity for learning, fellowship, and social action. By offering people these different ways to connect with the church, Anderson was able to establish a relationship with his parishioners. Today, Wooddale is one of the most popular churches in the Midwest.

Anderson is building a community of commitment. He understands what people want out of life. He speaks directly to them and taps a chord inside their hearts and minds. The church's mission was built on their shared values and goals. Their values and missions became the church's. This is critical. If leaders want people to support the goals of their organizations, they must make sure those goals are consistent with what people believe. And they must make it as easy as possible for people to "buy in." People are looking for a sense of belonging, but they will only join when they believe in the organization's mission and when they feel comfortable.

This brings up an important point about mutual expectations and reciprocal responsibilities. While Anderson is willing to go at least halfway to embrace people, he imposes a responsibility on members of his congregation in return.

"We all need to hold each other accountable for being mature citizens of the community. In our church, I will say that we need two hundred people to show up to build a habitat, and two hundred people will show up. Just as people need to hold leaders accountable, and people have a right to expect a lot out of the leaders, we have a right to expect a lot of them."

Over the last twenty years in running Wooddale, Anderson has gained maturity and wisdom. He now thinks it is time to share what he has learned. "I find the older I get, the more satisfaction I have in the success of other people. I'm less competitive and ambitious for my own achievements and take more and more delight in other people's successes."

Anderson has established a mentoring program with other churches. It is part of his attempt to develop other leaders. "I think God has given me the opportunity to have something far bigger than anything I ever dreamed of. I'm satisfied to the point where I want to see others succeed."

This is a man who is clearly dedicated to finding meaning in his own life and the lives of others. But even special people have problems. Anderson admits the downside of being overly dedicated to one's purpose. Despite all he has accomplished, he gets easily disappointed and discouraged. "I can have twenty people tell me I'm the greatest guy in the world, but if one person tells me I'm a jerk, I can't remember what the other twenty said. I get discouraged and disappointed, and I have to work on that. I've got to take care of myself more, because if I am not healthy, I am not of much use to anyone."

Anderson is an example of a mature man who knows how to build a healthy community. He articulates a reason for being, clarifies expectations for the people in the community, and knows how to knit together a cadre of relationships that are built around a common purpose. He has a realistic sense of himself, but a profound sense of purpose about his role in society. He does all he can to make a contribution to improve the lives of others. And he does it with a sense of humor.

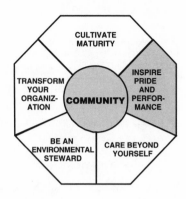

INSPIRING PRIDE AND PERFORMANCE

People want to be somebody, to feel important and make a contribution in the world. Whether you call that dignity, or a desire to achieve, it all comes down to having self-respect. A leader's job is to instill that sense of pride throughout the organization.

There is a link between people, pride, and performance. You simply cannot produce quality work unless you have quality people, people who feel good about themselves, their work, and their company. If employees are pessimistic, dissatisfied, or angry, it shows up in their work.

Successful leaders understand their greatest potential lies in the interaction between employees and their customers. And they know that employees end up treating their customers exactly the way the company treats them.

In a world where we look to ancient Chinese warlords and Attila the Hun for leadership advice, and *Fortune* magazine routinely celebrates "The World's Toughest Bosses," it might be surprising to discover that you can learn a lot about running a high-performance organization from a woman who heads a public transit authority. Most public-sector organizations fall short when it comes to inspiring pride and measuring performance. New Jersey Transit is an exception, at least it has been in the three years Shirley DeLibero has been there.

Before DeLibero became executive director of New Jersey Transit, which runs the state's bus and rail lines, NJT was anything but a model of efficiency. Schedules were rarely met, annual rate in-

SHIRLEY A. DeLIBERO
New Jersey Transit Corporation

TITLE: Executive Director

AGE: 57

FAMILY SITUATION: Single; 2 sons

EDUCATION: Associate Degree in Business Administration, American Institute of Management; Associate Degree in Engineering, Wentworth Technical Institute

HISTORY: 19 years in electronic manufacturing industry, starting as assembly-line worker; Superintendent and Project Manager, Massachusetts Bay Transportation Authority (1978–81); Assistant General Manager, Washington, (D.C.) Metropolitan Area Transit Authority (1982–87); Deputy Executive Director, Dallas Area Rapid Transit (1987–90); appointed to present position 1990

SPECIAL INTEREST: Growth and development of minority youth

HONORS AND SPECIAL ACCOMPLISHMENTS: Recipient, American Society of Civil Engineers (N.J. chapter) Service to the People Award (1993); Transportation Person of the Year Award, Metro Network Chamber of Commerce (1993); Outstanding National Transportation Award for Excellence in Management, Texas Association of Minority Business Enterprises; New Jersey Board of Governors of the National Conference of Christians and Jews; Board of Governors, Cathedral Healthcare Systems, Inc.; Board, Rutgers National Transit Institute

BUSINESS: Public transportation

NUMBER OF EMPLOYEES: 9,000

BUDGET: $775 million

FACTS: The New Jersey Transit Corporation, the third-largest public transit agency in the nation, carries 170 million passengers annually and covers 5,325 square miles.

creases were a certainty, and the only thing worse than the system's on-time performance was its high prices. The focus of the agency was not on operations, and there was little sense of urgency.

DeLibero and her organization have changed all that. On-time performance is now better than 90 percent. After several years of decline, ridership has climbed to 273,000 daily (third-highest in the country), and last year the agency came in nearly $6 million under budget. In addition, there has been a noticeable improvement in the attitude of employees.

Credit for this dramatic turnaround rests firmly on DeLibero's shoulders. She has created an organization that reflects her personality. She is a proud, demanding person—not only of others, but of herself as well. She celebrates her blue-collar roots. She began as an assembly-line worker in an electronics plant and got her first transportation job—supervising the rehabilitation of Boston's streetcars—because she knew about electronics. She then went on to run transit systems in Washington, D.C., and Dallas, before arriving in Newark.

DeLibero is proud of her operational background. And she is obsessed with people and their performance. Those two things are interrelated, and they are central to DeLibero's business strategy.

"People want to be somebody. They want to be the best at what they do," says DeLibero. "They want to perform. They want to accomplish goals. They want to understand how they are contributing to the organization. They want to know how they are performing. If people feel good about themselves and their performance, it shows."

DeLibero is her own best example. Her sense of pride is linked to her performance—every day.

"I came here without a contract, for two reasons," she says. "The board sets policy and I implement it. It's important that we both understand our roles and that a contract isn't necessary to bind either one of us. If I didn't do my job they should be able to get rid of me with no payouts and vice versa. It's all about performance. The board and I have worked well over the past three years."

Her point is a good one. Leaders can't hype performance, or oversell it. They must prove exactly how good they are. Linking pay to performance is popular these days. And it should be. People should be rewarded for their actual performance on the job. And leaders are no exception.

But DeLibero has an extra reason for wanting to be judged on what she does. As an African-American woman in a macho work culture, she has always wanted people to look at her performance and competence, and not her color or gender. Having a sense of dignity and self-respect is important, she says, but you still must know the "difference between self-confidence and arrogance. That difference is performance. If you're going to let people know how good you are, you also have to back it up with results. People have to see proof, or they will dismiss you as arrogant."

DeLibero takes pains to point out that she doesn't think she knows it all, talking openly about areas where her skills are not strong.

"I don't want a whole lot of Shirleys. I don't want a lot of people who know what I know. People tend to hire people like themselves, so they can look good. That way, when a new employee says, 'I think we should do this,' they can say, 'Oh, no, we tried something like that four years ago, and it didn't work.' I don't do that. I hire to my weaknesses. I want people who know what I don't. When I went looking for a chief financial officer, I went out to get a person who knew all about bonding and insurance, how to do cross-border leasing, and all the other financial areas I don't know. I know budgets inside and out. But I don't know how you get somebody from Japan to buy our refurbished rail cars for a lot of money, so that they can get tax breaks. I went out and hired someone who knew all these things."

But still, when asked about her abilities, there is no false modesty. "I have frequently said, 'I may not be the best in this business, but there's no one better.' I don't think of that as being cocky, because I sincerely feel I am the best in the business."

That kind of pride is essential. If performance is the business goal at New Jersey Transit, pride is the means of achieving it. As much as DeLibero is obsessed with performance, she is equally committed to the people side of the business, in order to instill that pride in her organization.

Very few people deliberately set off to do a bad job; people have a natural inclination toward quality. People who feel important, who feel good about themselves, are more likely to produce quality and excel. DeLibero knew that when she took over New Jersey Transit. If she could get people excited and proud about their jobs and the company, she knew they would do better. This was not something she could dictate. Real pride is inspired from within, as people begin to feel they can truly make a difference. When this happens, they develop pride in themselves. Suddenly the trains are on time, the customers are smiling, and performance soars.

"If you take care of your people, they'll take care of the product," DeLibero says. "If you care about them, it increases their personal pride, and they put that self-respect right back into the work. I really believe it, because I have seen it work over and over again."

DeLibero believes strongly in touching the people out in the field. She manages by walking around, because she knows that people want to be treated as if they are more than numbers. They need to be appreciated for being human. That is a feeling DeLibero remembers from her days on the assembly line, and it is a feeling she carries with her as executive director.

She creates organizational pride in a number of ways. For example, she sends employees handwritten notes after they have done particularly good jobs, or if something dramatic has happened in their lives. She always sends a condolence letter when a parent dies. The feelings are reciprocated. When DeLibero's mother died, she received scores of notes and cards and some thirty of her employees traveled to Boston for the funeral on their own time.

Because she understands that employees need to touch, interact, and understand their leaders, she'll hold staff meetings out in the field, in a bus or train, if the local facility is not big enough. In fact, DiLibero will invite the field employees to be part of the staff meeting, so they'll understand how decisions are made.

And because she believes a public transportation system is the lifeline to the community, DeLibero has placed radios in every New Jersey Transit bus, so that her drivers can alert the police to suspicious activity they see along their route. It's a program that she calls "Transit on Patrol," and it grew out of conversations DeLibero had with members of the New Jersey Transit police force, during her daily workouts in the police officers' gym. The program allows the bus drivers to serve both as community ambassadors and guardians and it has had huge payoffs.

"About three weeks ago, a bus driver was on his route, and there were two guys attempting to steal a car," DeLibero recalls. "It was clear that was what they were doing, because one guy was trying to open the door, while the other one was under the hood. Our bus driver immediately called it in. Well, the guys had gotten in the car, and were just about to drive away, when the police arrived. The community really loves us."

And that, of course, is another way employees can feel good about the jobs they are doing. When the community feels an employee's sense of pride in her job, there is added incentive to keep doing a fine job and a higher sense of morale.

DeLibero reinforces this kind of positive attitude by handing out lapel pins celebrating record-breaking performance, and by placing posters everywhere. Some of the posters vividly chart the dramatic turnaround the organization has made. Others display the vision statement that DeLibero and her employees helped create: "Our mission is to provide safe, reliable, convenient, and cost-effective transit service with a skilled team of employees dedicated to customers' needs and committed to excellence." Every employee has a wallet-sized version of the credo.

Has all this fostered pride in the organization? It sure has. "I took a train the other day, and while I was on the platform talking to some of our customers," DiLibero says, "the conductor came up to me and said, 'You better hurry up and get on board. This train waits for no one. Our on-time performance was horrible yesterday; it was down to 84 percent, and we've got to get it back up, so let's go."

Keeping the organization under a microscope, constantly measuring how well it is doing, is not something that many public agencies do. Indeed, many leaders of firms in the private sector fail here as well. Not DeLibero. She constantly posts New Jersey Transit's operating numbers for everyone—her employees, board of directors, the public, and the press—to see, letting employees know the good news and the bad. Everyone can tell at a glance what percentage of trains ran on time last week, or how long the average bus has been out of service for an overhaul. She calls these reports "Vital Signs," because they show the numbers that are vital to the agency.

But while DeLibero doesn't have any problems disclosing all the numbers, some of her employees did at first.

"Some of them used to get upset, but I told them not to worry about it," DeLibero explains. "It's the truth. And if we didn't do a good job last month, if we didn't perform as we should have, we should face up to that fact. Some employees will say it isn't fair, that people don't know all the effort we are putting in. And I tell them they're right, our customers don't know, and they don't care. They don't really care that Joe Smith stayed here around the clock fixing the catenary. All they know is that they had to wait an hour for their train. And that's the only thing that is important. The numbers show we have to get better."

But notice how DeLibero is using the numbers in all her comments. She isn't using them as a way to criticize her employees, pointing out how badly they are doing, subtly underscoring that their poor performance is the reason she is the boss and they're not. Rather, DeLibero, like many leaders of today's healthy companies, is using the numbers as a teaching tool: Here is where we are; this is where we want to go.

DeLibero is committed to making those numbers improve. Everything she does, from setting goals to talking to employees, is designed to do that. She knows that as those numbers improve not only will the organization benefit, but employees will benefit as well.

There is no doubt that DeLibero is demanding. But because she has made clear what she expects, and because she inspires pride in the work they do, the employees respond positively, instead of becoming resentful. They know she wants what's best for the organization, and because she has held herself to such a high standard, she has fostered a feeling that "we are all in this together." That allows her employees to forgive her on days when she is overly abrupt, makes a mistake, or is feeling down. DeLibero points out there are days she can use that forgiveness.

"It's tough to be strong and upbeat all the time in front of everybody," she says. "There are days when you just don't have it, when you are tired of the politics and the frustrations. But your employees expect the executive director to be able to deal with everything, to smile and be happy all the time."

DeLibero understands herself well. She knows her strengths—the ability to hire well-motivated employees and create a family atmosphere that shows she cares about her employees. But she also knows her weaknesses. She's too opinionated, has little tolerance for incompetence, and tends to take things personally.

Because she understands herself well, she knows that she needs her employees to be as forgiving of her as she is of them, on bad days. DeLibero makes sure she doesn't take advantage of that relationship, by admitting when she makes a mistake.

"A lot of people feel that's a weakness. To me, it's a strength. I want people to admit their mistakes and say what they are going to do to correct them. I have a lot of respect for people who do that, because we are all human, and we all are going to make mistakes. I think people understand that, and can even tolerate that.

"But I'll get on your butt if you sit there and become defensive about your mistakes and start explaining why it really wasn't your fault. I'm going to give you responsibility, but I am going to demand accountability in return. I am not going to tell you how to get the work done; everybody has their own style. But I am going to tell you what I want you to accomplish."

By fostering individual and organizational pride, Shirley De-Libero was able to transform New Jersey Transit from a mediocre government agency to a high-performance organization. She did it by understanding that proud people produce better products. Customers expect a lot these days. They want quality, value, and reasonable price all wrapped in one. Customers also want to be treated fairly and with respect. Proud employees know how to do that. And Shirley DeLibero knows what it takes to help them. Her human touch, coupled with her high-performance demands, creates terrific results.

CARING BEYOND YOURSELF

Some leaders are too narrow in their perspectives. They are too pre-occupied with self-interest and short-term profits, measuring their success and self-worth solely on how much money they make.

Successful leaders have a longer and broader perspective on business and life. They measure their success not just in terms of how much money they have, but also by their contribution to society. To them, profit is not a right but a reward, given to them from society for creating something of value, and for being a responsible corporate citizen.

This sense of social responsibility isn't imposed upon a corporation. It starts inside the leaders—leaders who are generous people, who are concerned about others and the circumstances that surround them. By caring beyond themselves, these leaders find a deeper sense of gratification and self-fulfillment. They are thankful for the opportunities they have been given and want to give something back.

As a result, they see a broad role for business within society. They know companies cannot be islands of self-interest. As partners in the community, businesses must share their talent and resources to help serve public needs, work on social issues, and help build healthier communities.

This is not only the right thing to do, it is good business.

Nobody would have blamed James Rouse if he had decided to work full time on his backhand. After all, given all that he had accomplished, everyone agreed Rouse was entitled to take it easy once he turned sixty-five.

No one had ever labored harder. Rouse came of working age during the depression. He parked cars seven days a week to put himself

---

JAMES ROUSE
The Enterprise Foundation

TITLE: Founder-Chairman

AGE: 81

FAMILY SITUATION: Married; 3 children

EDUCATION: L.L.B., University of Maryland Law School (1937)

HISTORY: Founded The Rouse Company (1939), which has developed over 50 regional shopping centers; founded Columbia, Maryland, a planned community (1967); recreated Faneuil Hall in Boston (1976); developed Inner Harbor in Baltimore (1980); founded Enterprise Foundation (1981); retired as Chairman of Rouse (1984)

HONORS AND SPECIAL ACCOMPLISHMENTS: Member, President Eisenhower's Task Force on Housing (1953), and President Reagan's Task Force on Private Sector Initiatives (1982); Chairman, National Housing Task Force (1988); member emeritus, Board of Trustees, Johns Hopkins University; board member: The Points of Light Foundation, One to One Foundation World Times, Inc.; honorary lifetime member, American Planning Association, American Institute of Architects, American Institute of Landscape Architects; *Fortune* magazine Business Hall of Fame

BUSINESS: Assisting cities in providing fit and affordable low-income housing

HEADQUARTERS: Columbia, Maryland

FACTS: Since 1987 the Enterprise Social Investment Corporation, a subsidiary of the Enterprise Foundation, has raised more than $917 million from corporate investors for producing over 40,000 housing units.

---

through law school at night. After beginning life as a mortgage banker, Rouse became a real-estate developer. Quickly his name became synonymous with innovative urban development projects, as the company chose historic, and often deserted, sections of cities to house their efforts. From Norfolk to Boston, if you mentioned the city was bringing in The Rouse Company, you knew new stores would be opening and hundreds of thousands of people over the course of a year would be flocking to a renovated part of town. All you have to do is look at the Inner Harbor project in Baltimore, or Manhattan's South Street Seaport, to see the stunning effects of Rouse revitalization achievements.

But Rouse went even further. He created an entire new city— Columbia, Maryland—from scratch, and it was a stunning success. Columbia is now the prototype everyone examines closely, when they are thinking of creating a totally planned community anywhere in the world.

So, if the elder statesman of the real-estate industry, after working for forty-nine years, had wanted to take it easy upon reaching the company's mandatory retirement age of sixty-five, everyone would have understood. Everyone that is except Rouse.

"I like to fish, and I like to play tennis, and I like to do a lot of other things," Rouse says from the office that houses his second career. "But I had no intention of making those things a way of life. I've always felt that the person who really retires, completely separating himself from that in which he has been engaged, is making an extraordinary judgment on what his life has been. He's saying that he's spent his whole life on something that wasn't worthwhile. It seems to me that the more natural response upon reaching 'retirement age' was to say, Gee whiz, now that I've had this experience, what can I do with it?"

And that is exactly what he did. Rouse applied the organizational and management skills he had learned in the profit-making world to the nonprofit one. Rouse is now founder-chairman of the Enterprise Foundation, which "brings together all available financial and technical resources and partners" to produce affordable housing for the poor. Working in 150 locations and with 500 neighborhood groups nationwide, the foundation has helped produce over 40,000 homes and 21,600 jobs for "hard-to-employ" people during the last 14 years.

Recognizing that people's needs go beyond housing, the foundation helps develop ways to link human services with housing. The idea is to give people a hand, in climbing out of poverty and into the middle class. "If we don't take care of our cities, they will disintegrate further, and we will all suffer," Rouse says simply.

What is now going on in Sandtown is a wonderful example of how Rouse, who refuses to take a paycheck from the Enterprise Foundation, acts out his vision and philosophy.

Sandtown is a neighborhood of 72 square blocks, comprised of 5,000 largely dilapidated dwellings, in downtown Baltimore. It is home to 10,000 people, 22 percent of whom are unemployed. Sandtown is, unfortunately, a fairly typical inner-city environment. Some 40 percent of the residents are high school dropouts. The local hospital serves as the family doctor, and sits in the epicenter of the section known for both drugs and violence in Baltimore.

While Sandtown is the kind of place most people will do anything to avoid, it is exactly the kind of place the Enterprise Foundation seeks out. It has formed a partnership with the residents, city agencies, and private businesses to rebuild the neighborhood. Money is being poured into the schools, with a special emphasis on trying to increase the graduation rate. Training and job-placement programs are being introduced, as are health and family services. Police patrols have been stepped up. "Eventually," says Rouse, "Sandtown will be a neighborhood where people will grow, raise families, and be productive participants in the mainstream of American life."

What kind of man devotes the second part of his life to something like Sandtown? Obviously, Rouse is a successful businessman who has been able to translate his skills to the private sector. But he is more than that. He is a man with far-sighted vision, warmth, and humanity, who has abiding faith in the basic rightness and purpose of mankind.

"I am obsessed with horror and hope," he said. "The horror is the lives of the people living on the bottom of the American city, and the hope, the bright hope, is that this need not be, and can be corrected. Americans can either become more selfish, or more concerned about serving others.

"I can't be expected to think much about things that are totally beyond my knowledge and awareness. I probably won't wake up worrying about the rain forests, unless I have some reason to be affected by environmental causes. But I can be expected to get up and be concerned about the life of my employees, about the life of people in the city, about crime, and be concerned about the things that are causing it.

"One of the greatest threats to America today is the wretched, miserable, threatening conditions in which the poor live in our cities," he adds. "Whether it's joblessness, homelessness, drugs, crime, school dropouts, unwed mothers, or the breakdown of the family, all of these conditions, which people talk about when they discuss the decay of our cities, are real. And the situation is getting worse. The number of people in poverty was 24 million in the 1970s, 28 million in the 1980s, and 34 million today."

The problem is daunting. But not so daunting as ever to depress Rouse. One of the most distinguishing aspects of this eighty-one-year-old is his positive outlook, not only about himself but about people, business, and society in general. No matter what the situation, he always asks, "What would it be like if it worked? And how do you get from here to there?"

Rouse is convinced he acquired this positive attitude as a result of "having the advantage of coming to adulthood during the depression."

"My family had lost everything. They foreclosed on our house in 1930, when I was sixteen, and that same year, both my mother and father died," Rouse recalls. "And it was the damnedst thing, but I had the clear sense that I could handle this. I remember thinking, 'I'm strong; I'm intelligent, and this is good for me.' "

As a result of this internal strength and his inherent optimism, Rouse has spent his whole career searching for solutions that are best for people.

"We had a set of goals at Rouse that were very specific and very motivating," he says. "First was to improve the urban life in America. Second, to provide for the growth of individual people within the company. The company is its people. And the final goal was to make a profit. And remember, we were a public company. Every year at the shareholder meeting I would explain our goals, and stress that they were listed in order of importance. I told our stockholders if we met the first two, the profits would take care of themselves, and they did.

"At Columbia [the planned community in Maryland] we had four goals: first, to respect the land; second, to build a real city, not just a better suburb; third was to provide a life of growth for man, woman, and family; and fourth was to make a profit. And we did, Columbia has been an unbelievably profitable adventure for The Rouse Company."

All these goals, Rouse says, emerged out of his way of thinking, and have their roots in values and purpose, not in a search for making money.

"Profit prostitutes purpose," Rouse says. "Profit is not a right.

Profit is a reward that society gives the corporation. There's no natural right to be a corporation. It's a contract that individuals make

THE WISDOM OF JAMES ROUSE

- Approach the world confidently, optimistically, and with brilliant expectations. The world is full of opportunities.

- Pay no heed to the no sayers, the preachers of gloom, the heavy-hearted. Their pessimism creates nothing, builds nothing, supports nothing.

- When you face a problem, don't fight it—look beyond it. What ought to be can be, when we have the will to make it so.

- When life gives you lemons, make lemonade. Making lemonade is one of the most important responsibilities of leading.

- Don't let money become a sole measure of success. Money and possessions are important, but they should not command your life.

- Don't hang on longer than you are needed. It's too easy for people at the top to persuade themselves of their indispensability.

- Believe in the good life, the good family, the good community. Plan it, build it, produce it.

with people in business who provide goods and services. Profit should be seen as the reward that somebody receives for doing that extremely well. The better you do it, the better your profits. Profit as a goal distorts that whole process.

"Instead," he adds, "the goal should be operating your business or profession with the primary goal of serving its natural market."

What comes through, when you hear Rouse talk, is his broad perspective on life. He is an "enlightened capitalist," someone who defines his business mission around social purpose, and builds his business with a conscience, investing time and money in socially responsible causes. He appreciates the enormous value of reputation capital, and he wants to leave the world a better place than he found it.

This is in stark contrast to the typical, unhealthy leader. That person tends to think being in charge is an entitlement, and only looks at the next quarter's fiscal results, and the company's current stock price. He is self-serving, withdrawn from community life, lacking in empathy, and has a short-term perspective on what both he and his company should be accomplishing.

But, many executives counter, I have to be this way. My job is to maximize the return to my shareholders. That is how I am judged by Wall Street.

That is too narrow a perspective, Rouse argues. First, he says, chief executives have a responsibility to all of the company's *stake*-holders—employees, the community, customers, and suppliers, in addition to *share*holders. Second, there is nothing stopping leaders from donating part of their company's profits.

When it comes to giving back to the community, the message from the man who has advised every President since Eisenhower about urban issues is simple: "Corporations willingly spend money on research and development because it deliberately leads to profits. But this whole field of the lives of your people, the impact that you have on your environment and on your circumstances, is another kind of research and development, which, if you paid attention to it, would not only produce greater profits, but would also give you, your employees, and your shareholders greater gratification. There is a whole world you're missing. Give yourself to purposes beyond self. Fulfillment, happiness, and success are almost never found in self-service and self-concern."

"That's been a myth that a lot of corporate executives operate under," says Rouse. "For years corporate executives have said, 'I don't have the right to give the shareholders' money to charitable causes, except in the very limited cases where it benefits the company. As a result, business is outrageously non-generous compared to the capacity it has. Total corporate contributions to charities average 0.9% of pre-tax earnings. Individuals give over 2 percent. And the corporate number is even worse than it appears, because of every $1 corporations give to charities, they get to deduct 50 cents.

"What we need in America is a national campaign to increase corporate giving, to make it so fashionable, so important, and so much a part of belonging to a corporate system that you would be ashamed to be the head of a corporation that isn't giving 2 percent, 3 percent, or 5 percent of earnings before taxes."

Is Rouse advocating good works at all costs? No. "I think there is such a thing as being irresponsibly generous, and that you can give beyond the capacity of the enterprise to produce enough to give," he says. "If that happens, pretty soon you've sunk the enterprise. There's a balance in these things that's subtle, but it's always there."

Still, he stresses that the corporation needs to look beyond its own four walls.

Rouse understands that he is asking people to think differently about what being in business really means. "Profit is the measure of success in American business today. When somebody comes along and enlarges that goal, and becomes known for it and is celebrated for it, he's still looked upon as a little bit abnormal. People give him praise, but they also tend to laugh at him."

Despite that, Rouse expects more people will respond to his approach in coming years, in order to resolve some of society's problems. He believes they won't do it out of altruism. Rather, they will do it because it is smart business.

"They need to be wise, they need to be articulate, they need to be open, and they're going to need to have faith, and by faith I mean belief in something beyond themselves."

Rouse knows that companies are part of the larger community, and that everyone within that community will thrive if companies recognize their responsibility to the larger community. The workplace is a central institution for making that happen. It is not an island of self-interest and short-term profit, but rather a bridge that links us all together and shapes and supports the lives of people and their communities.

Says Rouse: "If The Rouse Company and American business is to fulfill its reason for being—and perhaps even its right to be—it must stop looking upon the city as an accident to be splinted and bandaged and shot with anesthesia, and start seeing it instead as people in trouble, yearning for the leadership, the management skills, the technical knowledge, the resources of manpower, talent, and capital that business knows how to bring to a problem or an opportunity. America needs bold images of a society that works for all its people. We are the wealthiest country in the world, with the greatest problem-solving and management capability in the history of man. It has to be possible for us to fashion a society that works."

BEING AN
ENVIRONMENTAL STEWARD

We are all dependent on our environment. The true leader is committed to preserving and restoring his surroundings.

He starts with a deep appreciation for the environment—its beauty, resources, and limitations. His systemic view of life helps him see how each part of the ecosystem is connected to every other part.

As an environmental steward, the leader wants to pass on to his children an ecologically sound place to live. His long-term view of the world makes him concerned about the planet's sustainability.

In the workplace, this kind of leader sets an example by speaking out for the environment. He engages in ecologically sound business practices that ensure that every aspect of production, manufacturing, and even the disposal of his products protects the environment. But the leader cannot do this alone. So he educates his employees and customers about environmental responsibility.

The business rationale for acting this way is clear. Being an environmental steward leads to greater efficiency within the organization and more goodwill outside of it.

It's a typical morning at the Aveda Corporation in suburban Minneapolis.

Horst Rechelbacher, the founder and chairman of the company that manufacturers shampoos and cosmetics made almost exclusively of natural herbs, other plants, and flowers, is about to address a meeting of five hundred of his employees.

The employees, some of whom have biked to work, dropped a child off at the company-sponsored day-care facility, or have just

HORST M. RECHELBACHER
Aveda Corporation

TITLE: Chairman and founder

AGE: 54

EDUCATION: Left school at age 14

HISTORY: Began his career as an apprentice hairdresser; became stylist at age 17, and started his own company at age 22; owned 6 shops and a beauty school in 1970s when he began formulating plant-based personal-care products; established Aveda in 1978

SPECIAL INTEREST: The environment

HONORS AND SPECIAL ACCOMPLISHMENTS: sponsor of Aveda U.S. Environmental Film Festival; first signatory to CERES (environmental) Principles; Board, Business for Social Responsibility; established Give to the Earth Foundation

BUSINESS: Manufacturer of cosmetics and environmental-care products

NUMBER OF EMPLOYEES: 460

REVENUES: Privately held

FACTS: Aveda's 700 products are sold in more than 25,000 salons around the world. 25 full-time chemists and plant specialists investigate new products and formulations.

come from the company's organic restaurant, gather inside the company's environmentally sound facility, which has lots of windows to take advantage of solar heating and cooling. Aromas from the company's products fill the air. Environmental messages, such as "Have you hugged your planet today?" can be seen throughout the warehouse.

Rechelbacher brings everybody up to date on sales, the new salons that have taken on the company's line, and what the company's various environmental charities are up to, and everyone then goes back to producing the more than seven hundred products that the company is known for.

"Our mission at Aveda is to care for the world we live in, from the products we make to the ways in which we give back to society,"

Rechelbacher tells visitors who observe the morning ritual. "At Aveda, we strive to set an example for environmental leadership and responsibility, and we hope the rest of the world will follow that example."

Many of those visitors take one look at Rechelbacher, who is partial to wearing the latest style suits made from organically grown fibers created by his own daughter, and listen to him say such things as "You can no longer live for the present moment in the world. You've got to live for future generations," and they roll their eyes. When Rechelbacher adds that it is just as important for a CEO to take care of the environment as it is to take care of his shareholders, they just throw up their hands in frustration. What rubbish, is the most frequent response. Taking care of the environment is a nice afterthought, not an intrinsic part of a business, they tell Rechelbacher, fifty-four, who was receiving international acclaim as a hair stylist with clients such as Brigitte Bardot, Elke Sommer, and Jean-Paul Belmondo when he was seventeen.

Rechelbacher listens politely and then gives his response in terms that even the most skeptical business person can understand. "Our company is succeeding financially," he says from his office inside Aveda headquarters, which is located on sixty-five acres, complete with a huge pond filled with ducks and geese. "We are making good profits, and we're growing. Our products are now sold in 25,000 salons and free-standing lifestyle stores throughout the world, and we continue to successfully introduce eight or ten new ones a year. So we obviously are doing something right. It is clear that we're creating products the people like."

And what they like is the way Aveda, which means "knowledge of nature" in Sanskrit, does business. Some 95 percent of its products are made from "the purest forms and highest quality of ingredients," Rechelbacher says. Indeed, the company has trademarked the name "purefume" to symbolize the natural ingredients for its perfumes, for example. "We're working with about fifteen hundred species of plants and flowers, and of those, maybe eighty to ninety percent are grown organically," Rechelbacher adds. "We'd like to get to a point where all of the plants and flowers that we source are organic—no insecticides, no pesticides, no herbicides, no petrochemicals."

Until a few years ago, addressing environmental concerns was simply a matter of not breaking the law. Aveda was well out in front of most companies in embracing and integrating environmental concepts into all aspects of its business. That is what makes Rechelbacher so special.

Environmental concerns are an integral part of the business he has built, whether he is dealing with suppliers (they must carry his line exclusively so that they have the resources to educate customers about what makes Aveda unique), or purchasing (only from places where all natural ingredients are available) or public relations. Aveda gives heavily to environmental causes. Rechelbacher established the Give to the Earth Foundation, which researches and supports many environmental issues and funds various grassroots projects.

In short, environmentalism is part of every business decision Aveda makes. All this is a direct result of Rechelbacher. He was born in Austria to a shoemaker father and herbalist mother, and grew up quite poor. Rechelbacher quit school at age fourteen to apprentice in the local hair salon, and by seventeen he was based in Italy and had an international reputation.

In 1963, during a lecture series in the U.S., Rechelbacher was struck by a car driven by a drunk driver. Rechelbacher had no health insurance, and to make sure he paid his bill, the hospital where he was recovering from broken vertebrae took away his passport. To pay off his debt, Rechelbacher began working in Minneapolis. He quickly built up a chain of six hair salons and a beauty school. But the success of his second career came too fast, and by 1968 Rechelbacher decided to reorder his business and personal priorities, sold his business to employees, and immersed himself in holistic health—including Chinese and Indian herbal remedies.

Following a visit to India in the 1970s, he returned with a master Indian herbalist, who would become, and has remained, a company board member. Rechelbacher, who meditates daily, started Aveda in his apartment in 1978, mixing up the shampoos and cosmetics in his sink. He recorded sales of $1 million that first year, and has seen sales and earnings climb every year since.

Along the way, his views about the environment have never wavered. Rechelbacher believes that "the corporation is like a human body, because it's an ecosystem, where everything is related both internally and externally. All living things are interconnected. The liver functions as the liver, but symbiotically it is aligned to the heart and the brain and other organs. You cannot abuse or destroy one part of the ecosystem, and not have it affect other parts. As a result, to me the planet is my church. I'm clear that I'm here to provide service to all entities of life."

Rechelbacher has a systemic view of business. He believes that every aspect of development, production, manufacturing, distribution, and disposal is interrelated, and each can have an impact on the environment. He realizes we are collectively destroying the ecological infrastructure of our country, and we must think long and hard about how we produce and dispose of our products. He feels he is responsible from cradle to grave for whatever products he makes. Rechelbacher believes deeply that environmentalism is an individual and corporate responsibility.

Not surprisingly, Aveda is a leader in recycling: every communication is printed on recycled paper, using nontoxic soy inks, and all Aveda products are shipped in recyclable containers and boxes. Aveda's distributors work with their salons to maximize the amount of recycling in their area, and Aveda attempts to minimize the amount of packaging necessary for its products. "Recycling is a key ingredient in reducing the world's waste problem," Rechelbacher says. "Together, we can make a significant change for ourselves and generations to come."

Aveda has also been a leader in developing state-of-the-art research and development laboratories. Their trained staff of chemists, pure-fumers, and botanical technicians constantly search the globe, from the Atlantic rain forests to the Pacific seas, looking for new capabilities in plant properties. This commitment to use only plant species obtained from the wild or grown organically, without the use of hazardous pesticides or synthetic fertilizers, is a cornerstone to Aveda's business strategy. "Our goal is to eliminate petrochemicals from consumer goods," says Horst Rechelbacher.

And the company was the first to sign the CERES Principles (see page 350), guidelines drafted by a consortium of environmental groups, which outlines steps for corporations to follow in order to protect the environment.

"By adopting the CERES Principles, we affirm our belief that share-

Under Horst Rechelbacher's leadership, Aveda has been recognized and rewarded throughout the world for both its business excellence and environmentalism.

Aveda was the first corporate signatory of the CERES Principles, which were drafted by environmental groups.

1. **Protection of the Biosphere.** We will reduce and make continual progress toward eliminating the release of any substance that may cause environmental damage to the air, water, or earth, or its inhabitants. We will safeguard all habitats affected by our operations and will protect open spaces and wilderness, while preserving biodiversity.

2. **Sustainable Use of Natural Resources.** We will make sustainable use of renewable natural resources, such as water, soils, and forests. We will conserve nonrenewable natural resources through efficient use and careful planning.

3. **Reduction and Disposal of Wastes.** We will reduce and where possible eliminate waste through source reduction and recycling. Our waste will be handled and disposed of through safe and responsible methods.

4. **Energy Conservation.** We will conserve energy and improve the energy efficiency of our internal operations and of the goods and services we sell. We will make every effort to use environmentally safe and sustainable energy sources.

5. **Risk Reduction.** We will strive to minimize the environmental, health, and safety risks to our employees and the communities in which we operate through safe technologies, facilities and operating procedures, by being prepared for emergencies.

holders have a direct responsibility for the environment," Rechelbacher says, "We believe corporations must conduct their business as responsible stewards of the environment and seek profits only in a manner that leaves the earth healthy and safe. We believe that corporations must not compromise the ability of future generations to sustain their needs."

Rechelbacher believes that all businesses should adopt an "eco-

6. *Safe Products and Services.* We will reduce and where possible eliminate the use, manufacture or sale of products and services that cause environmental damage or health or safety hazards. We will inform our customers of the environmental impacts of our products or services and try to correct unsafe use.

7. *Environmental Restoration.* We will promptly and responsibly correct conditions we have caused that endanger health, safety, or the environment. To the extent feasible, we will re-dress injuries we have caused to persons or damage we have caused to the environment and will restore the environment.

8. *Informing the Public.* We will inform in a timely manner everyone who may be affected by conditions caused by our company that might endanger health, safety, or the environ-ment. We will regularly seek advice and counsel through dia-logue with persons in communities near our facilities. We will not take any action against employees for reporting dangerous incidents or conditions to management or to appropriate authorities.

9. *Management Commitment.* We will implement these Princi-ples and sustain a process that ensures that the Board of Directors and Chief Executive Officer are fully informed about pertinent environmental issues and are fully respon-sible for environmental policy. In selecting our Board of Directors, we will consider demonstrated environmental commitment as a factor.

10. *Audits and Reports.* We will conduct an annual self-evaluation of our progress in implementing these Principles. We will support the timely creation of generally accepted environ-mental audit procedures. We will annually complete the CERES Report, which will be made available to the public.

*Formerly the Valdez Principles

nomic" agenda, that is, they should not be solely motivated by short-term profits and should keep the ecology in mind as well. From the beginning there was that strong environmental commitment at Aveda, and a deep belief—instilled by Rechelbacher—that we are all connected to the environment. And that environment extends in-side the company, too. Just as people don't want the companies they work for to dump toxins into ground or water, they don't want their leaders—or colleagues—to poison the environment inside their organizations.

Rechelbacher is committed to having healthy, productive working relationships inside Aveda. There are two things he does to make that happen. First, he spends a lot of time on hiring, looking for people who are environmentally aware, have a creative sense of aesthetics, and have the right values. Second, he spends a lot of time studying how his organization functions.

Rechelbacher believes that it's too easy for someone to hide in typical organizations, to become, as he puts it, "invisible." And when that happens it is unhealthy for both individuals and the corporation.

To make sure that doesn't happen at Aveda, Rechelbacher has developed a process of doing work called "story boarding," which outlines in great detail each project, and people's roles and responsibilities within it. Part of this process is the use of "project commitment forms," which are filled out by project team members and outline tasks, timetables, and commitments to one another. These interactions take place face to face. Rechelbacher won't permit memos. Decisions and commitments are made in real time, to keep everyone focused on what needs to be done.

Today, other companies are becoming more aware of environmental issues. They are becoming more bottom-line issues, and investors, regulators, customers, and employees are expecting companies to be more environmentally aware.

While this is a new experience for most companies, it is old hat for Rechelbacher, who knows the payoffs from being an environmental steward are tangible as well as intangible. Internally, a focused and committed workforce helps generate greater efficiency, and therefore higher margins. And outside the company, the great responses Rechelbacher receives from customers, and the community, tells him that the company's approach to business is generating goodwill. He can see the payoff through increased customer satisfaction and loyalty and greater market share.

Says Rechelbacher: "We at Aveda are fortunate that our daily work is of service to the environment and all its species."

TRANSFORMING
YOUR ORGANIZATION

Once you have "downsized," and "reengineered" everything in sight, what can you do to take your organization to the next level?

There is only one answer: You must implement an effective people strategy. After all, once the fat has been trimmed away, and all the work processes have been realigned, the only remaining major asset a leader has to work with is his people.

This goes far beyond reengineering. Reengineering is a top-down exercise. Transforming your organization through people is one that goes in all directions. The transformation works one person, and one relationship, at a time.

Some people believe that the people side of the business is "the soft stuff" and has little to do with making money.

But the best leaders know profit and loss results are directly tied to the way people feel about the organization. To them, people's attitudes can work for or against them. They know the heart and soul of their work is to deliver results through people.

It was not a pretty sight.

Jack Callahan, a career veteran of Sears' Allstate Insurance Company, had just been named head of the Business Insurance unit in 1989, and what he discovered as he looked around was an absolute disaster.

Sears, Roebuck and Company took its Allstate unit public in 1993, and spun off its remaining 80 percent holdings to its shareholders in 1995. But back when it was a wholly owned subsidiary, the Business

JOHN D. CALLAHAN
Allstate Business Insurance

TITLE: Former President

AGE: 63

FAMILY SITUATION: Married; 4 children

EDUCATION: B.S. in Accounting and Finance, Bryant College

HISTORY: Over 35 years with Allstate companies. Spent his first dozen years learning the business in jobs from agent to manager. Regional management positions in the 1970s, nationwide responsibilities in the 1980s. Moved from personal lines to Business Insurance Group in 1989. Member of Allstate Board of Directors for 13 years; Chairman of Allstate's operations in Canada. Retired December 31, 1994

HONORS AND ACCOMPLISHMENTS: Board, Bryant College; Chairman, Business Advisory Council, School of Business Administration, University of Illinois at Chicago

HEADQUARTERS: Northbrook, Illinois

BUSINESS: Personal, Business, and Life insurance

NUMBER OF EMPLOYEES: 48,000

REVENUES: $21.5 billion

ASSETS: $61.4 billion

FACTS: Second-largest personal property and casualty insurer in the United States

CURRENT POSITION: Chairman and CEO of the Callahan Group

Insurance results were, to put it mildly, disappointing. America's second-largest property and casualty insurer had been created in 1978, and had not become profitable until 1986, and then just barely. Earnings were substantially below expectations. Morale was even worse. Some 70 percent of employees, according to internal surveys, were unhappy with their job and their company. That came as no surprise to Callahan.

"Employees used to call being transferred to Business Insurance 'the death sentence,' " he recalls. "It was the last step before you hit the grave. The situation was terrible."

It was Jack Callahan's job to turn it around.

The fact that he was given this tough assignment wasn't surprising. Callahan, who was trained in accounting and finance, had moved up quickly through the sales, marketing, human resource, and claims sides of Allstate. At each stop, he proved to be a quick study who was always willing to learn.

Earlier in his career, right after being named a regional vice president, Callahan was called to Allstate headquarters in Northbrook, Illinois, to explain how his region was doing. He put together an elaborate slide presentation to tell the story. At the end of the talk his boss threw him a curve. "He put his arm around my shoulder and said, 'Jack, your job is not to put on fancy presentations; your job is to change the numbers!' "

And "changing the numbers" became the focus of Callahan's life's work within Allstate. At each step along his career path, he improved performance by following a strategy that many of his peers found unusual: Callahan transformed each organization he inherited by focusing on the human side of the business. More than anything else, he invested time, effort, and money in the people who worked for him. Given the success he has achieved, Callahan is convinced that profit and loss at any company, especially in the information age, is directly attributable to skills and attitudes of its employees.

"People often say to me, 'You've worked in human resources. That's where you must have learned this soft stuff.' Honestly, it came from the experiences I've had in line assignments. I've learned the hard stuff—top-down/command and control—is the easy way. It's the soft stuff that's hard to do, but it's really what makes the difference."

Callahan came to this conclusion through trial and error. Mostly error, he concedes. There were places where he thought the turnaround was in place, only to discover later, after he left a new assignment, that his changes had never taken hold. A new manager would come and destroy his efforts by reverting to the old ways of managing people. From this experience, he realized that unless the transformation is institutionalized within the organization, it will never truly stick. And the only way to institutionalize change was to have a majority of people acting as owners of the business. And the only way to accomplish that is one person at a time, and one relationship at a time.

This doesn't mean that everyone needs to be on board to turn an organization around. Early on in his career, after constantly trying, Callahan realized that he could never get 100 percent of an organization to agree it has to change.

"But I discovered that's okay," Callahan says. "It turns out that about 35 percent represents critical mass, and my experience was that you automatically had about 20 percent with the 'change' mindset in place. So I set my goal at getting one convert a day. If you get to 35 percent of your employees, then the huge portion of the uncommitted will shift in your direction. While you can change the numbers relatively quick—say eighteen to thirty months—it will take four to six years to institutionalize the change process."

But Callahan does not go about setting a transformation in motion by edict. While issuing orders is certainly an expedient approach, he knows that change will not take hold, unless employees truly "buy in." That's why he concentrates on one employee at a time.

For Callahan, focusing on employees as the principal catalyst for transforming an organization makes sense in today's more competitive environment, and he is absolutely right.

"If you can provide the right tools and environment, if you focus on individual employees and give them a framework for success, and allow them to focus on the customer, you are bound to win," says Callahan. "If you focus on the people side of the business, you can create extraordinary results."

So focusing on employees was the place Callahan would start, as he tried to save Business Insurance. Naturally the first question was: Did Business Insurance have the talent to turn the unit around? Were there quality managers and employees, with the right attitudes and competencies, available to get the job done? Finding leaders with the intuitive skills, courage, commitment, and energy was the first order of business.

Callahan began meeting with managers within the division and kept hearing the same names mentioned over and over again when he asked, "If you were going to start another business insurance company across the street, who would you take with you?" There were thirty-five people who were on everybody's list. That convinced him that, while none of the thirty-five were among his sixteen direct reports, he had the talent to make the transformation work. His message to everyone who asked was simple: "We are going to bet everything on our people, and we are going to have to believe in them."

Having made that decision, the next step was to ask some of the newly identified leaders to join with the division's senior officers in developing a vision for Business Insurance. That vision would have to be driven by the realities of a rapidly changing marketplace. Callahan knew that Allstate would have to compete harder for customers, maintain higher levels of capital, reduce expenses, provide better service, and do it all at lower prices. In short, it would have to become a world-class company. To achieve that goal, the company would have to become realistic. It couldn't be the best in everything.

"We would have to stop being a generalist and learn to specialize," Callahan says. Specifically, the division would focus on small and mid-sized business owners whose needs fit best with Allstate's capabilities and distribution systems. But narrowing the business scope was just the beginning. Allstate Business Insurance would also become more selective about the kinds of business it would take on. Growth for growth's sake was out. Profitable growth would now be the number-one goal.

With the priorities established, it was time to share the vision with the other 15,000 employees, and create the environment that would help the division achieve its goals.

Callahan knew it was not going to be easy. Anytime you try to transform an organization, there will be bumps, tensions, and resistance along the way. But at least Callahan knew where he wanted Business Insurance to go. He drew up a chart to show people where the organization was and where it was headed. Callahan would be the tour guide.

Where we are	*Where we want to be*
Backward looking	Future oriented
Paternalistic	Professional
Company focused	Customer focused
Hierarchies	Teams
Authoritative bosses	Facilitators
Dependent employees	Empowered associates
Culture of entitlements	Culture of earning

To accomplish the kind of sweeping change he wanted, Callahan began developing new leaders at every level of the organization.

"Most of your existing managers will not be able to move from where you are to where you want to be," Callahan says simply. "To senior level people, paradise is locked up in the past. They are concentrating on survival and pensions, looking good in front of the boss, and all those other sins of management. They have the most to lose when things change. So, you bet your whole future on the people right below them, the second and third tier of managers.

Education and training become vital. Callahan sent out scores of articles about new concepts in teamwork, coaching, technology, and innovation, and he talked constantly with everyone about those ideas. In addition, he spent tens of millions of dollars on technology and training. Today, every employee must spend at least fifty hours a year in formal learning programs.

By 1991, the transformation had taken on a life of its own. Change was coming in all directions. People were becoming energized and had hope, and Callahan was starting to see a payoff. He had a critical mass, at least 35 percent of employees were on board, and he had put in place his new leadership system for success. The system, at its core, stresses the need to employ "eighteen success imperatives." (See page 359.)

THE EMPOWERED KNOWLEDGE WORKER

"Everything I did was designed to create knowledge workers," Callahan says. "The world, over time, has evolved from the harnessing of land, and then energy, and was now moving quickly in its pursuit to harnessing data. The data is turned into information, and then to knowledge. I long believed that we had entered a new age and while it was difficult to convince people back in the 1980s of what was happening, the reality of the Information Age was dawning on people as we entered the 1990s.

"The great breakthrough in our transformation was the realization that the only way we were going to make it in the twenty-first century was to be a world-class company. And, the only way you could accomplish that was through front-line knowledge workers supported by a highly skilled, fast-moving field support unit that was dedicated to the market realities of the new age. Incidentally, the

JACK CALLAHAN'S
EIGHTEEN SUCCESS IMPERATIVES

Vision. Vision is the ability to imagine what's beyond the horizon and make it real.

Leadership. Leaders are identified not by title, but by what happens to people, events, and actions around them.

Organization. Our organization is what we make it. It is flexible, and constantly evolving.

Diversity. Diversity is about the opportunity to learn from the broad mix of skills, knowledge, experience, backgrounds, and lifestyles.

Teams. Teams are the most powerful tool we have for creating change.

Quality. Quality is defined by our customers who tell us what it is, how to improve it, and whether we've delivered it.

Involvement. Involvement means being more than a spectator. It takes a willingness to be on the field—playing hard.

Initiative. Initiative is a "just do it" approach to getting the job done.

People Development. In today's rapidly changing business environment, our strongest competitive advantage is our people.

Education and Training. Our world is in constant motion, ever changing with greater velocity. The only way to master change is to be constantly learning.

Opinion surveys. The opinion survey enables us to assess where we are, so we can make midpoint corrections on our journey toward world class.

Communications. Communication is the exchange of ideas and information in support of a goal.

Recognition. Recognition is the regular celebration of accomplishment.

Coaching. Good coaches help us explore our capacity to grow.

Technology. Technology is the capacity to access and utilize information or knowledge.

Innovation. Innovation, an element of continuous improvement, encourages experimentation and risk taking.

Creativity. If you have asked yourself, "What can I do today to make this company and job better?" and then experience the energy and excitement of chiseling your ideas into something new and original, you have entered the world of creativity.

Trust. Trust is the glue that holds the other seventeen imperatives together. It is the sum of respect, openness, integrity, performance, and communications, and must flow in all directions.

field support unit was formerly called the home office. The name change was a real shock to the traditionalist," Callahan says.

"The challenge was how could we help the Knowledge Worker stand tall with knowledge, support, confidence, and trust? Communications, not traditional management, was the way to do that. For example, today we arm our catastrophe claim adjusters with lap tops, cellular phones and fax machines. Instead of having to go back to the hotel to telephone vendors about a repair job, they talk to them right on the job."

The approach paid off. By 1992 everyone could finally see increased customer satisfaction and growing profits. To underscore the link between good service, high value, and profits, Callahan introduced "gainsharing," to reward people for achieving aggressive goals and to get them to think like owners. It encouraged them to keep score and gave them a real stake in the business.

These improvements, however, happened during a relatively tranquil time in the industry. Later that year, Hurricane Andrew shattered that tranquillity for Allstate—and most other insurers. Despite that, Business Insurance managed to eke out a profit in 1992, but was able to share profits in 1993 and 1994.

Claims are "moments of truth" in the insurance industry, and the way Allstate Business Insurance handled the aftermath of Hurricane Andrew proved that Callahan had chosen the right course of action. Some 93 percent of customers who were affected by Andrew said they were "very satisfied" and none were "dissatisfied" with the way Allstate handled their claims.

By the end of 1993 everyone could see the plan had worked. The Business Insurance unit had lowered its combined ratio (losses plus expenses expressed as a percentage of premiums) by 17 percent, in just four years. The ROE (return on equity) was in excess of the targeted 16 percent in both 1993 and 1994. In 1994, one of its teams was a finalist in the Rochester Institute of Technology/USA Today Quality Cup Award; and Business Insurance was ranked among the best in the industry by independent insurance agents.

By the time Callahan retired in December of 1994, the transformation he created was fully entrenched. The managers he had trained were among the new change agents within the Allstate Insurance Company. Carrying on Callahan's legacy, they continue to

stress customer satisfaction, high value, competitive pricing, and the
need to give their employees the tools, training, and environment
necessary to get the job done right the first time every time. The
goal of creating a world-class organization—with world-class associates—remains.

LESSONS LEARNED

We can learn a lot from Callahan's experience.

- He leads by example. Callahan said the turnaround would be
  contingent on the performance of his employees, and he
  never wavered from that commitment.
- He laid out a clear vision of where he wanted to take the
  company, and he shared that vision with everyone. As messy
  as the transformation process was, Callahan never lost sight
  of what he was trying to accomplish.
- He was persistent and patient. He knew the transformation
  would take time, and he was confident enough in his decisions to let it happen naturally.
- He was realistic. He knew that most of the senior managers
  he inherited, the "old-timers" as he called them, would not
  be able to cope with the transformation process. He offered
  them training, coaching, and support, but realistically, he
  wasn't expecting much. "If one or two of them comes along,
  it's great, a real plus to the change process, but the odds of
  that happening are not high.
- He bet the future on second and third level managers. He
  promoted them quickly and gave them as much—and often
  a bit more—responsibility than they could handle. Then he
  rotated them quickly throughout the organization, so that
  they could gain a wide perspective, and establish a network
  throughout the organization. These moves produced a dramatic turnaround at Allstate.

Jack Callahan is a leader who utilizes many of the principles and
skills outlined in this book. He started out with a vision to transform
Business Insurance into a healthy, high-performing company. He

wanted it to become a world-class organization that people would be proud to work for. He had the courage of his convictions, patience, and a willingness to stick to his vision, despite the resistance around him. He created an environment where smart knowledge workers could partner with him to transform the organization.

Callahan has the ability to build great interpersonal relationships. He identified the best people, and brought out the best in them. He had great confidence in his people, set high standards, and empowered them to take on leadership roles.

In retiring from Allstate, Callahan takes pride in what his team has accomplished. He gets great satisfaction out of watching his people develop and accomplish their business goals. He knows their success is his success as a leader.

"As you develop people, a wonderful thing occurs. All of a sudden, you're getting the *discretionary effort,* that voluntary piece that comes when people have the confidence, commitment, and trust. And that's when a company takes off. Instead of workers coming to the job and, at best, feeling satisfied with pay, benefits, and working conditions, you get people who feel good about what's happening and are willing to give a performance above and beyond what we expect."

PUTTING WISDOM
TO WORK

PUTTING WISDOM

TO WORK

"I have come to believe that wisdom is not understanding the complexities of the universe. Wisdom is
understanding the simple things, the interpersonal-
relationship things, and practicing them—not just
reading them, not just agreeing with them, but practicing them."

DON SODERQUIST
WAL-MART

You have just met thirty-six of the most innovative leaders of our
time. They are leading people who are making a difference. While
different in background, gender, education, and race, they all have
one thing in common: These leaders have a special insight into
themselves. They are casting light, not shadows, on the people
around them, and in the process they are building successful enterprises, and leaving the world a better place than they found it.

None of these leaders is perfect. That isn't surprising. We are all
imperfectly human, searching for meaning in our lives, while trying
to make our unique contribution in the world.

Leading people is hard work. It is messy, idiosyncratic, and highly personal. It is full of tensions and trade-offs, celebrations and disappointments. Anytime you lay out a large vision with strong values you inevitably invite people to challenge you. Your employees and customers have high expectations that you practice what you preach. And they have every right to. Some people take advantage of your situation. They accuse you of hypocrisy when you are too demanding or disagree with them. Others simply resist change. There are even times when being a good leader can cost you your job. Learning how to deal with this is part of learning how to lead. We are all students in this classroom of life and the road to success is always under construction.

After having read this book it should be clear that we are all in the midst of reinventing ourselves and our organizations. The leaders you have met are excellent examples of people who are transforming the way they think, act, and operate their businesses. And they are doing this from the inside out.

I have found it helpful to think about this transformation process as a series of concentric circles that start inside the leader and move outward toward creating value for the enterprise. As the diagram below shows, the leader starts with some basic assumptions about human nature and organizational life. These assumptions influence

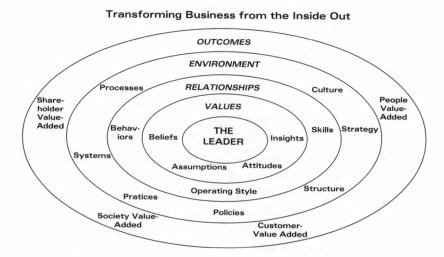

Transforming Business from the Inside Out

his values and beliefs about people and organizations. He develops an operating style and builds relationships with others that reflect these basic beliefs. From there the leader creates a work environment of strategies, systems, and practices that grow naturally out of these philosophies. When this is done well, all the stakeholders—employees, customers, shareholders, and society—benefit.

Each of the eight principles in this book can be understood through this inside out process. Think about the principle of trust, for example. A leader starts with the assumptions that people have a right to know what is going on inside the business and that open dialogue will lead to better solutions. As a trusting and trustworthy leader, he believes that the majority of people will do their best if given a chance. He values openness and authenticity. He communicates about the business, tells the truth, rewards honest feedback, and shares the financials with everyone in the firm. People appreciate his honesty and reciprocate with respect and responsible behavior. They begin to feel a sense of ownership in their work and develop a broader understanding of the business. It shouldn't be surprising that a business run this way makes fewer mistakes, has greater efficiencies, and produces smarter solutions.

HOW WELL ARE YOU LEADING PEOPLE?

The first step to leading people is to know where you stand on each of the eight principles. See if you can answer these questions honestly.

Vision
- Do you paint a picture of the whole enterprise?
- Have you created a common purpose with your employees?
- Do they engage in outcome thinking?
- How are you navigating the change process?
- Are you building a high-performance culture?

Trust
- Do you share yourself and the numbers in the business?
- Are you developing deep listening skills?
- Are you predictable and consistent?
- Have you opened all the doors?

Participation
- How well do you unleash people's potential?
- Are you building adult partnerships?
- Are you nurturing a team environment?
- Do your employees feel like owners?
- Is there a winning attitude?

Learning
- Are you nurturing your own personal development?
- Do you know your strengths and shortcomings?
- Are you being mentored and are you mentoring others?
- Are you tapping into people's discretionary effort?
- Is your company a learning organization?

Diversity
- Have you confronted your own biases and prejudices?
- Are you cultivating both your male and female sides?
- How well do you manage individual differences?
- Are you creating a culture of respect?

Creativity
- Are you discovering people's strengths and managing around their weaknesses?
- Do you know where the pockets of creativity lie?
- Are you developing people-centered technologies?
- Do you reward good people managers?

Integrity
- Do you promote institutional fairness?
- Do you foster ethics and entrepreneurship?
- Do you show courage and promote courage in others?
- Do you put your integrity into action?

Community
- Have you created a healthy community?
- Are you inspiring pride and performance in others?
- Do you care beyond your own self-interests?
- Are you an environmental steward?
- Are you committed to transforming your organization?

As you answer these questions you will get a better sense of how well you are leading people.

The next challenge is to take yourself on an inside-out journey to discover how you think about yourself, relate to others, and operate your business.

UNDERSTAND YOURSELF AT A DEEPER LEVEL

Learning to lead starts with getting to know yourself. You must first dig deep and get your own house in order before you can lead others.

Each of us carries emotional baggage around from childhood. What mental models do you hold about yourself and others? What are your greatest fears and most vivid aspirations? In what ways do you sabotage these aspirations? What values and principles really matter to you? You need to bring these thoughts and attitudes to the surface and understand how they influence your day-to-day behavior.

We also carry a picture in our mind of what we consider to be an ideal healthy leader. If your picture matches the eight principles in this book, which principles are your strengths and which are your shortcomings? How are they reflected in your words and actions? If you were to write your own chapter in this book what would your story be about, and what would the overarching principle say?

You want to strengthen your leading capabilities by understanding yourself at a deeper level and closing the gap between your ideal and your current performance.

PRACTICE POSITIVE ONE-ON-ONE RELATIONSHIPS

Numbers are easy. It's relationships that are hard.

Relationships are messy. People are always bumping up against one another. It is critical that you become agile in managing the space between people. The best leaders build relationships one at a time.

You can start by understanding your external self, the part of you that people see on a daily basis.

- What is your basic demeanor and operating style?
- What do people typically like and dislike about your personality?
- How comfortable are you with interpersonal relationships?
- Are you authentic and honest with others?
- Can you make demands on people and do you keep your commitments?
- Are you caring and respectful of others?
- How comfortable are you with the dark side of relationships—the side that's full of conflict, competitiveness, anxiety, resentment, and self-interest?
- Do you react differently with different groups of people?

Examining your relationships is an excellent way to assess your ability to lead. Some of us interact positively with certain types of people. Others know the right way to act, but lack the necessary interpersonal skills. Still others deal badly with crises, and we all know people who are simply blind to their own shadows. Where do you stand on this continuum?

The best way to improve your relationship skills is to find people to practice with. Ask them for feedback and listen carefully to what they have to say.

DEVELOP A DIVERSE LEADERSHIP TEAM

The most successful organizations develop a strong, diverse leadership team at the top. This is important because no one person can master all the necessary leadership skills. The team will always be stronger if there are diverse talents sitting around the table. Your job as the leader is to identify and leverage those differing talents into a whole that is greater than the sum of its parts.

On your team you will need all eight leading principles represented. So the first step is to assess the team's strengths and weaknesses. The key is to capitalize on people's strengths and manage around their weaknesses.

This requires that you understand your team members as well as yourself. Each person must be viewed as a complex human being with his own unique values, aspirations, and motivations. Each has her own temperament, learning style, prejudices, and resistances. Knowing people at a deeper level will help you navigate through the inevitable complexities of team dynamics and organizational life.

DIAGNOSE THE HEALTH OF YOUR ORGANIZATION

To build a high-performance company you must assess the current health of your organization. Does your organization operate like a muscular, aerobically fit athlete or a vitamin-deficient, homebound anorexic? Are your employees, customers, and shareholders undermining each other, or do they work well together as a balanced team? The key is to examine the gaps between your vision and your current performance.

The best way to do this is by assessing your company's strengths, weaknesses, threats, opportunities, and areas for improvement. Use a combination of interviews, focus groups, audits, and surveys. Analyze your work environment to see whether its values, policies, systems, and structures are aligned with your vision. Conduct a survey of your stakeholders to identify their satisfactions and concerns. Conduct an employee survey and follow it up with interviews so you can feel the very pulse of your organization.

As you assess the health of your organization you will appreciate the multiple causes of business problems and solutions, and the fact that everything operates as one system. The health of this system has a direct effect on employee commitment and performance, and ultimately the company's success.

BUILD A MATURE, ADULT WORKFORCE

Traditionally, we have underestimated the extent to which the new workplace requires a very different kind of adult employee-partner. Just as leaders must reinvent themselves, so must the people following their lead. People must share the responsibilities for an organization's success.

Leaders must first paint a picture of the ideal employee. The best candidates are mature, principle-driven adult partners who are hardworking team players, and committed to their own development. Here is a list of responsibilities we have found to be important in employees.

- Listens well, respects the confidence of information, and communicates with honest dialogue.
- Contributes ideas, takes responsibility for decisions, searches for new and better ways to work, and assumes leading roles.
- Understands the mind of the customer, sees their role in the customer chain, and anticipates and meets customers' needs.
- Commits to life-long learning, shares knowledge, learns from mistakes, and develops multiple competencies.
- Brings his unique beliefs, talents, and experiences to the workplace; works effectively with the prevailing culture; values the differences and uniqueness of others; censures discrimination and prejudice.
- Observes the policies and practices of the organization, and shares responsibility for improving work relations.
- Gives full value in her work, understands and supports the company's goals, and accepts the organization's multiple stakeholders.
- Shares commitments and burdens, recognizes that individual security is directly linked to long-term success of the organization.
- Adapts to new technologies, learns how to use new tools, supports innovation and technological changes.
- Takes personal health seriously, observes safety rules, shares the cost of managing health and illness; actively seeks optimum fitness for work.
- Strives to achieve high levels of quality, ethical behavior, and customer satisfaction.
- Actively seeks to balance their commitment to work, family, and personal needs.
- Shares public responsibilities as active citizens, environmental stewards, and volunteers for social good.

Create a Culture of Leaders

Today, the world is too complicated, change is too swift, and the issues too technical to expect any leader or team of leaders to solve every problem. That is why the best organizations create a culture of leaders.

The first step is to develop an organization-wide process for assessing these leaders. This is done best by assessing strengths and shortcomings, and developing feedback systems so everyone can learn how well they are performing. Feedback should come from all directions—top management, team members, customers—in all forms.

Next, you should develop an organization-wide leadership development program to help each leader learn and grow. Each leader should have a developmental plan based on the feedback systems and have access to a full program of education and coaching.

The goal is to develop a rich pool of leaders at all levels, who will be change agents inside the company.

BUILD A HEALTHY, HIGH-PERFORMANCE ORGANIZATION

Your ultimate challenge is to build a healthy, successful enterprise—one that is values-based and vision-driven internally, and customer-based and market-driven externally. You are the chief people officer in the firm.

People are the leading indicators inside your business. How they are led, and the environment you create, will predict what happens to the business over the long term.

Your goal is to strengthen your organization's capability—to increase the competence, commitment, and creativity of your people. This will require a top-down, bottom-up strategy. It will require managing costs and developing assets at the same time. And it will require transforming your culture until your leading principles are reflected and reinforced in the policies, practices, and systems of your organization.

- Do leaders walk their talk?
- Do people believe in the leader's principles?
- Do they use them to guide the way they lead and work?
- Are the leading principles used in how people are recruited, valued, managed, developed, and rewarded?
- Are they reflected in your selection, performance management, career development, and compensation systems?

This is all part of developing an integrated approach to leading people.

BE WISE ABOUT LEADING CHANGE

Leading people is always about leading change. Every person, at every company, from the shop floor to the executive suite, is always in whitewater conditions and there is turbulence ahead. Many of our change and reengineering efforts have failed. When this happens, we typically blame outsiders for causing the change or we accuse the insiders for resisting the change. But success or failure generally has to do with how leaders manage the change.

Many of us are unwilling or unable to deal with the complexity of change. Some people feel angry, fearful, or resentful when they confront it. Others deny these feelings altogether. But as change stays constant around us, we must all learn how to survive and thrive in it.

We all resist change. It is a human phenomenon as we seek control and predictability in our lives. We put up protective barriers and turn down the noise in order to survive. People need time to work through the change process. Some people resist change more than others, and many of us experience multiple, overlapping changes at the same time. None of us move through change at the same pace, in the same way. Nor are we motivated by the same things. All of this suggests that the leader needs to pay special attention to why and how people deal with change.

During any organizational transformation, leaders cannot reengineer people's commitment. They must build it one person, one relationship at a time. And if the goal is to help people feel engaged and committed to the organization's future, then people will need to feel respected, understood, listened to, and valued along the way. Otherwise, they will likely sabotage the change effort.

LEARN TO FOLLOW YOUR LEADERS

We are all leaders and followers. As we become better leaders we also learn to become better followers. In time, we begin to expect more from our own leaders.

What is it like for you to work with your current leaders? Are you inspired and challenged in their presence? Or do they criticize you and deplete your energy? As you examine your own leader more closely, and look around at other leaders, you may gain an added appreciation for what you have. If that's the case, give your boss some feedback. He or she is probably starving for recognition and will enjoy your honesty.

If you are not so fortunate and happen to work for a dysfunctional manager, you might consider doing something about it. With a boss who lacks people skills, it is important to evaluate his ability to hear candidly feedback, and then make a decision about whether it's safe to talk openly with him. In many cases, our fears of retaliation are greater than the reality of what would actually happen. But this is not always the case, so be careful. Some people find it easier to approach a thin-skinned leader with a group of colleagues. Others decide to work more independently. Or you may simply decide that you are unwilling to work in this type of environment anymore.

BROADEN YOUR MEASURE OF SUCCESS

What we measure is what we treasure. Today, managerial accounting omits from its accounts, and accountability, large portions of behaviors and outcomes that we associate with leading people. Labor is still viewed as a cost of production. We end up measuring some of these costs of mismanaging people on the balance sheet. There are other costs that are simply invisible to the accountant's eyes. Here are some examples:

- Underinformed employees
- Lack of urgency and initiative
- Limited new ideas and innovations
- Underdeveloped products and markets
- Excessive absenteeism and accidents
- Costly disputes and grievances
- Negative public image
- Lack of employee commitment and goodwill
- Tampering and sabotage
- Comformity and overcompliance
- Stress-related work compensation claims
- Underperforming technologies
- Angry, alienated customers

- Excessive health and disability costs
- Decaying communities and environments

It is important to remember that people are both appreciating assets to be developed and depreciating costs to be contained. And as knowledge, relationships, and the ability to learn and adapt become paramount factors of productivity and wealth creation, new ways of measuring and accounting for intangible "soft" assets are needed.

Consider these questions as you measure your organization's success:

- Do you have a clear sense of your business?
- Are you attracting, satisfying, and retaining the right customers?
- Do employees have the right skills, knowledge, and abilities?
- Is the work culture conducive to learning and innovation?
- Do you have a positive reputation in the community?
- Are you adapting and thriving amidst change?
- Have you designed the appropriate organization structure?
- Do you maintain an enthusiastic and committed workforce?
- Is there a shared mindset inside the company?
- Are your work processes efficient and effective?
- Are all your stakeholders delighted?

A new way of leading is emerging—one that is slowly, quietly, and decisively transforming our organizations. After reading this book I hope you are as optimistic and inspired as I am. My dream is that more people will see these possibilities and change the way they lead and work. If they do, we can move one step closer toward creating healthy enterprises that are good for all of us.

Never before have our challenges been so great and the need for responsible leaders been so profound.

We can all be part of this transformation. Each of us has within us enormous potential to lead. And each of us can take a stronger role in leading our families, schools, workplaces, and communities.

Successful enterprises know how to excel and compete. They make the most of their resources—their financial, marketing, and technological capabilities. But it's their people that make the deciding difference; they are the engine for growth and productivity.

Mature, wise leaders make it all happen.

NOTES: PART 1

1. Towers, Perrin. "Executives Rank People-related Issues Far Below Other Business Priorities." Press release, January 19, 1995.

2. Hall, Jay. "Americans Know How to Be Productive If Managers Will Let Them." *Organizational Dynamics*, 1993.

3. "Why Managers Derail." A Report from Center for Creative Leadership, 1994.

4. Leimbach, Michael. "Business Performance, Employee Satisfaction and Leadership Practices." Wilson Learning Corporation, 1994.

5. MacDuffie, John Paul, and Krafcik, John. "Integrating Technology and Human Resources for High-Performance Manufacturing." In *Transforming Organizations*, ed. by Thomas Kochan and Michael Useem. New York: Oxford University Press, 1992, pp. 210–26.

6. Huselid, Mark. "Human Resource Management Practices and Firm Performance." Mimeograph, IMLR, Rutgers University, June 15, 1993.

7. U.S. Department of Labor. "High Performance Work Practices and Firm Performance," 1993.

8. Ibid.

9. Ibid.

10. Corporate Social Responsibility and the Bottom Line: Financial Performance. Internal memo from Business for Social Responsibility, April 1994.

11. Kravetz, Dennis. *The Human Resources Revolution.* San Francisco: Jossey-Bass, 1988.

12. Cutcher-Gershenfeld, Joel. "The Impact on Economic Performance of a Transformation in Workplace Relations." *Industrial and Labor Relations Review* 44:2. January 1991. pp. 241–60.

13. Kruse, Douglas. *Profit Sharing: Does It Make a Difference?* Kalamazoo: Upjohn Institute, 1995.

14. Corporate Social Responsibility and the Bottom Line: Financial Performance. Internal memo from Business for Social Responsibility, April 1994.

15. Kotter, John, and Heskett, James. *Corporate Culture and Performance.* New York: Free Press, 1992.

APPENDICES

THE RESEARCH

This project is the culmination of ten years of work studying healthy leaders and the high-performance organizations they run. In the first phase of research, we explored the link between human development and corporate performance with business executives, labor leaders, academic scholars, and consulting experts. We then identified a set of factors we hypothesized to be critical to organizational success.

In phase two, we set out to test those hypotheses through the development and use of various assessment tools and the creation of a learning network of real world companies struggling to meet real world challenges. One observation was the powerful role that leaders have on the health and performance of their organizations.

So in phase three we set out to capture the insights and experiences of healthy leaders, so we could understand better how to build healthier, successful enterprises.

We asked business leaders, consultants, scholars, and association executives to nominate people. We scanned the country for leaders who were leading healthy enterprises and "walking their talk" in relationships with others. We generated a list of over two hundred leaders from all walks of life—business, unions, government, non-profits, museums, sports teams, community agencies, religious organizations, and associations. After studying the list and talking with leaders, we eventually chose the thirty-six found in this book.

To understand their organizations' culture, we reviewed a variety of company documents: mission and values statements, annual reports, policy and program descriptions, videos, speeches, company brochures, awards, articles, in-house magazines, corporate handbooks, business memos, and personal biographies. Then we conducted with each leader an in-depth face-to-face interview, in which we explored issues such as personal values, business challenges, people strategies, fears and frustrations, critical business incidents, and leadership philosophies.

Each interview was transcribed and the entire package was analyzed. We identified an overarching principle for each person, and a new conceptual framework emerged from this investigation.

HEALTHY COMPANIES INSTITUTE

The Healthy Companies Institute was founded as a not-for-profit organization in 1991 with a multiyear grant from the John D. and Catherine T. MacArthur Foundation. Its mission is to explore the critical links between people and organizational performance. The work is guided by three questions: How can we unleash people's talents, energy, creativity, and commitment? Where and how do people create the most value for the organization? What investments in people will really make a difference in organizational performance? Since its inception, we have gained many valuable insights about the relationship between people and performance.

Services available through Healthy Companies Institute:

- Learning Network. Leading-edge companies learn together about leading, developing, and motivating people to optimize organizational performance. Founding members are AT&T, Allstate, Motorola, Herman Miller, and Office of Personnel Management, among others.
- Learning Sessions. Workshops and dialogues available on topics related to people measurement, healthy organizations, and organizational renewal.

- Publications. Newsletters, reports, books, and case studies available.

For further information call 202-234-9288.

HEALTHY COMPANIES GROUP

The Healthy Companies Group, a consulting firm, was founded in 1988 to work with leaders and their teams to create healthy, high-performance organizations. Our special expertise is the "human side" of business. We are a national team of thoughtful, proven, and diverse professionals with broad business backgrounds and expertise in organizational renewal, leadership development, human-asset management, and people measurement.

Our clients include many Fortune 500 corporations, entrepreneurial growth companies, hospitals and health-care providers, associations, media and nonprofit organizations in the U.S. and around the world.

Consulting services available through Healthy Companies Group:

- Leadership. This consulting practice helps to build strong, wise leaders at all levels of the organization. Our services include leadership assessment, executive development, leadership coaching, leadership systems, dialogues, and strategic and board-level retreats and conferences.
- Organizational Renewal. This consulting practice helps to build healthy, high-performance enterprises by strengthening the organization's capacity to learn, solve problems, and work together. Our services include renewal projects, organization assessments (surveys and audits), and strategic development.
- Performance Measurement. This consulting practice helps to measure the success of the enterprise and renewal efforts. Our services include stakeholder surveys, performance measurement audits, and strategic measurement integration.

For more information call 202-234-0100.

INDEX